FEDERAL AGENTS

FEDERAL AGENTS

THE GROWTH OF FEDERAL LAW ENFORCEMENT IN AMERICA

Jeffrey B. Bumgarner

Westport, Connecticut
London

Library of Congress Cataloging-in-Publication Data

Bumgarner, Jeffrey B.
Federal agents : the growth of federal law enforcement in America / Jeffrey
B. Bumgarner.
   p. cm.
Includes bibliographical references and index.
ISBN 0–275–98953–4 (alk. paper)
1. Law enforcement–United States. I. Title.
HV7561.B86 2006
363.20973—dc22   2006014288

British Library Cataloguing in Publication Data is available.

Library of Congress Catalog Card Number: 2006014288

ISBN: 0–275–98953–4

First published in 2006

Praeger Publishers, 88 Post Road West, Westport, CT 06881
An imprint of Greenwood Publishing Group, Inc.
www.praeger.com

Printed in the United States of America

The paper used in this book complies with the
Permanent Paper Standard issued by the National
Information Standards Organization (Z39.48–1984).

10 9 8 7 6 5 4 3 2 1

This book is dedicated to my wife Kathy and my sons Jack, Alex, and Carl. Thanks for patiently enduring another book project. Okay, boys—time to play "tackle."

This book is also dedicated to the men and women who have chosen to serve their country as federal law enforcement officers and agents. They have my heartfelt gratitude for the unending vigilance they exhibit in protecting the Homeland.

Contents

Preface

Generally speaking, there are few subjects that have captured the attention and imagination of the American public to the degree that police work has. A examination of the programming on television and movies that are produced each year reveals that a persistently recurring theme is the crime drama. The story lines are usually variations of the same formula. The hero cops, who are flawed in many ways personally and perhaps professionally, nevertheless rise to the occasion to successfully investigate the crimes they are confronted with and dispense justice upon the evil-doers. Often, the heroes of these stories are local law enforcement officers. Bust just as often, they are federal agents. To be sure, Americans are fascinated with federal law enforcement.

One need not look only to Hollywood to find an interest in law enforcement generally and federal law enforcement specifically. In fact, the nation's colleges and universities provide ample evidence of this interest. Today in the United States, criminal justice is one of the fastest growing majors on college campuses throughout the country. Schools that do not possess criminal justice majors are rushing to develop such programs, and those with criminal justice or related programs in place find themselves in a never-ending cycle of hiring faculty to keep up with the student demand. For every newly minted Ph.D. graduate in criminal justice, there are 1.3 criminal justice faculty positions around the country needing to be filled.

For all the effort expended to develop the discipline of criminal justice and its various sub-disciplines, there is a conspicuous void in the field relating to federal law enforcement. There is no shortage of texts that deal with policing generally, and with community policing specifically. There are plenty of books, articles, and courses addressing juvenile justice, probation, and corrections. In recent years, there has been a significant advancement of literature in the area of terrorism and homeland security. But there is virtually nothing in the criminal justice literature that deals with the federal law enforcement community in a general sense. This fact is especially surprising given that surveys of criminal justice majors consistently show a high interest in federal law enforcement as a career. Regarding criminal justice majors, studies show that as many as two-thirds of these students have an interest in a law enforcement career and two-thirds of those are specifically bent on securing a position in federal law enforcement.

Federal law enforcement has always been a good career choice for college students. Federal law enforcement agencies have historically required higher levels of training and a college education. They also began using professional and scientific policing and investigative techniques long before even the most progressive state and local agencies started to do so (except perhaps for the Berkeley Police Department under August Vollmer). In addition, federal law enforcement has shown itself to be leader in progressive employment practices. According to the U.S. Justice Department, of the 90,000 sworn federal law enforcement officers in the United States in 2002, 15% were women and 32% were minorities—proportions well in excess of those found in state and local law enforcement generally.

Given the sustained—and even *growing*—interest in federal law enforcement among the American public, among high school and college students, and even among academicians conducting related studies in policing or homeland security, the need for general information about federal law enforcement is acute. As a part of an effort to meet that need, readers of this text will receive an overview of the history of federal law enforcement and the limitations of federal police power. Further, readers will gain an understanding of the current, disparate, and sometimes dysfunctional state of federal law enforcement today. If one were to begin reading this book with the belief that the Federal Bureau of Investigation and perhaps a couple of other well-known agencies comprised the whole of federal law enforcement, that belief would certainly be abandoned by the book's completion.

In short, this book amounts to an accumulation of basic but useful information regarding one of the most vital subsets of America's criminal justice system—the federal law enforcement community. It is my hope that *Federal Agents* will begin to fill the hole relating to federal law enforcement inside the otherwise increasingly well-developed discipline of criminal justice.

CHAPTER 1

The United States Constitution and Federal Police Power

THE DECENTRALIZED NATURE OF AMERICAN LAW ENFORCEMENT

Probably the single most unique characteristic of American law enforcement, when compared with law enforcement in other countries—including democratic ones—is its decentralized nature. American law enforcement is not a single, large system of law enforcement. The reason for this is because American government in general is itself based on the concept of decentralization.

In the United States, there is one national government; but there are also 50 sovereign state governments. Existing under the authority of state governments are literally thousands of county, municipal, and special district governments. Most of these governments employ full-time law enforcement officers whose responsibilities are to police the particular geographic boundaries of the employing government.

When one thinks of any American law enforcement agency, the question of jurisdiction is unavoidably prominent. *Jurisdiction*, for our purposes, is defined as the authority a law enforcement agency has to enforce particular laws in particular political and/or geographic boundaries and to do so coercively (i.e., using force), if necessary.

There is no law enforcement agency in the United States that has total jurisdiction; in other words, no agency has the authority to enforce all American laws in all American places. The question of an agency's jurisdiction is always one of breadth and depth.

Many people in the United States believe that the Federal Bureau of Investigation (FBI) is the premier law enforcement agency in the United States and that it has the broadest police powers of all law enforcement agencies. During the Cold War with the Soviet Union, the FBI and the KGB (the Soviet secret police) were often spoken of as if they were equivalent forces in competing countries. This perception was incorrect, however. Unlike the FBI, the KGB had total police power; the FBI did not and does not.

While it is true that the FBI and other federal law enforcement agencies have very broad geographic jurisdiction—throughout the United States and its territories—the laws that they have the authority to enforce—specifically, federal laws—tend to be rather narrowly focused. As powerful and prestigious as the FBI is thought to be, an FBI agent has no law enforcement authority beyond that of any other private citizen to make an arrest, for example, for drunk driving, because such laws are state laws. In other words, federal law enforcement has geographically broad jurisdiction—but only for federal laws (as a general rule), so it is also shallow. The exceptions to this rule center on federal agencies that have a general police function for their geographic jurisdiction, such as on Indian reservations or in the national parks. Those authorities of such agencies will be discussed later in the book.

The conditions of local law enforcement are quite different. A police officer in a town of 500 people can make an arrest within that town for virtually any criminal law that is broken—federal, state, or local. However, that officer is generally limited geographically to his or her municipality. The town may only be a square mile in area. Given that there are over 3.5 million square miles in the United States, the reach of the officer's jurisdiction is significantly limited. The officer has no geographic breadth.

In the United States, police powers are intentionally limited in breadth and depth so that no single law enforcement agency or government jurisdiction has too much power. Further, there is a premium on local control. Police agencies with the greatest scope of powers tend to be local. Americans and American politicians have historically been more inclined to bestow greater law enforcement authority on agencies over which citizens have the greatest control, through elected official (mayors, city council members, sheriffs). In the town of 500 people mentioned earlier, it is safe to say that any citizen could contact the police chief and voice a grievance with relative ease. It would be much more difficult for that same citizen to get an audience with the FBI director.

Today in the United States, there are 12,666 local police departments. There are also 3,070 sheriff's departments. Further, 49 states maintain some type of uniformed state police or state patrol organization; Hawaii is the lone exception. The decentralized nature of American law enforcement provides some advantages and significant disadvantages. These advantages and disadvantages mirror those identified by political scientist Thomas Dye,[1] which accrue generally to American government entities.

The primary advantage of decentralized law enforcement in the United States has already been mentioned—the dispersion of power. Our system of government is purposefully federal. Federalism is the form of government where power is divided between the national and state governments, with each state maintaining its sovereignty in relation to other states. The federal model extends to local jurisdictions within each state. By dispersing police power across thousands of governmental entities in the United States, the risk of unchecked tyranny by government using its enforcement apparatus is greatly diminished.

Another advantage of the decentralized nature of American law enforcement is that law enforcement efforts are more manageable and efficient—at least locally. As it is, a common complaint among police officers relates to the bureaucratic hassles and red tape associated with their jobs. This complaint's merit would be significantly compounded if decisions affecting local law enforcement operations had to pass a gauntlet of scrutiny from bureaucrats stationed in state capitals located many miles away or in Washington, D.C.

Akin to the benefit of manageability is accountability and responsiveness to the public. Even though some police organizations are very large in comparison to others, there is no national police force within which officers and managers can bury themselves and their actions to avoid public scrutiny. The chain of command for all law enforcement agencies in the United States ultimately leads to a civilian public official who is accountable to regular citizens. Given the decentralized nature of law enforcement, the relative influence of individual citizens on police practice and strategies in their communities is greater than if there were fewer and larger police agencies around the country.

Still another advantage of decentralized law enforcement is that there is an opportunity to observe many different ways of policing and to identify best practices within the profession. With so many local and state law enforcement agencies independent of each other, there are likewise many examples of successes and failures of police work.

Innovations that work in a larger community do not necessarily work as well in a smaller one, and vice versa. Directed problem-solving approaches to policing in one county may be inappropriate in another because the problems from one county to another are different. Indeed, America's decentralized law enforcement structure affords communities the chance to tailor policing efforts to their own specific local needs.

While the advantages of a decentralized law enforcement structure in the United States are many, there are also significant disadvantages. One is the fact that the quality of police services from community to community and state to state is uneven. Some communities have police departments that are professional, well-trained, sufficiently staffed, and adequately funded, while others do not. Such disparities in the provision of public services have long fueled criticism of federalism. Critics point out that wealthier communities, counties, and states can deliver better, more professional police services than can impoverished locales.

Another disadvantage is the inability of the federal government to mandate to the states and local governments specific public policy in the area of policing. For example, if the federal government determines that community-oriented policing is a model worth implementing around the country, only a limited amount can be done by the national government to ensure that implementation of its suggested policy takes place. Typically, the federal government can provide or withhold funds or other benefits to encourage state and local governments to follow its lead, but it cannot simply require that its will be done around the country.

Yet another disadvantage of decentralized law enforcement is the disjointed response to public safety problems. A crime spree of burglaries might take place across several suburbs of a metropolitan area. Each suburb may have its own police department investigating its portion of the crime spree without realizing the larger picture. Unless a concerted effort is made between law enforcement agencies to coordinate information, communications, operations, tactics, and so forth, public safety problems that overlap jurisdictions may receive inadequate or disconnected attention.

A Fourth disadvantage is the potential for competition between agencies that can promote an intentional lack of cooperation. Although many scholars have written about "police culture," there exists, in fact, many police subcultures; each views the other subcultures with some suspicion. While a police funeral will surely bring all of law enforcement together, the typical relationships across subcultures can frequently be strained.

City officers might hold the county deputies in contempt for always showing up and interfering with city matters. State troopers may similarly feel a little irritation at city police personnel who always respond to accident scenes under the jurisdiction of the state police or patrol. City and county officers may be united in their dislike for cocky troopers who, among all of law enforcement, are most likely to give a fellow officer a ticket. And state, county, and local law enforcement all have a common enemy in the "Feds," as federal agents frequently act as if they know it all, steal cases and publicity, and sometimes investigate other police officers.

THE U.S. CONSTITUTION AND FEDERAL POLICE POWER

The United States Constitution does not grant the federal government general police power. Instead, the Constitution reserves police powers for the states. In light of the absence of an affirmative statement granting the federal government broad police power, the 10th Amendment seems to be clearly saying that law enforcement is a function of state government:

The powers not delegated to the United States by the Constitution, nor prohibited by it to the States, are reserved to the States respectively, or to the people.

Given that nowhere in the Constitution is there an article or clause that specifically envisions a broad police power to be held by the federal government, it is reasonable to conclude from the 10th Amendment that police power would be one of many responsibilities of the individual states making up the Union. After all, the States were indeed sovereign. Sovereign governments can police their own people as they see fit.

Yet at the same time, other parts of the Constitution do seem to imply the existence of federal police power to enforce some criminal laws. Consider the following portions of the U.S. Constitution:

Article III, Section 3:

Treason against the United States, shall consist only in levying War against them, or in adhering to their Enemies, giving them Aid and Comfort. No

Person shall be convicted of Treason unless on the Testimony of two Witnesses to the same overt Act, or on Confession in open Court.

The Congress shall have Power to declare the Punishment of Treason…

While treason is narrowly defined in the Constitution, it does nonetheless amount to a criminal offense expressly assigned to the federal government, through Congress' role as legislature (and presumably the President's role as chief executive), for investigation and prosecution.

There is also the Necessary and Proper Clause of the Constitution. The final sentence of Section 8 within Article I of the Constitution states that Congress has the power:

To make all Laws which shall be necessary and proper for carrying into the Execution the foregoing Powers, and all other Powers vested by this Constitution in the Government of the United States, or in any Department or Officer thereof.

The "foregoing Powers" refer to those explicit powers granted to Congress in Section 8, including the following powers:

- To regulate Commerce with foreign Nations and among the several States and with the Indian Tribes;
- To establish an uniform Rule of Naturalization, and uniform Laws on the subject of Bankruptcies throughout the United States;
- To provide for the Punishment of counterfeiting the Securities and current Coin of the United States;
- To define and punish Piracies and Felonies committed on the high Seas, and Offenses against the Law of Nations;
- To provide for calling forth the Militia to execute the Laws of the Union, and suppress Insurrections and repel Invasions.

Each of these powers implies a federal law enforcement function.

Further, the catchall phrase from the Necessary and Proper Clause, which gives Congress the authority to make laws that are needed for the carrying out of "all other Powers" granted to it, has been interpreted by some as giving the federal government a fairly broad police power. In fact, many point to the Preamble of the Constitution for instruction on the scope of the federal government's responsibilities, and by extension, the authority to carry out those responsibilities. The Preamble declares that the people of the United States in ordaining the Constitution, seeks to "…establish Justice, insure domestic

Tranquility, provide for the common defence, promote the general Welfare, and secure the Blessings of Liberty…" for present and future generations of Americans.

If the Preamble represents the purpose of the U.S. Constitution and the federal government it creates, then the Necessary and Proper Clause seems to suggest that Congress has considerable leeway to pass laws and create agencies that do those very things that the Preamble articulates—namely, establishing justice, keeping the peace, and protecting the welfare of Americans.

Critics of that position contend that the Preamble merely states the purpose of the Constitution. That is, it introduces the document; it does not serve as a clause of it. The Preamble is not legally binding, according to this view, because it is a statement of ideals, not of specific powers granted to specific recipients.

Still other elements of the Constitution that clearly envision a federal law enforcement role, however limited, are certain amendments found in the Bill of Rights. The Bill of Rights is the first 10 Amendments to the Constitution. Their quick inclusion in the Constitution was a compromise to get the Constitution adopted between pro-Constitution Federalists and the Anti-federalists, who were suspicious of federal power. The Bill of Rights primarily protects individuals from an overzealous national government, including in criminal justice contexts. This fact implies that the Framers envisioned the federal government engaged in criminal justice activities.

Consider the 4th, 5th, 6th, and 8th Amendments to the Constitution—all ratified in 1791.

4th Amendment – The right of the people to be secure in their persons, houses, papers, and effects, against unreasonable searches and seizures, shall not be violated, and no Warrants shall issue, but upon probable cause, supported by Oath or affirmation, and particularly describing the place to be searched, and the persons or things to be seized.

5th Amendment – No person shall be held to answer for a capital, or otherwise infamous crime, unless on a presentment or indictment of a Grand Jury, except in cases arising in the land or naval forces, or in the Militia, when in actual service in time of War or public danger; nor shall any person be subject for the same offence to be twice put in jeopardy of life or limb; nor shall be compelled in any criminal case to be a witness against himself, nor be deprived of life, liberty, or property, without due process of law; nor shall private property be taken for public use, without just compensation.

6th Amendment – In all criminal prosecutions, the accused shall enjoy the right to a speedy and public trial, by an impartial jury of the State and district wherein the crime shall have been committed, which district shall have been previously ascertained by law, and to be informed of the nature and cause of the accusation; to be confronted with the witnesses against him; to have compulsory process for obtaining witnesses in his favor, and to have the Assistance of Counsel for his defense.

8th Amendment – Excessive bail shall not be required, nor excessive fines imposed, nor cruel and unusual punishments inflicted.

In recent decades, the limitations imposed upon government vis-à-vis individual criminal suspects and defendants have been applied to state and local criminal justice actions through the amendments' incorporation into the 14th Amendment of the Constitution. The 14th Amendment specifically requires of state and local governments their conformance with due process. Since the adoption of the 14th Amendment in 1868, the U.S. Supreme Court has ruled in an accumulation of cases that the "due process" required of law enforcement at the state and local level encompasses the very notions contained in the 4th, 5th, 6th, and 8th Amendments.

However, in 1791, these amendments addressed the police powers of one government in particular—the federal government. Therefore, there can be little doubt in the existence of the 18th century supposition that the American federal government indeed possessed police power. Otherwise, there would be no need to describe under what conditions searches and seizures of suspects and evidence could take place (4th Amendment); the process requirements for charging and trying violators of federal crimes (5th and 6th Amendments); the right of criminal defendants in federal cases to have the assistance of counsel and to have their cases heard by an impartial jury (6th Amendment); and the conditions under which someone can be held in custody or otherwise punished prior to and after a conviction of a federal crime (8th Amendment).

The existence of federal police power notwithstanding, there is also little doubt that the power was thought to be more limited than that possessed generally by the states. The notion of limited federal police power was reinforced on many occasions in the Federalists Papers. The Federalists Papers were a series of essays written by James Madison (commonly considered the Constitution's chief author), Alexander Hamilton, and John Jay. These essays were written prior to the adoption of the U.S. Constitution and in support of that adoption.

In some cases, the authors of the Federalist Papers (all of whom took the pen name "Publius" when these essays appeared in newspapers) went to great lengths to remind Americans that this new Constitution, which granted significantly expanded powers to the federal government when compared to the Articles of Confederation that it would replace, was nonetheless sensitive to the sovereignty of the states. In other words, Madison, Hamilton, and Jay all held to the view that the Constitution would properly limit the role of the federal government and any inclination it had to become tyrannical; therefore, they argued, people had little to fear from the Constitution's adoption.

In *Federalist 41*, James Madison confronts the concern raised by many who opposed the proposed constitution. Many critics objected to Article I, Section 8, which first grants the federal government the power to tax so as to "...provide for the common Defence and general Welfare of the United States." Indeed, some of the same language of the Preamble appears in Section 8 to justify Congress' need to levy taxes and pay debts. What then follows are the many additional enumerated powers of Congress, including some of those with criminal justice implications that were mentioned earlier in the chapter.

Madison mocks the critics' concern by pointing out that the specified, enumerated powers listed in Section 8 are the embodiment of Congress' fulfillment of providing for the common defense and general welfare. In other words, according to Madison, common defense and general welfare are expressions with particular manifestations— namely those that are enumerated immediately after those expressions appear.

Madison wrote in Federalist 41:[2]

Some, who have not denied the necessity of the power of taxation, have grounded a very fierce attack against the Constitution, on the language in which it is defined. It has been urged and echoed, that the power "to lay and collect taxes, duties, imposts, and excises, to pay the debts, and provide for the common defense and general welfare of the United States," amounts to an unlimited commission to exercise every power which may be alleged to be necessary for the common defense or general welfare. No stronger proof could be given of the distress under which these writers labor for objections, than their stooping to such a misconstruction.

Had no other enumeration or definition of the powers of the Congress been found in the Constitution, than the general expressions just cited, the authors of the objection might have had some color for it; though it would have been difficult to find a reason for so awkward a form of describing an authority to legislate in all possible cases. A power to destroy the freedom of the press, the trial by jury, or even to regulate the course of descents, or the forms of conveyances, must be very singularly expressed by the terms "to raise money for the general welfare".

But what color can the objection have, when a specification of the objects alluded to by these general terms immediately follows, and is not even separated by a longer pause than a semicolon? If the different parts of the same instrument ought to be so expounded, as to give meaning to every part which will bear it, shall one part of the same sentence be excluded altogether from a share in the meaning; and shall the more doubtful and indefinite terms be retained in their full extent, and the clear and precise expressions be denied any signification whatsoever? For what purpose could the enumeration of particular powers be inserted, if these and all others were meant to be included in the preceding general power? Nothing is more natural nor common than first to use a general phrase, and then to explain and qualify it by a recital of particulars. But the idea of an enumeration of particulars which neither explain nor qualify the general meaning, and can have no other effect than to confound and mislead, is an absurdity, which, as we are reduced to the dilemma of charging either on the authors of the objection or on the authors of the Constitution, we must take the liberty of supposing, had not its origin with the latter.

Madison was also instructive in *Federalist 45*. In that article, Madison addressed the concern that the power of the states would be subordinated to the federal government. That was a grave concern for many Anti-federalists who found the Necessary and Proper Clause especially offensive in light of Article VI, which stated: "This Constitution and the Laws of the United States... shall be the supreme Law of the Land; and the Judges in every State shall be bound thereby, any Thing in the Constitution or Laws of any State to the Contrary notwithstanding."

Madison wrote in *Federalist 45*:[3]

Having shown that no one of the powers transferred to the federal government is unnecessary or improper, the next question to be considered is, whether the whole mass of them will be dangerous to the portion of authority left in the several States...

The powers delegated by the proposed Constitution to the federal government are few and defined. Those which are to remain in the State governments are numerous and indefinite. The former will be exercised principally on external objects, as war, peace, negotiation, and foreign commerce; with which last the power of taxation will, for the most part, be connected. The powers reserved to the several States will extend to all the objects which, in the ordinary course of affairs, concern the lives, liberties, and properties of the people, and the internal order, improvement, and prosperity of the State.

The operations of the federal government will be most extensive and important in times of war and danger; those of the State governments, in times of peace and security. As the former periods will probably bear a small proportion to the latter, the State governments will here enjoy another advantage over the federal government. The more adequate, indeed, the federal powers may be rendered to the national defense, the less frequent will be those scenes of danger which might favor their ascendancy over the governments of the particular States.

It is clear from the preceding passage—especially in the second paragraph—that Madison, who is by all accounts a key Framer of the Constitution and our present form of government, envisioned that general powers, including law enforcement powers, would rest with states, save for some national emergency exigencies such as war.

Earlier in the chapter, it was noted that many of the provisions of the Bill of Rights (i.e., the first 10 amendments) imply the existence of police power because certain amendments relate specifically to the criminal justice functions of government. Alexander Hamilton wrote *Federalist 84* to address, in part, that very subject. At the time that the Federalist Papers were written by Madison, Hamilton, and Jay, no Bill of Rights had yet been proposed. The promise of pro-Constitution federalists to adopt a Bill of Rights came later as a compromise for ensuring passage of the Constitution itself by indecisive state legislatures.

In Federalist 84, Hamilton reasoned against the inclusion of a Bill of Rights because it would imply powers of the federal government that do not exist. He wrote:[4]

The most considerable of the remaining objections is that the plan of the convention contains no bill of rights...

But a minute detail of particular rights is certainly far less applicable to a Constitution like that under consideration, which is merely intended to regulate the general political interests of the nation, than to a constitution which has the regulation of every species of personal and private concerns. If, therefore, the loud clamors against the plan of the convention, on this score, are well founded, no epithets of reprobation will be too strong for the constitution of this State. But the truth is, that both of them contain all which, in relation to their objects, is reasonably to be desired.

I go further, and affirm that bills of rights, in the sense and to the extent in which they are contended for, are not only unnecessary in the proposed Constitution, but would even be dangerous. They would contain various exceptions to powers not granted; and, on this very account, would afford a colorable pretext to claim more than were granted. For why declare that things shall not be done which there is no power to do? Why, for instance, should it be said that the liberty of the press shall not be restrained, when no power is given by which restrictions may be imposed? I will not contend that such a provision would confer a regulating power; but it is evident that it would furnish, to men disposed to usurp, a plausible pretense for claiming that power. They might urge with a semblance of reason, that the Constitution ought not to be charged with the absurdity of providing against the abuse of an authority which was not given, and that the provision against restraining the liberty of the press afforded a clear implication, that a power to prescribe proper regulations concerning it was intended to be vested in the national government. This may serve as a specimen of the numerous handles which would be given to the doctrine of constructive powers, by the indulgence of an injudicious zeal for bills of rights.

On the subject of the liberty of the press, as much as has been said, I cannot forbear adding a remark or two: in the first place, I observe, that there is not a syllable concerning it in the constitution of this State; in the next, I contend, that whatever has been said about it in that of any other State, amounts to nothing. What signifies a declaration, that "the liberty of the press shall be inviolably preserved"? What is the liberty of the press? Who can give it any definition which would not leave the utmost latitude for evasion? I hold it to be impracticable; and from this I infer, that its security, whatever fine declarations may be inserted in any constitution respecting it, must altogether depend on public opinion, and on the general spirit of the people and of the government. And here, after all, as is intimated upon another occasion, must we seek for the only solid basis of all our rights.

INTERSTATE COMMERCE

The power of the American federal government to engage in law enforcement activities has expanded considerably in practice since the late 18th century and the adoption of the U.S. Constitution. As already noted, there are many provisions of the Constitution that specifically envision a federal law enforcement role. For example, treason against the United States is a federal offense and requires Congress to craft punishments for that crime. The Constitution also speaks to Congress' power to regulate immigration and to pass tariffs. Those who would violate immigration or customs laws would necessarily be violating criminal laws that are the exclusive domain of the federal government.

Whether speaking of treason, immigration violations, or violations of import or export laws in order to circumvent tariffs, violators face federal prosecution. It is reasonable to conclude that law enforcement officials acting on behalf of the federal government (federal agents) should necessarily exist and be equipped with the power to bring violators of federal law to justice.

However, much of federal law enforcement today is not concerned with the issues mentioned here—or at least is not primarily concerned with them. The federal criminal code is extremely large and covers many types of criminal conduct that could not have been envisioned by the Constitution's framers.

The federal criminal laws of the United States are found primarily (but not exclusively) in Title 18 of the United States Code. Well over 100 chapters (see Appendix A) appear in Title 18. Each chapter relates broadly to an area of criminal law. Each chapter typically contains several sections, and each section deals with a specific criminal offense that could be investigated and adjudicated as a federal offense, regardless of whether comparable state laws exist that would address the same criminal conduct.

On what basis has the federal government (Congress) passed so many criminal laws that require tens of thousands of federal agents to enforce? For most of these laws, the constitutional nexus for their passage and enforcement is the Interstate Commerce Clause. As noted earlier, Article I, Section 8 of the Constitution gives Congress the power to regulate commerce with foreign countries as well as among and between the states of the Union. This power has become the primary basis for the federal government's involvement in criminal matters. In some cases, the criminal statutes adopted and enforced by the federal government can be rather obscure.

Consider Section 1821 of the federal criminal code (18 USC 1821). It reads:

Whoever transports by mail or otherwise to or within the District of Columbia or any Possession of the United States or uses the mails or any instrumentality of interstate commerce for the purpose of sending or bringing into any State or Territory any set of artificial teeth or prosthetic dental appliance or other denture, constructed from any cast or impression made by any person other than, or without the authorization or prescription of, a person licensed to practice dentistry under the laws of the place into which such denture is sent or brought, where such laws prohibit;

(1) the taking of impressions or casts of the human mouth or teeth by a person not licensed under such laws to practice dentistry;

(2) the construction or supply of dentures by a person other than, or without the authorization or prescription of, a person licensed under such laws to practice dentistry; or

(3) the construction or supply of dentures from impressions or casts made by a person not licensed under such laws to practice dentistry.

Shall be fined under this title or imprisoned not more than one year, or both.

Congress has determined it necessary and proper to regulate the practice of dentistry through this statute by insisting that those engaged in the business of providing dentures are licensed. Every American state also has laws regulating the practice of dentistry. Many proponents of limited federal government argue that it is the respective states where such laws should originate. Nonetheless, in an effort to help maintain high standards of dental practice, Congress made it a federal criminal offense to engage in dispensing dentures without a license (ironically, the licensing process is itself a state-level process).

Commonly present in federal criminal laws is language similar to that which appears in the opening sentence of the above statute: "Whoever…uses the mail or any instrumentality of interstate commerce…" There is no provision for regulating the quality of dentures or the licensing of dentists in the Constitution. However, Congress is permitted—indeed expected—to regulate the mail and interstate commerce. To the extent that the dispensing of dentures involves interstate commerce, Congress has seen fit to legislate the matter. Because it has done so by creating a criminal law, the enforcement of this statute is part of the job of federal law enforcement.

Of course, not all federal criminal laws are as obscure as the statute just described. Many criminal laws of the United States are intended to accomplish things that are considered more urgent and serious. However, even noble and well-intentioned federal criminal laws must have roots in federal authority; further, it is not always the case that the power to regulate interstate commerce is sufficient to trigger proper federal authority.

In 1990, Congress passed the Gun Free School Zones Act. Title 18, Section 922 was amended to make it a federal felony-level crime to knowingly possess a firearm while inside a school zone. A "school zone" was defined as that area within 1,000 feet of the grounds of a public, private, or parochial school. Proponents of this legislation noted that Congress had the authority to pass the law because of the power to regulate interstate commerce that was granted to it by the Constitution.

But when 12th grader Alfonso Lopez was arrested at his high school for carrying a concealed handgun and was charged federally under the Gun Free School Zones Act, his attorney disputed the authority of the federal government to even pass such a law into existence. The Supreme Court heard Lopez' contention in 1995 and ruled that Congress indeed exceeded its authority in passing this law. Therefore, the Gun Free School Zones Act was ruled unconstitutional.

At the time, Bill Clinton was President of the United States. Gun control was one campaign issue that President Clinton had ran upon—and indeed delivered. His administration vehemently defended that statute. Despite this effort, the Supreme Court ruled in a 5-4 decision that the law was unconstitutional. Chief Justice William Rehnquist, author of the majority opinion, summarized the logic behind the government's defense of the statute:[5]

Possession of a firearm in a school zone may result in violent crime and that violent crime can be expected to affect the functioning of the national economy in two ways. First, the costs of violent crime are substantial and, through the mechanism of insurance, those costs are spread throughout the population. Second, violent crime reduces the willingness of individuals to travel to areas within the country that are perceived unsafe.

It was further argued that the fear of guns in schools distracts students from learning. The government's position was that: "…the presence of guns in schools poses a substantial threat to the educational cational process, in turn, will result in a less productive citizenry. That, in turn, would have an adverse effect on the Nation's economic well-being. As a result, the Government argues that Congress could rationally have concluded that [the Gun-Free School Zones Act] substantially affects interstate commerce."

In other words, the government believed that if students fail to learn, then they may fail to graduate and succeed later in life. If that happens, the failures will result in an adverse impact on the economy—not only in their own states, but also in other states that never benefited from the interstate commerce these students would have engaged in had they been successful and made positive societal contributions.

Five Supreme Court justices ruled that this logic, if upheld, would permit the federal government to connect any and all issues for which there was a desire to regulate to the Interstate Commerce Clause. The Court wrote:[6]

To uphold the Government's contentions here, we would have to pile inference upon inference in a manner that would bid fair to convert congressional authority under the Commerce Clause to a general police power of the sort retained by the States. Admittedly, some of our prior cases have taken long steps down that road, giving great deference to congressional action.… The broad language in these opinions has suggested the possibility of additional expansion, but we decline here to proceed any further. To do so would require us to conclude that the Constitution's enumeration of powers does not presuppose something not enumerated,...and that there never will be a distinction between what is truly national and what is truly local...This we are unwilling to do.

The Supreme Court in this case determined that there were limits to the federal government's role in matters of criminal justice—particularly when the rationale for the government's involvement is rooted in notions of interstate commerce.

In the Lopez case, several justices chose to write opinions that concurred with or dissented from the majority opinion written by Chief Justice Rehnquist. All of the opinions in this case referred back to the 1824 case of Gibbons v. Ogden. In that case, the United States Supreme Court under Chief Justice John Marshall ruled that the Commerce Clause of the Constitution conferred broad authority upon Congress to regulate commercial matters.

At issue was the fact that the State of New York had granted certain individuals the right to operate their steamboats in New York waters. A steamboat operator from New Jersey who did business between New York and New Jersey challenged the New York law that required him to pay special operating fees while other select individuals paid nothing.

Gibbons v. Ogden did not relate to criminal justice. The case genuinely related to commerce. But the Supreme Court for the first time provided the Interstate Commerce Clause of the Constitution with a dynamic characterization. The language in the Court's decision was used in future cases as the basis for arguing for the authority of Congress to regulate matters beyond mere trade occurring between the states.

Chief Justice Marshall wrote for a unanimous court in defining what interstate commerce essentially means. He wrote:[7]

The subject to be regulated is commerce;...it becomes necessary to settle the meaning of the word. The counsel for the appellee would limit it to traffic, to buying and selling, or the interchange of commodities, and do not admit that it comprehends navigation....Commerce, undoubtedly, is traffic, but it is something more: it is intercourse....The mind can scarcely conceive a system for regulating commerce between nations, which shall exclude all laws concerning navigation....

The subject to which the power is...applied, is to commerce "among the several States." The word "among" means intermingled with. A thing which is among others, is intermingled with them. Commerce among the States, cannot stop at the external boundary line of each State, but may be introduced into the interior.

It is not intended to say that these words comprehend that commerce, which is completely internal, which is carried on between man and man in a State, or between different parts of the same State, and which does not extend to or affect other States. Such a power would be inconvenient, and is certainly unnecessary.

Comprehensive as the word among is, it may very properly be restricted to that commerce which concerns more States than one. The phrase is not one which would probably have been selected to indicate the completely interior traffic of a State, because it is not an apt phrase for that purpose....The genius and character of the whole government seem to be, that its action is to be applied to all the external concerns of the nation, and to those internal concerns which affect the States generally; but not to those which are completely within a particular State, which do not affect other States, and with which it is not necessary to interfere, for the purpose of executing some of the general powers of the government. The completely internal commerce of a State, then, may be considered as reserved for the State itself.

It is the power to regulate, that is, to prescribe the rule by which commerce is to be governed. This power, like all others vested in Congress, is complete in itself, may be exercised to its utmost extent, and acknowledges no limitations other than are prescribed in the Constitution. These are expressed in plain terms, and do not affect the questions which arise in this case, or which have been discussed at the bar. If, as has always been understood, the sovereignty of Congress, though limited to specified objects, is plenary as to those objects, the power over commerce with foreign nations, and among the several States, is vested in Congress as absolutely as it would be in a single government, having in its Constitution the same restrictions on the exercise of the power as are found in the Constitution of the United States.

The language of the Chief Justice Marshall's opinion provided ammunition for both sides of the Lopez decision. Commerce is not merely "traffic"...it is "intercourse." Further, the ability to regulate it is a power of Congress "complete in itself." But also, the power to regulate commerce does not extend to those matters with only internal relevance to a particular state. Such matters, even those affecting commerce, are left to the states themselves, according to the Gibbons decision, as long as there is no affect on other states.

In the end, Congress' willingness to rely on the Interstate Commerce Clause of the Constitution to enact legislation—including criminal laws and other statutes that create the executive police agencies that enforce those laws and statutes—has usually been the result of political rather than judicial processes. When the American people have put political pressure on their elected representatives to do something, something has usually been done. This fact was no doubt envisioned and sanctioned (at least somewhat) by John Marshall when he concluded in the Gibbons decision:

"The wisdom and the discretion of Congress, their identity with the people, and the influence which their constituents possess at elections are, in this, as in many other instances, as that, for example, of declaring war, the sole restraints on which they have relied, to secure them from its abuse. They are the restraints on which the people must often they solely, in all representative governments."

CHAPTER 2

Federal Law Enforcement Takes Root in America (1700–1850s)

A number of significant events occurred during the 18th century and early 19th century that are relevant to the growth of federal law enforcement in America. Chief among these events was the creation of a distinct American government. In 1776, the fledgling would-be country known as the United States of America declared its independence from Great Britain. The United States went on to win that improbable independence by fighting a war with Great Britain that raged from 1775 to 1783.

The new nation that was the United States went on to adopt a confederation form of government through the Articles of Confederation. That document provided for a very weak federal government and strong, sovereign states, which is the nature of any confederation government. The parts are more powerful individually than the whole. Thus, there was little need for federal law enforcement; the federal government had virtually no authority to create laws that would need to be enforced.

After a half-decade of operating under this arrangement—an arrangement in which states routinely ignored the treaties negotiated by the federal government and in which federal officials could only hold their breath in hope of payment of salaries (because the federal coffers were perpetually low)—the United States in 1789 adopted the present Constitution (without the amendments). The Constitution created a government with federalism as its foundation. That is, the new form of government provided for a viable, but limited, national government that would share power with the sovereign states. Further, in matters where the federal government would be involved, the federal government, its laws, and certainly the Constitution, would be supreme. Now there would be a need for some amount of police power exercised at the federal level because there would clearly be federal laws needing enforcement.

During the same period of time (late 1700s and early 1800s), significant changes in the nature of law enforcement occurred in the United States and abroad—particularly in Great Britain. Despite fighting a war of independence with Mother England and another war with that country in 1812, the United States embraced much of England's legal traditions and government practices when it crafted its own laws and government apparatus.

THE ORIGINS OF LAW ENFORCEMENT INSTITUTIONS

From the late 13th century through the 18th century, England and its colonies utilized the Parish-Constable Watch system of law enforcement.[1] Under this system, each parish or town would appoint at least two unpaid constables, usually selected by lot. Constables in turn selected night watchmen to assist them in their duties. When a constable or night watchman, later called a bailiff, would come across a crime in progress, the practice was to call out to anyone and everyone who could hear him. In fact, English law made it a crime in its own right for an able-bodied citizen to ignore the "hue and cry" of a night watchman. English law further required citizens to keep weapons in their homes for the purpose of rendering such assistance.[2] These same citizens were also expected to join a posse, if necessary, to capture offenders. Posses were led by the chief law enforcement official in the shire (county). This official was known as the "shire reeve," from which the word "sheriff" is derived.[3]

In the 1700s, particularly after the advent of gin, which was amazingly cheap for an intoxicating beverage, English urban areas became frequent sites of riots. Criminal justice scholar Frank Schmallager notes that huge numbers of people living in London's industrial ghettos began binges of drinking and rioting to drown out their social and economic hardships—which were legion. The night watchmen proved to be woefully incapable of dealing with the riots. In fact, the watchmen became targets of mob violence to the point of frequently being beaten for sport.[4]

The alternative to the watchmen when things were out of control was to call upon the military. Under the English Riot Act, troops could be called out "in aid of the civil power."[5] In one encounter after another, the military was used to quell riotous disorder. The military customarily put an end to each riot with the finesse of a sledgehammer. For example, in 1818, British soldiers were called out to put down a riot in Manchester, England. In the process of doing so, they killed 11 civilians and wounded 500.

It was after the Manchester riot, and others with similar results, that British politicians began to seriously look at the option of forming a police force to handle civil disorder. After all, the objection to creating a police force because it would constitute fielding troops in the streets was negated by the fact that real troops were frequently fielded because of the lack of a police force.

Probably the single most significant event in police history— certainly in British and American police history—was the British passage of the Metropolitan Police Act of 1829. This piece of legislation, submitted to Parliament by Home Secretary Sir Robert Peel, created the first modern police force. Samuel Walker[6] described a "modern police force" as one employing full-time officers who engage in continuous patrol of fixed beats for the purpose of preventing crime.

Immediately after the Act's passage, the Metropolitan Police Force (commonly referred to as the "Met," then and now) was formally established. The Met employed nearly 1,000 officers. Within a year, over 3,300 officers were working for it. Officers were equipped with a uniform, a short baton, and a rattle, which was to be used to raise an alarm when necessary. The rattle would eventually be replaced by a whistle. Each constable, nicknamed "bobbies" in honor of Robert Peel, was issued a number that they wore on the collar, thus making them immediately identifiable to the public.[7]

In the United States, modern police departments arose under remarkably similar circumstances as those existing in Great Britain. From the 1830s to the 1870s, there was an unprecedented amount of civil disorder occurring throughout the industrial United States. Very few cities escaped serious rioting and mob violence. The civil upheaval was often rooted in ethnic fighting due to the massive influx of immigrants during that time period. There was also violence rooted in economic hardship, resulting in banks and businesses being ransacked by angry customers or employees.[8]

As had been the case in England, there was no continuous police presence in most of America's urban centers in the early 19th century. The night watch was largely the only official mechanism in place, short of troops, to confront the frequent outbreak of mob violence—and it was only available at night.

In one major city after another, the response was the same. Police departments began to be formed throughout the middle of the 19th century in America's urban centers to keep the peace. Although American police forces were modeled after London's metropolitan force, there were some significant differences between the English and American models.

Chief among the differences was the political orientation of American police. The Met was a creation of the national government in England, while America's police departments were installed by city governments acting under the auspices of sovereign state authority. This made American police officers much more a part of the political machinery than their federally created London counterparts. Police officers were usually recruited by political leaders of a given ward or precinct, and they served at the pleasure of the political leadership. An excellent example of this—although outside of the time frame that is the focus of this chapter—is the Cincinnati Police Department. In that city, after an election in 1880 in which the party in power changed, 219 of the 295 members on the police force were dismissed. Six years later, after another political power shift, 238 of the 289 patrolmen and 8 of 16 lieutenants were removed.[9]

Federal law enforcement in the United States, however, was not as subject to the political whims of local officials. In this sense, federal law enforcement officers—although few in number and limited in scope of power—possessed greater freedom to be professional, much like the members of the British Metropolitan Police.

THE FIRST FEDERAL LAW ENFORCEMENT OFFICERS

There is actually some debate over just who the first federal law enforcement officers were. Depending on who one talks to, the oldest federal law enforcement agency in America is either the U.S. Customs Service (now the U.S. Immigration and Customs Enforcement), the U.S. Coast Guard, the U.S. Postal Inspection Service, or the U.S. Marshals Service. In fact, some might even argue that the Federal Protective Service, the U.S. Park Police, or the U.S. Capitol Police is the oldest federal law enforcement agency. Ultimately, the determination is not that important. Each of these entitities had a role in early American law enforcement—or at least their ones that were predecessors did.

In the late 18th century and early 19th century, federal law enforcement was organized around mission just as it is today. At that time, broadly speaking, federal law enforcement agencies were concerned with essentially four missions: taxes and tariffs, the postal system, securing public facilities, and the judicial system (with miscellaneous duties attached).

TAXES AND TARIFFS

Many federal law enforcement agencies today trace their heritage back to the mission of enforcing tax and tariff laws of the young American nation-state. These agencies include the Bureau of Immigration and Customs Enforcement (which includes the investigative elements of U.S. Customs), the U.S. Coast Guard, and the Internal Revenue Service.

The importance of revenue collection for the United States after gaining its independence cannot be overstated. After the Revolutionary War, the United States was nearly bankrupt due to war-related debt. Further, a few years of operation under the Articles of Confederation exacerbated the inability of the United States to pay down its debt. Although the states were thriving, their contributions to federal coffers was anemic. The financial health of the United States was in critical condition. America would have to find a way to effectively collect revenues.

In a general sense, things began to turn around with the ratification of the new Constitution, which allotted real (albeit limited) power to the federal government. In fact, where the federal government had a role assigned to it by the Constitution, the federal government's authority would be supreme over the states. One such assigned role was the determination of how imports and exports would be taxed.

On July 4, 1789, President George Washington signed into law the Tariff Act of 1789. This legislation authorized the federal government to collect duties for goods coming into the country from other nations. Later that month, Congress passed a law that established what would become the Customs Service.[10] That law also established the official ports of entry to the country. This, the Fifth Act of Congress, created the first federal agency, Customs.

Customs, by that statute, was an agency created to "regulate the Collection of Duties imposed by law on the tonnage of ships or vessels, and on goods, wares, and merchandises imported into the United States".[11] The law provided for 59 collection districts and over 100 ports of delivery. For each district, a presidentially appointed "Collector" was authorized, along with an appropriation for 10 naval officers and 33 surveyors to aid in collection efforts. This new customs organization was to be housed under the authority of the Secretary of the Treasury.

This Customs agency was the chief provider of federal funds during the nation's first 125 years. Through the taxes on imports and exports, the salaries of the nation's military and civilian employees were paid. In fact, the collection of customs-related taxes was so effective that the national debt was paid off by 1835.[12]

In 1792, 80% of all Treasury Department employees—500 in all—were working in the offices of Collectors. A Customs House could be found in many cities and in every state. Some ports of entry were more important than others. By the middle of the 19th century, the customs revenues collected in the City of New York alone amounted to 75 percent of all customs revenues collected and forwarded to the Treasury Department annually.[13]

Interestingly, Customs represented the only armed naval force of the United States until 1798, when Congress created the Department of the Navy. In 1790, Congress passed legislation that authorized the construction of 10 warships to be used for enforcing tariff and trade laws, and for preventing smuggling and piracy. This branch of the U.S. Treasury Department's customs operation came to be known as the Revenue Cutter Service—the direct ancestor of the United States Coast Guard.[14]

Coast Guard historians are quick to point out the significance of the Revenue Cutter Service in the overall collection efforts of the Treasury Department. During the first 10 years of service, the taxes on imports and exports rose from $52 million to $205 million; much of the increase in collection is thought to be due to the efforts of the cutters.

Many in the United States were not terribly happy with armed warships infringing upon their abilities to engage in free trade. In one example, the State of South Carolina (always independent-minded) attempted to nullify tariff laws in 1832. Five revenue cutters were sent in to Charleston harbor to ensure that vessels carrying goods from foreign ports were subject to the tariffs and that customs collectors had an opportunity to do just that—collect. President Andrew Jackson made it known that the cutters would not hesitate to use force and that any who would shed "a single drop of blood...in opposition to the laws of the United States" would be hanged.[15]

The Revenue Cutter Service also participated in the law enforcement function of fighting pirates. For example, in 1819, the cutters *Alabama and Louisiana* fought and captured the pirate vessel *Bravo*, which was commanded by Jean LaFarge, a lieutenant of the famous pirate Jean Lafitte. These two cutters also destroyed the pirate stronghold of Patterson's Town on Breton Island, Nova Scotia.[16]

Still another law enforcement duty of the young Revenue Cutter Service was the interception of contraband. In modern America, contraband is usually understood to mean illegal drugs or weapons. In the late 18th and early 19th century, contraband was chiefly illegally imported slaves. The United States had banned the uses of American vessels in the slave trade in 1794 and outlawed the introduction of any new African slaves in 1808 with the Anti-Slave Trade Act. In 1794, revenue cutters were given the task of preventing slave runners from getting to American shores with their illegal passengers/cargo, who had been kidnapped or sold on the continent of Africa. By halfway through the 19th century, several hundred would-be slaves were freed by Treasury officers assigned to these cutters, and numerous slave traders were captured and prosecuted.

POSTAL SERVICE

The U.S. Constitution gives the federal government the exclusive right to establish and regulate a national postal system. However, the first American postal system even pre-dates America's independence. In 1753, Benjamin Franklin was appointed Postmaster General of the colonial postal system. In 1772, he created the position of "surveyor," a position designed to assist with the regulation and auditing of postal functions. These surveyors, whose titles in 1801 would change to "special agents," are considered the ancestral lineage of the modern day Postal Inspection Service. Given that Postal Inspectors trace their history back to 1772, the Postal Inspection Service officially claims to be the oldest American law enforcement agency.[17]

In 1789, after the adoption of the Constitution, Congress temporarily established a national post office and formally created the Office of Postmaster General. At that time, there already were 75 post offices and about 2,000 miles of post roads that had previously existed under the postal systems of the American colonial and confederation governments. The Postal Service was permanently established as an agency of the United States by 1792. At that time, postal employees included the Postmaster General, a few surveyors, an Inspector of Dead Letters, and a couple of dozen post riders.[18]

In 1830, the Postal Service created an Office of Instructions and Mail Depredations. The role of that office was to serve as the investigative and inspection/audit branch of the Postal Service. The special agents in that office, and even the surveyors that preceded them, had a significant law enforcement role. From colonial times in the early 1770s until the middle part of the 1800s, postal officials pursued those engaged in embezzlement in the post offices and those who would rob mail riders and mail stagecoaches, steamboats, and trains. By 1853, the number of special agents working for the Post Office was 18, with each assigned to specific territories. These agents carried firearms and executed law enforcement powers as agents of the federal government.

SECURING PUBLIC FACILITIES

Today, there are a number of federal police agencies that serve as a security force for facilities operated and controlled by the federal government. These agencies include, but are not limited to, the Federal Protective Service, the U.S. Park Police, the U.S. Capitol Police, the U.S. Supreme Court Police, and the Uniformed Division of the Secret Service. All of these agencies can trace their respective missions back to the late 1700s.

In December of 1790, Congress convened for the first time in Philadelphia. Prior to that, the capital of the United States had been New York City. However, the United States government would temporarily move to Philadelphia until a new capital city, Washington DC, was sufficiently constructed to house the American government. Through the Residence Act of 1790, the United States government would be located in Philadelphia for 10 years while public buildings were constructed in the District of Columbia.[19]

Also in 1790, Congress appointed a commission to consider, among other things, how to protect the growing inventory of real property—whether under construction or completed—controlled by the newly empowered federal government. In that year, the commission hired six night watchmen to protect the buildings in Washington DC that would eventually become home to America's national government when the seat of power was moved from Philadelphia to the District of Columbia. Specifically, the buildings included those that would house the President, Congress, and several other public offices when the transfer of the nation's capital from Philadelphia to Washington DC took place.

By 1802, the commission's responsibility over the federal buildings was assumed by a superintendent. The overseeing of the watchmen's protective activities was transferred to the superintendent's office. In 1816, the superintendent's office was abolished and replaced with the Office of the Commissioner of Public Buildings. In 1849, when the Department of the Interior was established, the Commissioner of Public Buildings was transferred organizationally to that department.[20]

Washington DC became the capital of the United States in November of 1800. However, construction of public buildings continued for two and half decades after that. Throughout that time, the Capitol Building and its grounds were guarded by a single watchman at any given time. Several incidents in the 1820s, however, drew attention to the need for more security personnel.

The Capitol Building's rotunda was completed in 1824. With the completion of the rotunda, many more visitors came to the Capitol. This increase pushed the ability of the lone watchman to keep the facility secure to its limit. Additionally, in 1824, Washington DC was visited by dignitaries from France and other countries. These visits demonstrated the need for increased protective services. In 1825, there was a fire in the Capitol Building's library—an area generally left unattended. And in 1828, President John Quincy Adam's son was beaten in the Capitol rotunda. All of this led to an Act of Congress that extended the City of Washington's police protective duties to the Capitol Building and its grounds.[21]

On April 29, 1828, Congress created a police force for the Capitol Building and the immediate area around it. The duties of the Commissioner of this newly created force were explained in the statute:

"...that it shall be his duty to obey such rules and regulations, as may be, from time to time, prescribed by the Presiding Officer of either House of Congress, for the care, preservation, orderly keeping, and police of those portions of the Capitol and its appurtenances, which are in the exclusive use and occupation of either House of Congress, respectively; and, that it shall also be his duty to obey such rules and regulations, as may, from time to time, be prescribed by the President of the United States, for the care, preservation, orderly keeping, and police, of the other Public Buildings and Public Property, in the City of Washington, and the Commissioner and his assistants are hereby authorized and empowered to use all necessary and proper means for the discharge of the aforesaid duties; and the Commissioner and the assistants of the Commissioner shall receive a reasonable compensation for their services, to be allowed by the Presiding Officers of the two Houses of Congress...".[22]

This early Capitol Police force was given the authority to protect the grounds of the Capitol under the direction of the House of Representatives and the Senate, and to protect other public buildings controlled by the Executive branch under the direction of the President.

Initially, officers who worked for the Capitol Police did not wear uniforms and received very little formal training in duties related to law enforcement. Of course, in 1828, it was rare to find anyone involved in law enforcement, other than the military itself, who had received police training as such. In the case of the Capitol Police officers, their jurisdiction was sufficiently limited that training wasn't a significant priority. Indeed, they regularly engaged in non-police duties, such as serving as tour guides of the Capitol for visitors. They frequently relied on supplemental support from the Washington DC auxiliary guard to deal with public gatherings and to keep the peace.[23]

The experience of the Capitol Police serves as an early example of jurisdictional limitations, overlap, and confusion. The City of Washington, being a federal district, derived its authority from the federal government. In addition to watchmen authorized by Congress for the protection of public buildings, the city government was eventually given authority to extend its routine, municipal law enforcement function to federal property. In 1834, Congress declared that "the regulations of the city of Washington for the preservation of the public peace and order, be extended to all the public buildings and grounds belonging to the United States within the city of Washington whenever the application of the same shall be requested by the commissioner of the public buildings".[24] The language of this statute now enabled routine offenders—such as vagrants, disorderly persons, and others—to be treated routinely. The police would no longer need to use the cumbersome process of charging them with federal trespass. As soon as the law was passed, the commissioner of public buildings requested that city law enforcement regularly and routinely aid the federal watchmen with keeping public order and foiling crime on federal properties.[25]

For the remainder of the first half of the 19th century, federal and local authorities worked closely together to provide protection to the public buildings in the District. During that time, federal police agencies such as the Capitol Police and what would become the U.S. Park Police under the Interior Department began to evolve and professionalize as legitimate, uniformed police service providers.

THE JUDICIAL SYSTEM

The fourth and broadest mission of federal law enforcement in the late 18th and early 19th centuries was to support the judicial system. In other words, some agency with law enforcement powers had to necessarily exist in order to serve and enforce the processes and decisions of the federal courts. This mission fell on the U.S. Marshals Service.

The U.S. Marshals Service was created through the Judiciary Act of 1789. The historian of the U.S. Marshals Service claims that this organization was the first bone fide federal law enforcement agency; unlike postal surveyors, customs personnel, or even early public buildings watchmen, the offices of U.S. Marshal and deputy marshal were the first to be created with law enforcement as the office holder's primary function.[26]

The Judiciary Act of 1789 was one of the most important pieces of legislation in all of American history. While the Constitution described a judiciary branch in the form and substance of the U.S. Supreme Court, it also assigned to the legislative branch the authority to establish and set jurisdiction for federal lower courts. Thus, in the Judiciary Act of 1789, the form of America's federal courts system was defined and set into motion. This includes the establishment of district courts that would serve as courts of original jurisdiction and the federal appellate courts—known as circuit courts of appeal.

In 1789, 13 federal judicial districts were created. Each state constituted a single federal judicial district, except for the district of Maine, which was part of Massachusetts until it became a state in 1820. Additionally, the territory of Kentucky was allotted a federal judicial district of its own. Kentucky became a state in 1792.

The authors of the Judiciary Act of 1789 clearly understood that the federal courts had a role in both criminal and civil matters. Section 9 of the Act states:

And be it further enacted, That the district courts shall have, exclusively of the courts of the several States, cognizance of all crimes and offences that shall be cognizable under the authority of the United States, committed within their respective districts, or upon the high seas; where no other punishment than whipping, not exceeding thirty stripes, a fine not exceeding one hundred dollars, or a term of imprisonment not exceeding six months, is to be inflicted; and shall also have exclusive original cognizance of all civil causes of admiralty and maritime jurisdiction, including all seizures under laws of impost, navigation or trade of the United States, where the seizures are made, on waters which are navigable from the sea by vessels of ten or more tons burthen, within their respective districts as well as upon the high seas; saving to suitors, in all cases, the right of a common law remedy, where the common law is competent to give it; and shall also have exclusive original cognizance of all seizures on land, or other waters than as aforesaid, made, and of all suits for penalties and forfeitures incurred, under the laws of the United States. And shall also have cognizance, concurrent with the courts of the several States, or the circuit courts, as the case may be, of all causes where an alien sues for a tort only in violation of the law of nations or a treaty of the United States. And shall also have cognizance, concurrent as last mentioned, of all suits at common law where the United States sue, and the matter in dispute amounts, exclusive of costs, to the sum or value of one hundred dollars. And shall also have jurisdiction exclusively of the courts of the several States, of all suits against consuls or vice-consuls, except for offences above the description aforesaid. And the trial of issues in fact, in the district courts, in all causes except civil causes of admiralty and maritime jurisdiction, shall be by jury.

In addition to district and circuit court judges, the Judiciary Act of 1789 also established the office of the United States Attorney—which still exists in every one of the 94 judicial districts present today. The U.S. Attorney in any given judicial district was required to be educated in the law. His duties were to "prosecute and conduct all suits in such Courts in which the United States shall be concerned and to give his advice and opinion upon questions of law when required by the President of the United States and when requested by the Heads of any of the Departments, touching any matters that may concern their Departments".[27]

Still another office created by the Judiciary Act of 1789 was that of United States Marshal. Each district would have one. The duties of the United States Marshal in each district, and any deputies, were clearly defined in the statute and mirrored the duties of local sheriffs. The relevant sections of the Act that relate to the U.S. Marshals are found in Sections 27, 28, and 29 which state:

SEC. 27. And be it further enacted, That a marshal shall be appointed in and for each district for the term of four years, but shall be removable from office at pleasure, whose duty it shall be to attend the district and circuit courts when sitting therein, and also the Supreme Court in the District in which that court shall sit. And to execute throughout the district, all lawful precepts directed to him, and issued under the authority of the United States, and he shall have power to command all necessary assistance in the execution of his duty, and to appoint as there shall be occasion, one or more deputies, who shall be removable from office by the judge of the district court, or the circuit court sitting within the district, at the pleasure of either; and before he enters on the duties of his office, he shall become bound for the faithful performance of the same, by himself and by his deputies before the judge of the district court to the United States, jointly and severally, with two good and sufficient sureties, inhabitants and freeholders of such district, to be approved by the district judge, in the sum of twenty thousand dollars, and shall take before said judge, as shall also his deputies, before they enter on the duties of their appointment, the following oath of office: "I, A. B., do solemnly swear or affirm, that I will faithfully execute all lawful precepts directed to the marshal of the district of _____ under the authority of the United States, and true returns make, and in all things well and truly, and without malice or partiality, perform the duties of the office of marshal (or marshal's deputy, as the case may be) of the district of, during my continuance in said office, and take only my lawful fees. So help me God."

SEC. 28. And be it further enacted, That in all causes wherein the marshal or his deputy shall be a party, the writs and precepts therein shall be directed to such disinterested person as the court, or any justice or judge thereof may appoint, and the person so appointed, is hereby authorized to execute and return the same. And in case of the death of any marshal, his deputy or deputies shall continue in office, unless otherwise specially removed; and shall execute the same in the name of the deceased, until another marshal shall be appointed and sworn: And the defaults or misfeasances in office of such deputy or deputies in the mean time, as well as before, shall be adjudged a breach of the condition of the bond given, as before directed, by the marshal who appointed them; and the executor or administrator of the deceased marshal shall have like remedy for the defaults and misfeasances in office of such deputy or deputies during such interval, as they would be entitled to if the marshal had continued in life and in the exercise of his said office, until his successor was appointed, and sworn or affirmed: And every marshal or his deputy when removed from office, or when the term for which the marshal is appointed shall expire, shall have power notwithstanding to execute all such precepts as may be in their hands respectively at the time of such removal or expiration of office; and the marshal shall be held answerable for the delivery to his successor of all prisoners which may be in his custody at the time of his removal, or when the term for which he is appointed shall expire, and for that purpose may retain such prisoners in his custody until his successor shall be appointed and qualified as the law directs.

SEC. 29. And be it further enacted, That in cases punishable with death, the trial shall be had in the county where the offence was committed, or where that cannot be done without great inconvenience, twelve petit jurors at least shall be summoned from thence. And jurors in all cases to serve in the courts of the United States shall be designated by lot or otherwise in each State respectively according to the mode of forming juries therein now practised, so far as the laws of the same shall render such designation practicable by the courts or marshals of the United States; and the jurors shall have the same qualifications as are requisite for jurors by the laws of the State of which they are citizens, to serve in the highest courts of law of such State, and shall be returned as there shall be occasion for them, from such parts of the district from time to time as the court shall direct, so as shall be most favourable to an impartial trial, and so as not to incur an unnecessary expense, or unduly to burthen the citizens of any part of the district with such services. And writs of venire facias when directed by the court shall issue from the clerk's office, and shall be served and returned by the marshal in his proper person, or by his deputy, or in case the marshal or his deputy is not an indifferent person, or is interested in the event of the cause, by such fit person as the court shall specially appoint for that purpose, to whom they shall administer an oath or affirmation that he will truly and impartially serve and return such writ. And when from challenges or otherwise there shall not be a jury to determine any civil or criminal cause, the marshal or his deputy shall, by order of the court where such defect of jurors shall happen, return jurymen de talibus circumstantibus sufficient to complete the pannel; and when the marshal or his deputy are disqualified as aforesaid, jurors may be returned by such disinterested person as the court shall appoint.

Through the sections of the Judiciary Act of 1789 just presented, U.S. Marshals and their deputies, as sworn officers, are empowered to serve writs and processes of the federal courts, to deputize others to aid them in the execution of their duties, to take control of and deliver prisoners to justice, and to notify (and compel as necessary) citizens of their obligation to serve on juries if they have been so summoned by the court.

The legislation gave U.S. Marshals broad power—essentially any power necessary—to perform their duties. This certainly included the power to carry firearms (even where firearms might have been prohibited), the power to make arrests, and the power to conduct searches and seizures pursuant to court-approved warrants.

Historian Frederick Calhoun described the responsibilities of the nation's first marshals in his seminal work, *The Lawmen* (1989): "They served subpoenas, summonses, writs, warrants, and other process issued by the courts; made all the arrests; and handled all the prisoners. They also disbursed the money, paying the fees and expenses of the court clerks, U.S. attorneys, jurors, and witnesses. They rented the courtrooms and jail space and hired the bailiffs, criers, and janitors".[28] In essence, the U.S. Marshal in each district served as the court administrator.

In addition to covering the expenses of other court personnel, Marshals were empowered to exact fees of their own for their services. U.S. Marshals and their deputies were not salaried federal employees. Much like the office of sheriff at the county level, they collected fees for process serving and fugitive apprehensions. That was how they were financially compensated. In colonial times and before, a 10% commission against fees and taxes collected by the local sheriff was determined to be reasonable. For federal marshals, similar percentages probably prevailed, but fees also varied according to duty or function.[29]

While not necessarily true of their deputies, the U.S. Marshal in each district was generally well-to-do and needed little extra income to begin with. U.S. Marshals, as appointments of the President of the United States, were usually connected politically to the President's party. They were typically successful attorneys or politicians. Being financially secure was to some extent a job requirement, because appointed marshals and their deputies had to post a $20,000 bond as insurance against improper fee collection or fraud.[30]

Certainly federal marshals were responsible for executing orders of the judiciary. But marshals had responsibilities to the other branches of government as well. The Federal Bureau of Investigation did not exist in the 1700s and 1800s. It was the marshals and their deputies who served as general law enforcers for the federal government and the criminal laws of the United States.

In the 18th and 19th centuries, federal marshals were used to enforce the tax laws of the United States. In 1794, the refusal by many Pennsylvanians to pay a federally imposed tax on whiskey resulted in court summonses for 75 whiskey distillers.[31] U.S. Marshal David Lenox accompanied tax inspector John Neville, as marshals were often called to do, in order to serve a summons upon a Pennsylvania farmer and distiller named William Miller. Dozens of people rose up to resist Lenox and Neville on behalf of Miller; Marshal Lenox and Inspector Neville were even captured by the mob for a time but eventually escaped. By then, 500 so-called "whiskey rebels" were now positioned with Miller in opposition to the tax and to the court summons requiring his presence before a judge in Philadelphia. The rebellion was eventually put down by federalized militia troops activated by President Washington himself.

Similarly, U.S. Marshals and their deputies were called upon to enforce the Alien and Sedition Acts of 1798. The Alien Act gave the president broad powers to deport any foreign national who was deemed to be dangerous to the United States. Further, in times of war, such aliens could be imprisoned rather than deported if it was determined that they were loyal to the enemies of the United States. Marshals, rather than military officials, were used to investigate and arrest foreign nationals accused under that law, which was the nation's first anti-espionage and anti-spying criminal statute.

The U.S. Marshals were extremely busy investigating and enforcing the provisions of the Alien Act during the War of 1812. During the war between the United States and Great Britain (1812–1815), the U.S. Marshals and their deputies worked closely with the United States State Department to register and monitor nearly 12,000 British citizens then living in the United States. Many British citizens were arrested for providing military and logistical intelligence to British forces that had invaded American soil.[32]

The Sedition Act of 1798 did not target foreign nationals, but rather American nationals. The enforcement of this law was thus far more controversial than the enforcement of the provisions of the Alien Act. Sections 1 and 2 of the Sedition Act state:

SEC. I Be it enacted...,That if any persons shall unlawfully combine or conspire together, with intent to oppose any measure or measures of the government of the United States, which are or shall be directed by proper authority, or to impede the operation of any law of the United States, or to intimidate or prevent any person holding a place or office in or under the government of the United States, from undertaking, performing or executing his trust or duty; and if any person or persons, with intent as aforesaid, shall counsel, advise or attempt to procure any insurrection, riot. unlawful assembly, or combination, whether such conspiracy, threatening, counsel, advice, or attempt shall have the proposed effect or not, he or they shall be deemed guilty of a high misdemeanor, and on conviction, before any court of the United States having jurisdiction thereof, shall be punished by a fine not exceeding five thousand dollars, and by imprisonment during a term not less than six months nor exceeding five years; and further, at the discretion of the court may be holden to find sureties for his good behaviour in such sum, and for such time, as the said court may direct.

SEC. 2. That if any person shall write, print, utter. Or publish, or shall cause or procure to be written, printed, uttered or published, or shall knowingly and willingly assist or aid in writing, printing, uttering or publishing any false, scandalous and malicious writing or writings against the government of the United States, or either house of the Congress of the United States, or the President of the United States, with intent to defame the said government, or either house of the said Congress, or the said President, or to bring them. or either of them, into contempt or disrepute; or to excite against them, or either or any of them, the hatred of the good people of the United States, or to excite any unlawful combinations therein, for opposing or resisting any law of the United States, or any act of the President of the United States, done in pursuance of any such law, or of the powers in him vested by the constitution of the United States, or to resist, oppose, or defeat any such law or act, or to aid, encourage or abet any hostile designs of any foreign nation against the United States, their people or government, then such person, being thereof convicted before any court of the United States having jurisdiction thereof, shall be punished by a fine not exceeding two thousand dollars, and by imprisonment not exceeding two years.

In effect, the Sedition Act of 1798 made criticism of the United States government and its officials a criminal offense punishable by large fines and imprisonment. Odious as this law was, it was the responsibility of U.S. Marshals and deputy marshals to enforce it. Further, criminal investigation of alleged violations of this statute was the responsibility of the marshals. Allegations needed to be investigated— particularly the truthfulness or validity of the criticisms alleged to have been made—because the truthfulness of one's statements was an affirmative defense to this charge. During the two and a half years that the Sedition Act was in effect, 25 people were arrested for violating it, ten of whom went on to serve prison sentences. In most cases, those convicted of this crime were politicians and newspaper publishers campaigning against Federalist policies.[33]

In addition to the Alien and Sedition Acts, U.S. Marshals were called upon to investigate and arrest violators of many other federal criminal statutes, including those against the counterfeiting of federal coin and currency. That responsibility would eventually be transferred to the U.S. Treasury Department and its Secret Service, but in the late 1700s and early to mid-1800s, the Secret Service did not yet exist. Thus, the job belonged to the marshals.

U.S. Marshals also investigated and arrested violators of slave trade laws. By 1808, it was no longer legal to import slaves from other countries. Legislation was passed in 1819 and 1820 to toughen the anti-slave trading laws. In fact, legislation passed in 1820 designated slave trading as a variant of piracy and made it a capital offense. Section 5 of this statute states:[34]

Sec. 5. And be it further enacted, That if any citizen of the United States, being of the crew or ship's company of any foreign ship or vessel engaged in the slave trade, or any person whatever, being of the crew or ship's company of any ship or vessel, owned wholly or in part, or navigated for, or in behalf of, any citizen or citizens of the United States, shall forcibly confine or detain, or aid and abet in forcibly confining or detaining, on board such ship or vessel, any negro or mulatto not held to service by the laws of either of the states or territories of the United States with intent to make such negro or mulatto a slave or shall on board any such ship or vessel, offer or attempt to sell, as a slave, any negro or mulatto not held to service as aforesaid, or shall, on the high seas, or any where on tide water, transfer or deliver over, to any other ship or vessel, any negro or mulatto not held to service as aforesaid, with intent to make such negro or mulatto a slave, or shall land, or deliver on shore, from on board any such ship or vessel, any such negro or mulatto, with intent to make sale of, or having previously sold, such negro or mulatto, as a slave, such citizen or person shall be adjudged a pirate; and, on conviction thereof before the circuit court of the United States for the district wherein he shall be brought or found, shall suffer death. [Persons forcibly confining, detaining, or aiding to confine or detain negroes, etc., on board vessels, etc. declared pirates, and to suffer death.].

Marshals worked closely with personnel manning revenue cutters and took custody of those interdicted under this statute.

As noble as it was for U.S. Marshals to foil the efforts of slave traders, they were also called upon to enforce controversial fugitive slave laws. This responsibility hit its zenith with the passage of the

Fugitive Slave Act of 1850. Under the auspices of this statute, U.S. Marshals and their deputies were responsible for capturing slaves who had escaped from southern slave states into the North and non-slave territories. Upon capture, the slaves were to be returned to their rightful owners by the marshals.

The marshals were met with considerable hostility in northern states as they tried to enforce fugitive slave statutes. State and local governments frequently refused to cooperate with marshals engaged in this duty. Many cases exist of local governments refusing to permit their police officers and jailers to assist the marshals in capturing and holding fugitive slaves until their return to the South could be arranged. In fact, in 1854, Deputy U.S. Marshal James Batchelder was shot and killed in Boston by rioters who sought to free a fugitive slave in Batchelder's custody.[35]

The period of the 1790s through the 1850s was an exciting time in the United States, because the very form and substance of American government was created and molded. While significant philosophies, legislation, and events guided the nation from a fledgling existence into a viable nation-state with worldwide influence, interesting things were happening on the law enforcement front as well. Congress grappled, through legislation, with the protection of the mail system, the protection of public buildings, the credibility of tax laws, and the general protection of the Republic. In doing so, Congress paved the way for what would become an interesting ancillary of federal power—the growing influence, scope, and size of the nation's federal law enforcement apparatus.

CHAPTER 3

Go West, Young Man (1860–1920s)

The latter half of the 19th century and the early part of the 20th century was a time of incredible growth in the United States. The growth not only occurred economically and technologically, but also geographically. Twenty-nine states entered the Union during the 19th century, fifteen of which achieved statehood after 1850. Three more states entered the Union in the first decade and a half of the 20th century. During the 1800s, the nation's citizens chose in large numbers to march westward. The apparatus of government necessarily marched westward with them.

Herbert Johnson and Nancy Travis Wolfe[1] described the unique nature of law enforcement on the American frontier. It was on the American frontier that individuals rooted in Western civilization and culture met the primitive conditions of unbridled nature and the unwelcoming and war-fighting indigenous peoples. It was through America's westward expansion that the American people became most known to the world for their rugged individualism and can-do optimism.

But while law-abiding American pioneers faced down the twin threats of raiding, tenacious Indians and the geographic and climatic hazards of the Great Plains and mountain regions of North America, there was yet an additional threat that typically emerged to plague those choosing to settle in the West. That threat was lawlessness. Given the scarcity of law enforcement in the western territories, it is no wonder that crime was a genuine concern. As Johnson and Wolfe[2] noted, "...the institutions of government [in the West] were only recently established and law enforcement was thinly spread. At times, only a handful of federal marshals policed an entire territory that today might include several of the western states."

While law enforcement was sparse in the west, the criminal element was not. There was anonymity and freedom in migrating to the western territories. People with unsavory pasts could go west and start a new life without the baggage of having the authorities and the community aware of one's deficit in character.[3]

During the late 1700s and early 1800s, the U.S. Marshals were the primary face of federal law enforcement. Their law enforcement responsibilities were the most plentiful among the federal agencies and their authority was the broadest. Throughout the second half of the 1800s, these characterizations remained true. The U.S. Marshals and their deputies were the primary representations of federal police power. And as suggested earlier, in many western territories they were the only representation of police power there was.

During the Civil War (1861–1865), the U.S. Marshals revisited their earlier role as guardians against espionage—a role previously honed during the War of 1812. However, this time they were on guard against rebellious Americans who no longer gave any deference to the marshals (if they had ever been inclined to do so in the first place).

What marshals faced was not unlike the uncooperative or even hostile behavior many people in northern communities displayed when U.S. marshals attempted to enforce fugitive slave laws. Marshals and deputy marshals during the Civil War found many so-called "neutral" territories to be hotbeds of Confederate sympathies. The U.S. Marshal for Southern California wrote in 1861: "Treason is rampant here in Southern California...We have bold daring Secessionists who are plotting in secret; our Sheriff and nearly all our county officers just elected disavow all allegiance to our Government and say that Jeff Davis' government is the only Constitutional government!".[4]

The United States Congress attempted to craft laws that would assist the Marshals Service in performing its duty of preserving the Union by fighting Southern subversives. In 1861 and 1862, Congress passed two separate confiscation acts. The first confiscation act read in part:[5]

Be it enacted by the Senate and House of Representatives of the United States of America in Congress assembled, That if, during the present or any future insurrection against the Government of the United States, after the President of the

United States shall have declared, by proclamation, that the laws of the United States are opposed, and the execution thereof obstructed, by combinations too powerful to be suppressed by the ordinary course of judicial proceedings, or by the power vested in the marshals by law, any person or persons, his, her, or their agent, attorney, or employé, shall purchase or acquire, sell or give, any property of whatsoever kind or description, with intent to use or employ the same, or suffer the same to be used or employed, in aiding, abetting, or promoting such insurrection or resistance to the laws, or any person or persons engaged therein; or if any person or persons, being the owner or owners of any such property, shall knowingly use or employ, or consent to the use or employment of the same as aforesaid, all such property is hereby declared to be lawful subject of prize and capture wherever found; and it shall be the duty of the President of the United States to cause the same to be seized, confiscated, and condemned.

Through that statute, and through the Second Confiscation Act, which was adopted on July 17, 1862, the federal government through its federal marshals was authorized to seize property and money and to deposit them into the federal coffers. In fact, the Second Confiscation Act also mandated the freeing of slaves from owners residing in states that were in open rebellion against the United States. Under that law, federal marshals were called upon to take custody of, and then free, many slaves in the South. This occurred long before President Lincoln delivered his Emancipation Proclamation.

After the Confederate rebellion was put down and the Civil War ended in 1865, U.S. Marshals were called upon to enforce a number of postwar statutes that were aimed at keeping the Southern states in check. They were also responsible for the enforcement of new provisions in the U.S. Constitution itself—namely:

- The 13th Amendment (1865), which outlawed slavery;
- The 14th Amendment (1868), which made freed slaves citizens and afforded them due process of law;
- The 15th Amendment (1870), which guaranteed former slaves the right to vote.

In 1866, the first Civil Rights Act was passed by Congress. The bill made it a federal criminal offense (albeit a misdemeanor) to deny the basic rights of citizenship to newly freed slaves. This legislation was vetoed by President Andrew Johnson—a Southerner. However, the Northern-dominated Congress was in no mood to placate a defeated South that had just waged a five-year war against the Union. Congress overrode President Johnson's veto (the first override of a presidential veto in American history), and the protection of blacks' civil rights became the latest jurisdictional responsibility of the U.S. Marshals.

During Reconstruction, most Southerners resented the perceived heavy-handedness of federal legislation. There was a sense that anything the federal government did in relation to the South was either punitive or exploitive in nature. In 1865, several Confederate Army veterans in Pulaski, Tennessee, formed a secret, fraternal organization. They called themselves the Ku Klux Klan. Initially, their activities were relatively harmless. They would parade through town in robes and with hooded heads as a lark. In short order, however, the Klan members used their secrecy and concealed identity as a cover for harassing and threatening local black residents.

The Ku Klux Klan quickly spread as an organization throughout the South and took on genuinely terroristic characteristics. On numerous occasions, Klan members physically attacked black families who dared to attempt to exercise their right to vote or otherwise participate in community processes. In 1868 alone, Ku Klux Klan members had murdered as many as 1,300 people—both black and white (mostly northern "carpetbaggers" and Southern Republicans, or "scalawags"). Congress responded by passing anti-Klan legislation. This included the Force Act of 1870 and the Civil Rights Act of 1871. Those laws made it a federal criminal offense to wear masks or hoods that would disguise one's identity for the purpose of attacking or intimidating citizens on the basis of race, color, or prior condition of servitude.

It was the U.S. Marshals who were called upon to enforce these statutes. Between the late 1860s and 1877, over 7,000 Klan members in the South had been arrested by U.S. Marshals and their deputies.[6] During this same period, many deputy marshals lost their lives in the line of duty while enforcing federal civil rights laws.

While marshals and deputies confronted significant challenges in the South during Reconstruction, the challenges they faced in the frontier West were just as bad or worse. In addition to the criminal element that left the industrialized East and North for a fresh start in crime, the West contained many post-Civil War southern veterans who turned to crime for the first time—partly out of anger, partly out of economic desperation. The James Gang, with its leaders Jesse and Frank James, is probably the most infamous example. The gang left a trail of blood over several years of robbing banks, stagecoaches, and trains. In all cases, when the robberies involved federal money, federal property, or the U.S. mail, the U.S. Marshals had concurrent jurisdiction with the local authorities.

In the case of the Indian Territory, U.S. Marshals had broad law enforcement authority. Their mandate in the Western District of Arkansas (which covered the Indian Territory now known as Oklahoma) in the 1870s, was described as follows in a publication about federal law enforcement authority on Indian lands or for crimes committed by Indians:

U.S. Deputy Marshals for the Western District of Arkansas may make arrests for murder, manslaughter, assault, with intent to kill or maim, attempts to murder, arson, robbery, rape, burglary, larceny, incest, adultery, willfully and maliciously placing obstructions on a railroad track...These arrests may be made with or without warrant first issued and in the hands of the Deputy or the Chief Marshal.

Working in the Indian Territory was dangerous work for the U.S. Marshals. In the Oklahoma Territory, 103 deputy U.S. marshals were killed between 1872 and 1896. Crimes committed in the Indian Territory were adjudicated in Ft. Smith, Arkansas, in front of U.S. District Judge Isaac Parker, who sat on the bench there from 1875 until his death in 1896. Parker is famously known as the "hanging judge"— having sent 88 convicted criminals to the gallows.[7]

While general law enforcement authority in the West still primarily rested with county and municipal officers, marshals had broad authority where Indians were alleged to be involved in criminal activity. Further, given that it was difficult to engage in any sustained criminal activity without purposefully or inadvertently violating a federal crime, the marshals typically shared jurisdiction with sheriffs and town marshals when tracking down violent offenders on the frontier. In non-Indian territories that were unorganized (i.e., no formal territorial government had been established), the U.S. Marshals were the only law enforcement officers authorized to engage in general police duties.

As the marshals and deputy marshals enforced the law in the West and the South, the organizational structure of the Marshals Service back in Washington DC was simultaneously evolving. In July of 1870, Congress passed the "Act to Establish the Department of Justice".[8] That legislation created the U.S. Justice Department and, among other things, gave it the overarching authority to control federal law enforcement. The U.S. Marshals were reorganized to exist under that department. Later, in July of 1896, the fee system of compensation for marshals and deputies was replaced with set annual salaries as Justice Department employees.

While the marshals experienced bureaucratization (not necessarily a bad thing) in the latter part of the 19th century, other elements of the federal government were also evolving bureaucratically. A hallmark of the bureaucratic model for organization is the trend toward specialization. This trend in government would impact federal law enforcement as existing and new specialized agencies emerged as major players in exercising federal police power.

The latter part of the 19th century was certainly an important and dramatic period for the U.S. Marshals Service, which was placed under the Department of Justice during that time. However, this period was also a time of expansion for other federal law enforcement agencies. The most notable newcomer to the community of federal law enforcement during this time was the U.S. Secret Service.

In April of 1865, the United States Secret Service was created. In 2003, the Secret Service became part of the U.S. Department of Homeland Security. However, for most of its history, the U.S. Secret Service was a branch of the U.S. Department of the Treasury. Organizing the Secret Service under the Treasury Department made sense in light of the mission of the Secret Service at its founding—to fight counterfeiting. During the months after the Civil War, it was estimated that easily one-third of the monetary currency in circulation around the United States was counterfeit. The counterfeit tally might even have been as high as one-half of all money in circulation.[9]

Counterfeiting currency was relatively easy during the 1860s. At that time, hundreds of state banks existed around the country that were designing and printing their own paper notes. Counterfeiters had the option of either copying legitimate and existing notes, or creating entirely fictitious notes of their own. The Treasury Department estimates that there were approximately 4,000 varieties of counterfeit notes and 7,000 varieties of genuine notes from actual banks.[10]

In an effort to solve the problem of so many notes—legitimate and illegitimate—Congress passed three Legal Tender Acts in February and July of 1862 and in March of 1863, respectively. The first Legal Tender Act authorized the Treasury Department to issue $150 million in Treasury notes. The second and third Legal Tender Acts authorized $300 million more. It was as a result of the Legal Tender Acts that the United States began to print its own paper currency; green in color, the Treasury notes soon came to be known as "greenbacks".[11]

But adoption of a national currency did not put an end to counterfeiting—especially in the context of a chaotic Civil War occupying the federal government's attention. Soon after the issuance of these federal notes, criminals (in the North) and subversives (in the South) began to counterfeit them just as the bank notes had been counterfeited.

Until the creation of the Secret Service, the U.S. Marshals had the responsibility of tracking down counterfeiters of Treasury notes. But that organization—to the extent that the marshals were organized— was also preoccupied with the Civil War and the fight against espionage and other subversive activities. In 1865, at the recommendation of Treasury Secretary Hugh McCulloch, Congress passed and President Lincoln signed legislation creating the Secret Service as a bureau of the Treasury Department with the specific mission of halting counterfeiting. As daunting as the task was, the Secret Service had a very successful first year. By the middle of 1866, the Secret Service had closed down more than 200 counterfeiting operations. By 1875, the amount of counterfeit money in circulation had been so dramatically reduced that counterfeiting was considered a negligible problem.[12]

Interestingly, the term "Secret Service" was not created out of thin air in 1865. Allan Pinkerton, the famous 19th century detective who founded Pinkerton's National Detective Agency, actually used the term first. Pinkerton founded his company in 1850 and gained a national reputation for security work and for tracking down wanted criminals for reward. His company's motto, "We Never Sleep," was widely known throughout the country and was associated with the Pinkertons. In fact, the Pinkerton logo includes an open, all-seeing eye, a symbol which gave rise to the term "private eye" used still today to refer to a detective who works for private citizens.

During the Civil War, Pinkerton's popular profile was further enhanced when he uncovered a plot to assassinate President Lincoln. During the Civil War, the United States contracted with Pinkerton in the fight against the South. Pinkerton and a subset of his detectives formed what Pinkerton called the Secret Service. The job of Pinkerton's Secret Service was to spy on the Confederate Army for General George McClellan. After the Battle of Antietam, General McClellan was fired by President Lincoln for incompetence and for being unwilling to fight. Pinkerton, as McClellan's chief intelligence provider, was sacked with him. But the creation of an unofficial intelligence organization known as the Secret Service had laid the groundwork for naming the future organization. Thus, Allan Pinkerton has long been associated with the founding of the modern-day U.S. Secret Service.

Prior to and after the Civil War, Pinkerton and his detectives were well known for their security work. If someone or something needed protection, Pinkerton was who one would enlist in the cause. Today, the United States Secret Service is likewise known as the "go-to" agency for really important protection responsibilities. In fact, under current law, the Secret Service is the lead agency for ensuring security and safety at any events designated as "National Special Security Events." Such events include any large-scale events that could be targeted by terrorists (e.g., the Super Bowl, the World Series, and the Olympics).

However, when the Secret Service was created in 1865, its mandate related only to combating the counterfeiting and forging of government obligations and notes. In 1867, the Secret Service's jurisdiction was broadened to include the detection of persons committing fraud against the United States government. But still, as a law enforcement agency, it had no official responsibility to protect anyone or anything except the obligations of the Treasury.

The dignitary-protection duties of the Secret Service—for which it is primarily known today—began in 1894. Since the time the Secret Service had been created, two presidents had been assassinated—Abraham Lincoln in 1865 and James Garfield in 1881. In 1894, the Secret Service began to provide infrequent and informal protection to President Grover Cleveland. However, protecting the President or anyone else in government remained outside the realm of its official responsibilities for the Secret Service and the Treasury Department. In fact, in 1898, Secret Service Chief William Hazen was demoted because he had misappropriated Secret Service funds when he authorized payment for agents who were protecting President Cleveland and his family.[13]

The rationale for providing protection to President Cleveland was that specific threats had been made against him as a result of a Secret Service investigation. The subjects of the investigation—several Colorado gamblers— had threatened the President simply because he was the chief executive of the federal government and therefore the person to whom the Secret Service answered. Secret Service Chief Hazen assigned two agents from the Colorado investigation to the White House for the President's protection. The presidential detail was not a reach for power or an expansion of responsibility on the Secret Service's part; it was an extension of an existing criminal investigation. That investigation saw the first use of Secret Service agents for presidential protection duties.[14] Nonetheless, it was determined that Chief Hazen had exceeded his authority when he spent funds for that function.

In September of 1901, President William McKinley was assassinated by anarchist Leon Czolgosz while visiting the Pan American Exposition in Buffalo, NY. Prior to 1865, no presidents had been assassinated. Now, in the span of 35 years, three presidents had been murdered by assassins' bullets. Interestingly, at the time of McKinley's assassination, the President had been under the Secret Service's protection due to temporary, special permission granted to the agency. Three Secret Service agents and several police officers were assigned to President McKinley during the President's visit to Buffalo.

After the assassination, Congress turned to the Secret Service and informally requested that the agency provide protection for the President of the United States. By 1902, the Secret Service was providing full-time protection for the President. Two agents were assigned to the White House protection detail.

However, even though Congress now knew it had to do something for the permanent protection of the President, it was not a foregone conclusion that the Secret Service would be the agency this mission fell upon. After all, it had just failed to protect President McKinley. Some in Congress wanted the United States Army to be responsible for protecting the President. One Senate bill proposed in 1902, which made it a capital crime under federal law to assassinate or attempt to assassinate the President, included language that directed the Secretary of War "to select and detail from the Regular Army a sufficient number of officers and men to guard and protect the person of the President of the United States without any unnecessary display" and to "make special rules and regulations as to dress, arms, and equipment...of said guard".[15] In essence, the proposed legislation granted the Secretary of War the authority to create a plainclothes, secret service within the army.[16]

Many others in Congress opposed that proposal. They worried that protecting the President would become a pretext for creating a police state with the Army at the helm. When the Senate bill was considered by the House of Representatives, the House Judiciary Committee removed the language from the bill that authorized the Army to create a Presidential protective unit. The Judiciary Committee wrote in its report:[17]

[under the Senate version of the bill] the Secretary of War may detail every man and officer in the Regular Army, under the pretense of protecting the President, dress them to suit his fancy, and send them abroad among the people to act under secret orders. When such laws begin to operate in this Republic the liberties of the people will take wings and fly away.

The House Judiciary Committee went on to recommend instead that the Secret Service be given the responsibility for protecting the President. This recommendation was written into the House version of the bill. The House and Senate were not able to reconcile this and other differences and the proposed legislation and the bill simply died in Congress.

Finally, in 1906, Congress passed the Sundry Civil Expenses Act for 1907. Inserted into this legislation was a section in which Congress expressly gave the Secret Service the responsibility for protecting the President of the United States and provided funds to the Department of Treasury designated for that purpose. The controversy over whose responsibility it was to protect the President was finally resolved.

In 1906, not only did the Secret Service receive new legal jurisdiction to protect the President, but it began to expand its investigative domain under its broad, existing jurisdiction at the time to investigate fraud against the government. This expansion of its investigative domain would have long-term and far-reaching consequences, as we shall see later. One area in particular into which the investigative purview of Secret Service expanded was the area involving government lands in the West. In the early 1900s, the federal government was (and it still is, by the way) the major land owner in the western United States. Through fraudulent schemes, public land would be converted to the use of private citizens who would then sell the property off themselves as if they actually owned it. The Secret Service investigated several cases of defrauding the government through land schemes and returned millions of acres of public lands to the government. In fact, on November 3, 1907, Joseph Walker became the first Secret Service agent (or "operative," as agents were called at that time) killed in the line of duty while he was working on a land fraud case.[18]

However, in the early 1900s, the Secret Service wasn't the only agency with a law enforcement interest in public lands. In particular, the U.S. Forest Service became the chief land-management law enforcement agency and paved the way for others to follow. In 1891, Congress passed the Forest Reserve Act. That law permitted the President of the United States to set aside timber-covered public lands as federal forest reserves. The forest reserves would later be called national forests. Initially, the forests were controlled by the Department of the Interior. However, timber was an agricultural product. Timber was used for construction, paper, and other goods. Trees were farmed. Consequently, most of the expertise concerning the maintenance of the forests was found in the Department of Agriculture.

On February 1, 1905, President Theodore Roosevelt (commonly thought of as the first environmentalist President) signed into law an Act creating the United States Forest Service as an agency within the Department of Agriculture. According to the Forest Service, its mission then (and now) was to sustain healthy and productive forests and grasslands for present and future generations.[19] Of course, the Forest Service was not the only holder of public lands and wilderness.

In 1872, the federal government had established Yellowstone National Park as "a public park or pleasuring-ground for the benefit and enjoyment of the people".[20] In the 1890s, many more national parks were established for the enjoyment of the public, including Yosemite, General Grant, and Sequoia National Parks in California, and Mount Rainier National Park in the State of Washington. Unlike the forest reserves, the land set aside as national parks was not for harvesting. Also unlike the forests, the national parks were controlled by the Department of the Interior, not the Department of Agriculture.

On June 8, 1906, a little over a year after the creation of the Forest Service, President Roosevelt signed the Antiquities Act. This legislation further empowered the federal government to set aside lands for public enjoyment and educational purposes. The legislation specifically gave the President the authority "to declare by public proclamation historic landmarks, historic and prehistoric structures, and other objects of scientific interest that are situated upon the lands owned or controlled by the Government of the United States to be national monuments".[21] National monuments, like other parks for the public's use, were to be administered and protected by the Department of Interior.

The Antiquities Act also made it a crime to steal or destroy antiquities on public lands. Section 1 of the Act, codified into Title 16, Section 433, states:

Be it enacted by the Senate and House of Representatives of the United States of America in Congress assembled, That any person who shall appropriate, excavate, injure, or destroy any historic or prehistoric ruin or monument, or any object of antiquity, situated on lands owned or controlled by the Government of the United States, without the permission of the Secretary of the department of the government having jurisdiction over the lands on which said antiquities are situated, shall, upon conviction, be fined in a sum of not more than five hundred dollars or be imprisoned for a period of not more than ninety days, or shall suffer both fine and imprisonment, at the discretion of the court.

On August 25, 1916, Congress consolidated the various national parks and monuments under a single organization by creating the National Park Service as a part of the Department of the Interior. The National Park Service was primarily concerned with conservation and recreation. The Forest Service was primarily concerned with sound agricultural use of timberlands and grasslands. Both the Forest Service and the National Park Service controlled millions of acres of land throughout the United States. Protecting those lands through law enforcement became the responsibility of those agencies along with the other federal agencies that already had jurisdiction there (i.e., the U.S. Marshals and the U.S. Secret Service).

On March 3, 1905, Congress authorized employees of both the Forest Service and the National Park Service to exercise law enforcement authority under Title 16, Section 10, of the U.S. Code. Later, Congress separated the two agencies from each other in the statute, giving each agency specific law enforcement authority under Title 16, the portion of the U.S. Code that deals with conservation and natural resources.

For the Forest Service, Title 16, Section 559, states:

All persons employed in the Forest Service of the United States shall have authority to make arrests for the violation of the laws and regulations relating to the national forests, and any person so arrested shall be taken before the nearest United States magistrate judge, within whose jurisdiction the forest is located, for trial; and upon sworn information by any competent person any United States magistrate judge in the proper jurisdiction shall issue process for the arrest of any person charged with the violation of said laws and regulations; but nothing herein contained shall be construed as preventing the arrest by any officer of the United States, without process, of any person taken in the act of violating said laws and regulations.

Notice that the language granted every employee of the Forest Service law enforcement authority. In the early years, every employee was a generalist who might be called upon to grab a weapon and cite or arrest violators of law on forest lands. While this broad authority is still technically extended statutorily to all Forest Service employees, only law enforcement personnel actually exercise the authority under Forest Service rules and more recent legislation.

Law enforcement personnel in the National Park Service were empowered by Title 16, Section 1a-6. That statute states, in part:

...the Secretary of Interior is authorized to designate, pursuant to standards prescribed in regulations by the Secretary, certain officers or employees of the Department of the Interior who shall maintain law and order and protect persons and property within areas of the National Park System. In the performance of such duties, the officers or employees, so designated, may—

(1) carry firearms and make arrests without warrant for any offense against the United States committed in his presence, or for any felony cognizable under the laws of the United States if he has reasonable

grounds to believe that the person to be arrested has committed or is committing such felony, provided such arrests occur within that system or the person to be arrested is fleeing therefrom to avoid arrest;

(2) execute any warrant or other process issued by a court or officer of competent jurisdiction for the enforcement of the provisions of any Federal law or regulation issued pursuant to law arising out of an offense committed in that system or, where the person subject to the warrant or process is in that system, in connection with any Federal offense; and

(3) conduct investigations of offenses against the United States committed in that system in the absence of investigation thereof by any other Federal law enforcement agency having investigative jurisdiction over the offense committed or with the concurrence of such other agency.

Shortly after the turn of the last century, newly created land management agencies were legislatively equipped with specific statutory authority to exercise federal police power. But other federal law enforcement agencies were also beginning to appear. The Bureau of Internal Revenue (renamed the Internal Revenue Service in 1953) was created on July 1, 1862. For decades, the U.S. Marshals and, to a lesser extent the Secret Service, enforced tax laws in this country. However, on July 1, 1919, the Commission for Internal Revenue created the Intelligence Unit to investigate tax fraud.[22]

Six U.S. Postal Inspectors were transferred to the Bureau of Revenue under the Department of the Treasury. These six investigators were the first special agents of what would become the Criminal Investigative Division (CID) of the Internal Revenue Service. In fact, only a few years later, Treasury agents from that unit would play a pivotal role in prosecuting Al Capone and other prominent figures in organized crime who violated tax laws while violating liquor laws under Prohibition. Special Agents in the Intelligence Unit of the Treasury Department's Bureau of Internal Revenue quickly became known as the most highly trained and professional financial investigators in the world.

The second half of the 19th century and first decade of the 20th century was an exciting time for proponents of federal police power. This period of time saw the expansion of jurisdiction and the professionalization of U.S. Marshals. During those years the U.S. Secret Service and the investigations division of what would become the Internal Revenue Service came into being, and the federal government also gave newly created land management agencies law enforcement power for their employees.This period of time was also an opportunity for other, older federal law enforcement organizations to further define and refine their missions, and Congress granted greater statutory recognition of the law enforcement missions of the Postal Inspection Service, the Customs Service, the Capitol Police, and the U.S. Park Police.

However, despite the advancement of federal law enforcement during this period of time, nothing was more significant (in retrospect) than the transfer of eight Secret Service agents to the U.S. Department of Justice in 1908 to form a small investigative unit within the Justice Department. That was the meager beginning of the Federal Bureau of Investigation. The origin and development if this most famous federal law enforcement agency is the subject of the next chapter.

CHAPTER 4

Hoover's G-Men
Come of Age

THE FBI FROM INCEPTION THROUGH THE 1930s

By midway through the first decade of the 20th century, the United States Secret Service was well established as a law enforcement agency. In fact, if one was a government official in need of investigative or other law enforcement assistance, the Secret Service in many ways had replaced the U.S. Marshals as the agency to be relied upon. Moreover, the Secret Service appeared eager to expand its law enforcement jurisdiction. The marshals, on the other hand, were still overtly political in nature. Marshals were appointed and served at the pleasure of the President. Thus, the reliability of marshals and their deputies hinged, in part, on the degree to which political favor could be won by carrying out the assignment at hand.

In the early 1900s, a common practice for the Secret Service was to loan its operatives (agents) to other agencies for criminal investigative operations. Eventually, concern over this practice resulted in legislation forbidding it. Then, as now, many in Congress were concerned about an all-powerful federal police agency with its fingers in every aspect of government affairs. By loaning agents out, the Secret Service experienced mission creep that was troubling to many.

The name of the agency—"Secret Service"—probably didn't help. Members of Congress and the public at large were concerned about

America fielding a federal secret police agency not unlike those that exited in other countries possessing less deference for individual liberties. In fact, this very concern convinced Congress to create the Secret Service as a civilian-controlled agency instead of one that was controlled by the Army.

One of the departments that had come to regularly rely on contracted or loaned Secret Service agents, as well as contracted detectives from private companies such as the Pinkerton National Detective Agency, was the Department of Justice. A common characterization of this practice was that the Secret Service was engaged in "espionage" within the United States government. U.S. Representative Walter Smith of Iowa stated that "[n]othing is more opposed to our race than a belief that a general system of espionage is being conducted by the general government." And House Appropriations Committee Chairman James Tawney of Minnesota said that the Secret Service practice of loaning agents to the Justice Department and other agencies amounted to "a system of espionage in this country which is entirely inconsistent with the theory of our government" and was a way for agencies such as Justice to circumvent the will of Congress, which would "never authorize...a secret service bureau in every department".[1]

While Congress expressed its concerns over the presence of the Secret Service at the Justice Department, so did Attorney General Charles Bonaparte—but for different reasons. Bonaparte, who was appointed Attorney General in 1907 by President Theodore Roosevelt, was dismayed at the lack of control that Justice had over the Secret Service agents. But he didn't share Congress' concern about the expansion of federal law enforcement—he just wanted agents that belonged to the Justice Department. In the Annual Report of the Attorney General to Congress, Bonaparte wrote in 1907 of the need for the Department of Justice to have its own criminal investigators. His report states:[2]

The attention of the Congress should be, I think, called to the anomaly that the Department of Justice has no executive force, and, more particularly, no permanent detective force under its immediate control. This singular condition arises mainly from the fact that before the office of the Attorney-General was transformed into the Department of Justice a highly efficient detective service had been organized to deal with crimes against the Treasury laws, which force has been, in effect, lent from time to time to this Department to meet its steadily increasing need for an agency of this nature, without, however, being removed from the control of the Treasury Department. I note with pleasure the efficiency and zeal with which these officers have cooperated with the United States attorneys and marshals, as well as with the special representatives of this Department in the interest of their own special and appropriate duties. When emergencies arise requiring prompt and effective executive action, the Department is now obliged to rely upon the several U. S. marshals; if it had a small, carefully selected, and experienced force under its immediate orders, the necessity of having these officers suddenly appoint special deputies, possibly in considerable numbers, might be sometimes avoided with greater likelihood of economy and better assurance of satisfactory results. I venture to recommend, therefore, that provision be made for a force of this character; its number and the form of its organization to be determined by the scope of the duties which the Congress may see fit to intrust to it. It may well be thought wise to preserve the existing detective organization, especially in view of its highly creditable record and excellent service, and it is not in any wise my purpose to suggest a different view, but it seems obvious that the Department on which not only the President, but the courts of the United States must call first to secure the enforcement of the laws, ought to have the means of such enforcement subject to its own call; a Department of Justice with no force of permanent police in any form under its control is assuredly not fully equipped for its work.

In July of 1908, the Attorney General began to organize a detective bureau within the Department of Justice. He did so by transferring dozens of Justice Department employees as well as eight Secret Service agents into the new detective unit. On July 26, 1908, Bonaparte wrote a memorandum that was issued to all Justice Department personnel. The memo directed that all matters before the Justice Department that required investigative or law enforcement services were to be referred to Stanley Finch, the head of the new unit, from that day forward. Services to be delivered by bank examiners or by those connected to the naturalization service were excluded from Bonaparte's directive. Finch, whose title was "Chief Examiner" of the unit, is recognized today as the Federal Bureau of Investigation's de facto first director.

However, the creation of the Justice Department's detective bureau, which was done administratively (that is, without Congress' express approval or funding), was not uncontroversial. Many in Congress were upset with the prospect of Justice possessing a general purpose investigative agency. Indeed, Attorney General Bonaparte was called upon to explain the need for and legal justification of this new unit.

In January 1909, Attorney General Bonaparte submitted a letter to President Roosevelt outlining the need for the new investigative bureau he had created in the Department of Justice. Bonaparte noted that, as of that date, many departments (e.g., Interior, Agriculture, Treasury) had law enforcement bureaus within them. He also noted the limitations of using U.S. Marshals for criminal investigative purposes.

Bonaparte's vision was for a viable, professional cadre of special agents within the Department of Justice who would investigate matters under the department's jurisdiction. The Marshals Service, which also fell under the Justice Department, should be generally responsible for serving court process as its statutory authority under the Judiciary Act of 1789 prescribed. Attorney General Bonaparte, in defense of his administratively created investigative unit at Justice, wrote to the President in part:[3]

...There are at present in the Treasury Department, the Post Office Department, and the Departments of the Interior, of Agriculture and of Commerce and Labor, a large number of officers whose duties include the detection of offenses [created by] various criminal statutes on the United States and the collection of evidence for use in the prosecution of such offenders. These officers report to the heads of their respective Departments, are subject to discipline or separation from the service, and receive promotion only through him, and are subject to no direct control by the Department of Justice.

In the meantime, however, the position and duties of the Attorney General have been completely changed. By the Acts approved August 2, 1861, (12 Stat., 285) and June 22, 1870, (16 Stat., 162), the latter creating the Department of Justice, the Attorney General was given supervision and control over all United States Attorneys and Marshals; and by a result of a large number of successive statutes all tending with more or less of conscious purpose, of to the same end, the Department of Justice and the Attorney General, as its head, are now, in substance, the direct agency through which the President discharges his constitutional duty to "take care that the laws be faithfully executed" in all those cases in which proceedings, criminal or civil, in courts of justice constitute the necessary or appropriate means of enforcement. This constitutes already an extremely wide field or duty, and the tendency of Federal legislation has been to steadily increase the burdens and responsibilities of the Department of Justice ever since its organization in 1870.

By reason of this radical change and vast expansion of its duties, it has become, each year, more and more imperatively necessary that this Department should have some executive force directly subject to its orders. The actual arrest of persons charged with crime may, indeed, be required of the several Marshals as part of their duty to execute all civil and criminal process, and they can also be called upon to supply such force as may be needful for the protection of Federal officers in the discharge of their duties or the preservation of public order in localities under the jurisdiction of the United States; but the detection of crime, the collection of evidence, and the conduct of all forms of preliminary inquiries necessary for the enforcement of the law, are not duties imposed by law upon the Marshals or which they could be reasonably expected to discharge with efficiency. It is true that, as above noted, other Executive Departments are supplied with what may be fairly called detective agencies for certain limited purposes, as, for example, the punishment of counterfeiting or frauds upon the revenue, of offenses against the postal laws and of violations of various penal statutes; but a large and increasing residuum of cases exists in which the Department of Justice is obliged by law, and expected as a result of custom, to furnish such services itself; and by a curious anomaly, no specific provision has been made by law to enable it to discharge these difficulties...".

Although his arguments were compelling, there was no immediate push by Congress or the White House to legislatively endorse the existence of Bonaparte's investigative agency within the Justice Department.

In March of 1909, George Wickersham was appointed Attorney General by newly elected President Howard Taft. During his first month as Attorney General, Wickersham formally changed the name of the Justice Department's detective unit to the "Bureau of Investigation." Under Wickersham and his several successors during the next 20 years, the Bureau would flourish and its authority would expand considerably.

The years 1910–1935 saw the passage of significant federal legislation that broadened the jurisdiction of the Bureau of Investigation. In 1910, Congress passed the Mann Act, which barred White Slave trafficking. The law was significant for the Bureau of Investigation in that it expanded the agency's jurisdiction over interstate crime. Thanks to World War I and the concern over German sabotage and spying, Congress passed the Espionage Act of 1917, which empowered the Bureau of Investigation to confront subversives within the United States. That responsibility had belonged chiefly to the U.S. Marshals during prior wars.

As the 1920s approached, motor vehicles were becoming more common. State and county governments were creating road systems that made it easier to travel relatively large distances in automobiles. In October of 1919, Congress passed the National Motor Vehicle Theft Act, which made it a federal crime to bring stolen vehicles across state lines. The investigative responsibility relating to this act was given to the Justice Department and its Bureau of Investigation.

Early in 1932, one of the most infamous crimes in American history was committed, a crime that would shape the image and jurisdiction of the Bureau of Investigation profoundly. On March 1, 1932, the 20-month old son of aviation hero Charles Lindbergh was kidnapped from the Lindbergh home in Hopewell, New Jersey. An initial ransom note for $50,000 was left on the window sill of the nursery room where the toddler had been sleeping. Several other ransom notes would follow during the month of March with amended demands from the kidnappers. During this time, the Bureau of Investigation provided special agents to support the investigation of the New Jersey State Police. However, they were there only in an auxiliary capacity, because no federal law against kidnapping yet existed. In May of 1932, the toddler's body was found. The cause of death was determined by the coroner to be blunt force trauma to the head.

Eventually, in September of 1933, President Franklin Roosevelt would direct the Bureau of Investigation to cooperate with the kidnapping/murder investigation in any way it could. Roosevelt declared that the Bureau of Investigation would have exclusive federal jurisdiction to assist in the case. Through considerable criminal investigative effort, and with the assistance of modern and scientific investigative techniques spearheaded by the Bureau of Investigation, the kidnappers were identified and an arrest was made. German immigrant Bruno Hauptmann was convicted of kidnapping and murder in February of 1935 and sentenced to death. A little over a year later, he was executed in New Jersey's electric chair. In response to the public outcry in the wake of the crime and the Bureau of Investigation's important contributions to the resolution of the case, Congress passed the Federal Kidnapping Act in 1932, making kidnapping a federal crime when the act involves crossing state borders.

The Bureau of Investigation also gained prestige in the 1930s by investigating fugitive gangsters who were marauding from state to state throughout the midwestern United States. In 1934, Congress enacted several pieces of legislation that enhanced the authority of the Bureau's special agents to actually arrest gangsters and bank robbers who crossed state lines to avoid capture. It was through this legislation that Congress officially gave Bureau of Investigation special agents the authority to make arrests and carry firearms.[4] Also in 1934, Congress enacted the Federal Bank Robbery Statute, which made it a federal offense to rob a financial institution whose holdings were insured by the Federal government. During the 1930s, special agents of the Bureau killed or captured several notorious gangsters, including John Dillinger, "Pretty Boy" Floyd, "Baby Face" Nelson, "Machine Gun" Kelly (who coined the term "G-Men" for federal agents), and Ma Barker, Fred Barker, and Alvin Karpis of the Barker-Karpis gang.

Focusing the public's attention on the Bureau's crime-fighting efforts in the 1930s was the idea of then-director J. Edgar Hoover. Hoover was a master at leveraging the public's interest in gangland-style crime and the media to the Bureau's advantage. He created a "Public Enemies" list of criminals who were wanted by the Bureau of Investigation. Much fanfare could then be made through the media when one of these public enemies was captured or killed. One of the most sensational news stories in the 1930s was the killing by Hoover's agents of John Dillinger— dubbed Public Enemy #1— just outside of the Chicago Biograph Theatre on July 22, 1934. Having received information of his presence at the theatre, agents led by Special Agent Melvin Purvis surrounded the building. When Dillinger emerged from the theatre after the show, agents confronted him. Dillinger drew a pistol but was unable to get a round off. Agents opened fire and Dillinger was dead at the scene. The publicity the Bureau of Investigation received after Dillinger's death, and in the wake of several other high profile captures or killings, was pivotal in the public's recognition of Hoover's agency as *the* premier federal law enforcement agency in the United States.[5]

In 1935, the Bureau of Investigation was renamed the "Federal Bureau of Investigation." The name, abbreviated as "FBI", has remained intact to this day. Hoover, who was director longer than any other leader of the FBI, was also its most influential director. Hoover made many changes to the FBI in the pursuit of professionalism in law enforcement. Today, as a direct result of Hoover's leadership and philosophy, the FBI continues to be the standard bearer for police professionalism—not only to the federal law enforcement community, but to all of law enforcement around the country and even around the world.

THE FBI FROM THE 1940s THROUGH THE 1960s

In 1939, World War II broke out in Europe. Although the United States itself was not at war, an ally whom we supplied was (Great Britain). The FBI began to identify and keep track of suspected agents of the Axis powers (Germany, Japan, and Italy) who were present in the United States. When the United States entered the war in 1941, those foreign agents were arrested and either prosecuted or deported. Approximately 1,300 Axis-power intelligence agents were identified and apprehended by the FBI during the war.[6]

After the war concluded, the FBI quickly shifted its focus away from the defeated Axis powers to the victorious Soviet Union. In the 1940s and 1950s, many academics and other elites were self-identified Communists. Many others, including mid- and high-level government officials, privately sympathized with the Communist Party in the United States. The Federal Bureau of Investigation was given the lead responsibility for quashing the threat and influence of Communism in the country. Key pieces of legislation were passed during this period of time that empowered the FBI to do just that.

On June 28, 1940, the Smith Act was enacted into law. That law made it a federal crime to advocate the violent overthrow of the United States. It was a more pointed law than the Sedition Act had been a century and a half earlier. The language outlawed specific actions and speech that implicated violence. As a consequence, the speech banned under the Smith Act is not constitutionally protected, and the law, although amended, has survived to this day. The original Smith Act of 1940 stated in part:[7]

Sec. 2. (a) It shall be unlawful for any person—

(1) to knowingly or willfully advocate, abet, advise, or teach the duty, necessity, desirability, or propriety of overthrowing or destroying any government in the United States by force or violence, or by the assassination of any officer of any such government;

(2) with the intent to cause the overthrow or destruction of any government in the United States, to print, publish, edit, issue, circulate, sell, distribute, or publicly display any written or printed matter advocating, advising, or teaching the duty, necessity, desirability, or propriety of overthrowing or destroying any government in the United States by force or violence;

(3) to organize or help to organize any society, group, or assembly of persons who teach, advocate, or encourage the overthrow or destruction of any government in the United States by force or violence; or to be or become a member of, or affiliate with, any such society, group, or assembly of persons, knowing the purposes thereof.

Sec. 2. (b) For the purposes of this section, the term "government in the United States" means the Government of the United States, the government of any State, Territory, or possession of the United States, the government of the District of Columbia, or the government of any political subdivision of any of them.

Sec. 3. It shall be unlawful for any person to attempt to commit, or to conspire to commit, any of the acts prohibited by the provisions of this title.

The FBI utilized the Smith Act to pursue vocal Communist Party members in the media, government, and unions, as well as others who were loosely confederated, such as anarchists. While plotting or engaging in actual violence against United States institutions had long been a federal criminal offense via the federal conspiracy statute, the Espionage Act of 1917, and other statutes, the Smith Act enabled the

FBI to target individuals and organizations that stood behind the actual subversive individuals and provided technical and moral support to the cause of violent overthrow of the United States government.

Additionally, the Atomic Energy Act of 1946 gave the FBI the authority to root out non-violent Communists who held sensitive positions in government service. In particular, the Act equipped the FBI to determine the loyalty of federal employees who had access to state secrets relating to atomic energy and weaponry. Probably the most famous case involving the identification, arrest, and prosecution of federal employees whose loyalty was not with the United States was that of Julius and Ethel Rosenberg.

In 1949, the FBI learned that information about the construction of the atomic bomb at Los Alamos during World War II (code-named the "Manhattan Project") had been passed to agents of the Soviet Union's secret police—the KGB. Through the investigation, it was learned that an Army enlisted man assigned to Los Alamos during the war, David Greenglass, had facilitated the transfer of atomic secrets to the Soviets at the behest of his brother-in-law and sister, namely Julius and Ethel Rosenberg. The investigation determined that the Rosenbergs were longtime members of the Communist Party. Through the investigation, the FBI uncovered several civilian and military government officials in the United States who were part of the scheme to transfer technological information about atomic weapons to the Soviets.

In July of 1950, Julius Rosenberg was arrested by FBI agents for conspiring to transfer state secrets to a foreign power—a violation of the Espionage Act of 1917 and a capital offense. Ethel Rosenberg was arrested on similar charges in August of 1950. In March of 1953, the Rosenbergs were convicted of espionage and sentenced to death. Others implicated in the spy ring were also convicted and sentenced to lengthy prison terms. On June 19, 1953, Julius and Ethel Rosenberg were executed via the electric chair at Sing Sing Prison in Ossining, New York.

According to J. Edgar Hoover, who was still FBI Director at that time, the Rosenbergs had committed the crime of century. Indeed, the transfer of secrets relating to atomic weaponry was a grave national security breach, and the American public tended to agree with Hoover's assessment. In the wake of the Rosenberg case and others, the FBI began to receive additional resources from Congress for the purpose of detecting and countering the threat of Soviet espionage conducted in the United States.

When J. Edgar Hoover had become director in 1924, the Bureau of Investigation employed a total of 650 people, about 400 of whom were special agents. There were 30 field offices. By the mid-1950s, the FBI employed just over 6,000 special agents—many of whom were dedicated to the counterespionage mission. Approximately one decade later, the FBI employed over 6,700 special agents and an additional 9,300 staffers in support functions in 59 field offices—essentially in every major American city. Clearly, a world war and the emergence of Communism as a threat were not without benefit for the expansion of the power and jurisdiction of the Federal Bureau of Investigation.[8]

J. EDGAR HOOVER

John Edgar Hoover is indisputably the most famous federal agent in American history. At the helm of the FBI, he turned an upstart federal law enforcement agency with limited law enforcement powers into the most respected law enforcement organization in the world. His career was controversial at times because of his tactics. However, avoiding controversy would have been difficult in the contentious and complicated time periods during which he shepherded the agency.

J. Edgar Hoover was born in Washington, DC in 1895. He attended George Washington University and graduated with a master of laws degree in 1917. Soon after completing his degree, he joined the U.S. Department of Justice as a lawyer with the General Intelligence Division. Hoover was quickly identified in the organization as a reliable, outstanding agent and as a potential leader within the organization. During his first year with the division, Hoover was promoted to head the Enemy Aliens Registration Section.[9] That assignment was very important, because the United States had just entered World War I and indeed did have enemy aliens within its midst. German espionage was a real concern during that period. But so was Communism. The Bolshevik Revolution in Russia took place in October of 1917. After World War I ended in 1918, the so-called "Red Scare" ensued in the United States. The Justice Department, through Hoover's efforts, aggressively prosecuted and deported many foreigners with Communist ties who were attempting to subvert America's economic and political systems. In 1919, Hoover was promoted yet again. This time, he was assigned to head the General Intelligence Division within the Department of Justice. Hoover continued to build a reputation as an ardent and effective foe of Communism.[10]

In 1921, the General Intelligence Division at the Justice Department was organizationally moved under the Bureau of Investigation. At that time, Hoover was selected by Bureau of Investigation director William J.

Burns to be the Bureau's deputy director. Then, in 1924, Director Burns was forced to resign his position due to ineffective leadership and scandal. Hoover, at the age of 29 years old, was appointed as the Bureau's sixth director—a position he would occupy for nearly 50 years.

Hoover inherited an agency with limited federal authority and a wounded reputation, due to Burns' ouster. Burns had been caught up in the Teapot Dome scandal that touched many high-ranking officials in the administration of President Warren G. Harding. The Teapot Dome scandal involved the bribery of Harding Administration officials by oil companies in exchange for the rights to drill on federally controlled lands. In that scandal, the Bureau of Investigation under Burns sought to provide cover for the Harding Administration by attempting to discredit Sen. Burton Wheeler of Montana, who was leading the congressional investigation of the scandal.[11]

Hoover was not personally implicated in the scandal, even though Burns had been a longtime friend and mentor. Hoover quickly infused into the organization his values, including an affinity for a progressive law enforcement model and no tolerance for corruption and cronyism (despite having benefited from cronyism himself). Hoover vowed to not permit the Bureau or its agents to be vulnerable to outside political influence again. Pursuant to this goal, Hoover ran a very tight, regimented organization and tolerated no dissent.

The Bureau of Investigation had over 400 special agents when Hoover took the post of director. Many of them were fired by Hoover as incompetent or unqualified. Hoover made every effort to professionalize the Bureau. He began a program of background checks for all special agents in the organization. He also implemented a rigorous special agent academy training program and installed physical fitness requirements. In 1932, Hoover established the Bureau's crime laboratory for the purpose of assisting agents, through science, with criminal investigative efforts. Approximately 1,000 examinations, most involving handwriting and firearms analyses, were conducted by the FBI laboratory during its first year of operation.[12]

As mentioned earlier, the FBI became a part of American popular culture under Hoover's leadership. It was seen as the chief opponent to violent gangsters in the 1930s. The FBI was also seen as a key part of America's victory in World War II because of its counterespionage efforts. In the 1950s and 1960s, Hoover stepped up the FBI's Cold War efforts to thwart the influences of Communist sympathizers and spies in the United States. In the 1960s and 1970s, the FBI emerged as the lead agency to protect the civil rights of all citizens in the desegregated South.

Herbert Johnson and Nancy Travis Wolfe identified three broad areas of law enforcement improvement that can be attributed to J. Edgar Hoover:[13]

1. Personnel and Management:
   - Special agents were appointed based upon qualifications, not political loyalties.
   - Special agents were required to possess a college degree in law or accounting.
   - Discipline was uniform.
   - The character of the special agents was a job criterion (even off-duty).
   - Special agent training was specialized and rigorous.
   - Organizational structure was hierarchical, with field-level supervision (by the Special Agents in Charge of each field office).
   - Advancement was based upon qualifications.

2. Investigative Practices:
   - The work ethic of agents was characterized as persistent and results-oriented.
   - Special agents relied on advanced technology and science to solve crimes.
   - A forensic laboratory was created.
   - Extensive intelligence files that could be cross-referenced for investigative leads were maintained.
   - Specified investigative procedures that protected the rights of suspects were codified into policy.

3. Law Enforcement Liaison and Training:
   - The FBI National Academy was created in 1935 and taught modern law enforcement investigation and management techniques for state and local police officials.
   - The *FBI Law Enforcement Bulletin*, a professional journal, was created in order to provide legal and investigative updates in the field of law enforcement.
   - The fingerprint identification division was created in order to collect and classify offender fingerprints sent from law enforcement agencies around the country for use in identification of suspects in new cases.

While J. Edgar Hoover's legacy was primarily one of law enforcement professionalization and advancement, his reign as director was not without controversy. Today, most historians agree that Hoover kept secret files on potential opponents. Those files presumably contained information that could be used to blackmail his opponents into complying with whatever wishes or demands he may have had. He was even thought to have leveraged the sexual orientation and sexual practices of others for the benefit of the Bureau. Those about whom Hoover is suspected of having kept files include notable politicians over the years, civil rights activists such as Martin Luther King, and even President John F. Kennedy.

However, even Hoover's critics acknowledge that any leverage Hoover did possess (with or without secret files) was used for the benefit of the FBI rather than for Hoover himself. He loved the FBI and did everything in his power to protect it, develop it, and keep it on the forefront of advances in the field of law enforcement. To the extent that he accomplished that goal, all of law enforcement benefited.

THE FBI FROM THE 1970s TO THE PRESENT

The FBI remained engaged in the counterespionage effort throughout the Cold War, which ended with the fall of communism in Eastern Europe and the Soviet Union in the late 1980s and early 1990s. However, the FBI also became involved with many other high-profile types of cases. In the 1970s and 1980s, the FBI aggressively investigated domestic terror groups—on both the left and the right wings of the political spectrum. Groups advocating political violence in urban areas and on college campuses tended to be leftist/Marxist in their orientations. Such groups included the Black Panthers, the Weathermen, and the Symbionese Liberation Army—the group responsible for the kidnapping and brainwashing of Patty Hearst in February of 1974. Kidnappings and violent bank-robberies were commonly committed by these groups to raise funds for their antigovernment activities.

The FBI also redoubled its effort to investigate groups on the right-wing of the political spectrum. Those groups tended to be nationalistic or ethnocentric rather than ideological. Chief among them was the Ku Klux Klan (KKK) and its offshoots. White supremacy groups like the KKK were prevalent in the South, but many supporters moved into northwestern states, such as Idaho and the Dakotas, where sentiment against the federal government was already strong. Groups such as

Aryan Nations, the Aryan National Alliance, and the Order, received intense focus from the FBI and other federal agencies in the 1980s.

The FBI also treated public corruption and organized crime as major priorities during the 1970s and 1980s. In 1978, the FBI conducted a bribery investigation later dubbed "ABSCAM" by the media. For the investigation, the FBI created a fake corporation called Abdul Enterprises, Ltd. Special agents then posed as Middle Eastern businessmen affiliated with Abdul Enterprises who were seeking to procure favors from members of Congress. The investigation resulted in bribery convictions for six sitting members of Congress (one member of the Senate and five House members). Critics of that investigation note that it came dangerously close to entrapment—that is, enticing a person to commit a crime that he or she was not predisposed to commit. However, none of the convictions were ever overturned on that basis.[14]

The FBI also targeted the potential for bribery and corruption in the judiciary. "Operation Greylord" was one such example. In the early 1980s, the FBI investigated the Cook County, Illinois (Chicago) court system for corruption. By 1984, 92 public officials had been indicted by a federal grand jury. Most of the officials were eventually convicted of accepting bribes and abusing their public offices. The officials included 17 judges, 48 attorneys, 8 Cook County court officials, 8 local police officers, 10 deputy sheriffs, and a member of the Illinois state legislature.[15]

Beginning in the 1980s, continuing through the 1990s, and up to the present, the FBI has increasingly focused its attention on acts of terrorism. In the middle and late 1980s, several acts of terrorism were perpetrated against American citizens abroad. The most significant incident in the 1980s was the bombing of Pan American Airlines Flight 103 over Lockerbee, Scotland, on December 21, 1988. A total of 259 people on board and 11 people on the ground were killed. The FBI worked closely with British law enforcement officials and those in other countries to solve the case. In the end, it was determined that intelligence operatives of the Libyan government had committed the crime.

In the 1990s, the focus on terrorism continued in response to several high-profile incidents. In February of 1993, the World Trade Center in New York City was bombed by Middle Eastern terrorists living in the United States. In April of 1995, the Murrah Federal Building in Oklahoma City, Oklahoma, was destroyed with a truck bomb by antigovernment zealot Timothy McVeigh and other co-conspirators. That bombing killed 168 people. In 1996, the Khobar Towers military barracks for American airmen in Dhahran, Saudi Arabia, was truck-bombed, killing 19 Americans. Also in 1996, Olympic Park in Atlanta,

Georgia, was pipe-bombed during the Olympic festivities by another antigovernment zealot—Eric Rudolph (also responsible for bombing two abortion clinics and one gay night club). One person was killed and dozens were injured in Olympic Park. In 1998, the American embassies in Kenya and Tanzania were bombed, killing hundreds. In 2000, the USS Cole was struck by suicide bombers in a boat as the American naval vessel was anchored at the Port of Aden in Yemen for refueling. Nineteen sailors died in that attack. And then came September 11, 2001 and the second World Trade Center attack (killing 3,000). Before the year was out, Anthrax-laced letters killed five people.

A detailed explanation of the federal law enforcement response to terrorism by the FBI and other agencies appears in a later chapter. However, it is clear that the FBI has made counterterrorism its number one priority.

Not unexpectedly, the Federal Bureau of Investigation grew in size at the same time that its responsibilities grew. By the end of the 1980s, the FBI employed 9,600 special agents and over 13,000 support personnel. However, because of its growing list of duties—particularly in the realm of confronting terrorism and protecting national security—the FBI grew precipitously between 1993 and 2001, gaining nearly 3,000 special agents and 5,000 support staff. Today, the FBI has over 12,400 special agents and nearly 18,000 support personnel. Its annual budget exceeds $4 billion.[16]

The FBI has identified its top 10 priorities as a federal law enforcement agency as follows:[17]

1. Protect the United States from terrorist attack.
2. Protect the United States against foreign intelligence operations and espionage.
3. Protect the United States against cyber-based attacks and high-tech crimes.
4. Combat public corruption at all levels.
5. Protect civil rights.
6. Combat transnational and national criminal organizations and enterprises.
7. Combat major white-collar crime.
8. Combat significant violent crime.
9. Support federal, state, county, municipal, and international partners.
10. Upgrade technology to successfully perform the FBI's mission.

The first three priorities relate to the security of the United States, especially vis-à-vis threats posed from outside of America's borders.

Public corruption and civil rights investigations remain relatively high. However, organized crime, violent crime, and fraud trail toward the bottom of the list. Nowhere on the list is drug enforcement, which was identified as one of the top priorities for the FBI only a few years ago. The fact is that the FBI, even with expanded resources, is unable to be all things to all people. Antiterrorism operations are personnel-intensive. Special agents may be needed, for example, on a surveillance team covering one of a dozen suspected players in possible terror cell. Those agents are simply unavailable for assignment to other investigations.

In essence, the ordering of current priorities for the FBI poses many opportunities for other federal law enforcement agencies to take the lead. Over the years, the FBI worked very hard to secure operational jurisdiction in all areas of federal criminal law. Even while possessing exclusive jurisdiction relating to crimes such as bank robberies, kidnapping, and civil rights enforcement, it worked diligently to gain jurisdiction in areas already covered by other federal agencies, such as drug enforcement, smuggling, fraud against the government, and firearms and explosives violations. Indeed, the legal authority to do so has long existed under Title 28 of the United States Code, section 533 which states:

The Attorney General may appoint officials

(1) to detect and prosecute crimes against the United States;

(2) to assist in the protection of the person of the President; and

(3) to conduct such other investigations regarding official matters under the control of the Department of Justice and the Department of State as may be directed by the Attorney General.

This section does not limit the authority of departments and agencies to investigate crimes against the United States when investigative jurisdiction has been assigned by law to such departments and agencies.

Many in the federal law enforcement community outside of the Federal Bureau of Investigation, while taking solace in the last sentence of the above statute, believed their own agencies' reputations would rise after serious missteps by the FBI in recent years. The FBI received very serious criticism for its handling of the Ruby Ridge, Idaho, stand-off in 1992 and the Waco siege in 1993.

In August of 1992, an individual named Randy Weaver was indicted for a federal weapons violation. When he failed to show up for his court appearance, a federal magistrate issued an arrest warrant. The U.S.

Marshals Service sought to serve the arrest warrant on Weaver at his cabin, located in the mountains near Ruby Ridge in northern Idaho. In the woods near his cabin, deputy marshals came across Weaver, his teenage son Sammy Weaver, and family friend Kevin Harris. Both Sammy Weaver and Harris were carrying rifles. The deputy marshals and the Weaver party exchanged gunfire. When the shooting stopped, Deputy U.S. Marshal William Degan and Sammy Weaver were both dead.

At that point, Randy Weaver and Kevin Harris retreated to the cabin to join other Weaver family members. With the death of a federal law enforcement officer, the FBI asserted jurisdiction and took control of the siege. During the 10-day standoff before a surrender to authorities was negotiated, an FBI sniper accidentally shot and killed Vicki Weaver (Randy Weaver's wife) while she was holding her baby daughter. The FBI sharpshooter was later charged by the local county attorney with manslaughter under state law. However, the charges were vacated in federal court because the agent had been acting in an official capacity as a federal law enforcement officer at the time of the killing.

In an unrelated case less than a year later, the Bureau of Alcohol, Tobacco, and Firearms (ATF), part of the Treasury Department at that time, attempted to serve search and arrest warrants in February of 1993 on a compound controlled by a religious sect known as the Branch Davidians near Waco, Texas. The warrants related to violations of federal firearms laws. Scores of ATF agents surrounded the compound. When they attempted to gain entry, they were met with gunfire. After an intense firefight, four ATF special agents were dead and at least 16 were wounded. Six Branch Davidians had also been killed in the battle.

However, David Koresh (the sect's leader) and dozens of others, including women and children, remained inside the compound. Again, because federal law enforcement officers had been killed, the FBI asserted its jurisdiction as the lead agency and took control of the standoff. Negotiations for the sect's surrender went on for nearly two months. Finally, on April 19, 1993 (day 51 of the siege), the FBI moved in with armored vehicles and deployed tear gas in different locations of the compound's main building. At that time, a fire was started on the inside (presumably intentionally by sect members who preferred dying to arrest). The fire spread throughout the building. Nearly 80 people inside the compound, including 19 children, perished. Nine occupants fled the burning compound and were arrested.

The FBI had no shortage of critics after its handling of the sieges in Ruby Ridge and Waco. Members of the public and members of

Congress who were concerned about the growing powers of federal law enforcement saw these two incidents as further evidence that federal law enforcement, if unchecked, would get out of control. Investigations conducted by committees in both the House and Senate produced reports critical of the FBI and its management. And yet the FBI continued to receive increases in funding and expanded authority in subsequent years.

With a growing emphasis on national security matters, the FBI finds itself today in the position of having to retreat from some of the investigative areas it historically concentrated on (e.g., drug enforcement, smuggling, fraud). It remains to be seen whether other federal agencies will see the FBI's action as an opportunity to raise their own reputations in the eyes of Congress (since Ruby Ridge and Waco failed to do so) by picking up the slack.

CHAPTER 5

Overshadowed but Not Forgotten (Other Treasury and Justice Agencies)

Throughout the 20th century, federal law enforcement as a whole has grown substantially from its small beginnings. Over the years, a reputation for federal law enforcement has developed which attributes to it epitomized notions of police professionalism and of cutting-edge, highly trained, and technologically sophisticated criminal investigators and investigations. Certainly, the Federal Bureau of Investigation has emerged as the nation's premier federal law enforcement agency. This organization has the broadest federal law enforcement power, with statutory authority to investigate any federal crime concurrently with other authorized federal agencies as it sees fit. Further, the FBI possesses additional statutory authority to investigate some federal crimes alone.

Even so, the strong reputation of federal law enforcement was not built by the FBI solely. Many other federal law enforcement agencies contributed to this reputation. In fairness, though, the primary pillars on which the standing of federal law enforcement was built was not propped up by the collective sum of today's 70 or more federal law enforcement agencies. For most of this country's history, when anyone spoke of federal law enforcement, if one was not speaking of the FBI, then one was almost certainly speaking of one or more of the few agencies located in the Departments of Justice and Treasury.

In this chapter, those "other" Justice and Treasury agencies will be explored—particularly in so far as their respective missions have developed and evolved (often in the shadow of the FBI).

U.S. MARSHALS SERVICE

The United States Marshals Service is arguably the oldest federal law enforcement agency in America. As noted earlier, the Judiciary Act of 1789 assigned to the U.S. Marshals and their deputies only law enforcement-related responsibilities. U.S. Marshals were responsible for enforcing a wide range of federal criminal laws in the first century of the nation's existence. However, over many years, Congress has seen fit to bestow primary law enforcement jurisdiction for many federal criminal offenses upon other agencies. With the rise of the Federal Bureau of Investigation, the U.S. Secret Service, and many other enforcement organizations, relatively few of the Marshals' historical investigative responsibilities of decades past remain. So where has that left the nation's oldest federal law enforcement agency?

The United States Marshals Service remains one of the key law enforcement agencies in the U.S. Department of Justice. The Marshals Service acts as the federal sheriff. It still possesses a primary responsibility for serving the processes of federal courts (although many other federal law enforcement agencies have been granted permission to do so as well).

Today's U.S. Marshals Service employs over 3,300 marshals and Deputy U.S. Marshals throughout the United States and the U.S. Territories. When the Judiciary Act was passed in 1789, only 13 judicial districts existed. Today, U.S. Marshals serve in all of 94 federal judicial districts. This includes at least one district in each of the 50 states as well as districts in territories such as Guam, Puerto Rico, the Virgin Islands, and, of course, the District of Columbia. Many states have more than one district. In fact, New York City alone has three federal judicial districts.

Today, the U.S. Marshals Service is empowered with law enforcement authority under Title 18, Section 3053, and Title 28, Section 566. Title 18, United States Code, Section 3053 states:

United States marshals and their deputies may carry firearms and may make arrests without warrant for any offense against the United States committed in their presence, or for any felony cognizable under the laws of the United States if they have reasonable grounds to believe that the person to be arrested has committed or is committing such felony.

The language articulating the law enforcement authority of U.S. Marshals and their deputies mirrors the language found in 28 USC 566 and has been codified in one form or another since the 19th century. U.S. Marshals have broad law enforcement authority to carry firearms and to make arrests for *any* federal criminal law violation. However, 28 USC 566 goes on to define the U.S. Marshals Service's primary responsibility today.

Subsection (e) (1) and (2) states:

(1) The United States Marshals Service is authorized to
   (A) provide for the personal protection of Federal jurists, court officers, witnesses, and other threatened persons in the interests of justice where criminal intimidation impedes on the functioning of the judicial process or any other official proceeding; and
   (B) investigate such fugitive matters, both within and outside the United States, as directed by the Attorney General.
(2) Nothing in paragraph (1)(B) shall be construed to interfere with or supersede the authority of other Federal agencies or bureaus.

According to the statute, the Marshals Service is to provide federal court security and conduct fugitive-from-justice investigations. Further, the statute does not grant the Marshals exclusive jurisdiction in these areas. The statute instead recognizes concurrent jurisdiction in the matter of fugitive investigations, courthouse security, and court processes integrity by noting that the statute itself does not interfere with the lawful authority of other agencies authorized to engage in those activities.

In light of the authorities granted to the U.S. Marshals Service, the organization has carved out several modern-day law enforcement niches in the federal law enforcement community, even while sharing the authority to engage in some of these activities with many other federal agencies. The Marshals Service provides the following three primary federal law enforcement services:[1]

1. Service of court processes and warrants
2. Court security
3. Prisoner transport and custody.

According to the U.S. Justice Department, the U.S. Marshals Service arrested over 36,000 federal fugitives wanted on federal warrants in 2004. This amounted to 55% of all federal arrest warrants executed in that year. Additionally, deputy U.S. marshals made over 31,000 state arrest warrants through their participation on fugitive task forces.

The arrest of fugitives is perhaps the most well-known of the services provided by the Marshals Service, but there are many others. Annually, U.S. Marshals serve hundreds of thousands of civil and criminal subpoenas, summonses, and other court orders. In 2004, pursuant to federal court orders, the U.S. Marshals seized assets for forfeiture totaling $964 million.[2]

As a part of the Marshals' court security operations, the agency protects over 2,000 federal judges and magistrates at more than 400 court facilities around the nation. The Marshals Service also deploys 4,500 contracted court security officers (CSOs)—most of whom are retired police officers. The Marshals Service is also responsible for protecting federal witnesses and jurors. The agency manages the federal government's famous Witness Protection Program. Since 1971, the U.S. Marshals have relocated and provided new identities for 7,700 witnesses and over 9,800 family members of witnesses.[3]

The U.S. Marshals Service is also responsible for the custody and care of all persons convicted of a federal crime who have not yet been sentenced and then placed in the custody of the Bureau of Prisons. On any given day, the Marshals Service has custody of nearly 50,000 such federal prisoners. The Marshals Service is also responsible for transporting all federal prisoners to and from their court appearances. They also contract with local and county law enforcement agencies for the provision of holding facilities for federal prisoners who are under arrest and awaiting trial.

The Marshals' system of prisoner movement, known as the Justice Prisoner and Alien Transportation System (JPATS), was responsible for nearly 300,000 prisoner movements in 2004, including more than 175,000 prisoner movements by air.[4]

No longer the generalist federal law enforcement agency it once was, the U.S. Marshals Service has achieved a reputation of excellence in delivering the services discussed here, for which it is well-known and well-regarded in the federal law enforcement community today.

IMMIGRATION AND NATURALIZATION SERVICE

The U.S. Justice Department's Immigration and Naturalization Service, or INS for short, no longer exists as such. In March of 2003, the agency was transferred to the newly created Department of Homeland Security along with 21 other federal agencies. The rationale and other details of this transfer will be addressed in a later chapter. The transfer notwithstanding, the Immigration and Naturalization Service was, for

100 years, the agency responsible for enforcing the nation's immigration laws. Some of these laws were strictly administrative or civil in nature; others triggered criminal penalties when violated. One thing is certain: The crafting and enforcement of the nation's immigration laws, which proved to be so necessary in the late 19th century, resulted in one of the largest segments of the federal law enforcement community today.

The INS traces its roots back to the Immigration Act of 1891. Prior to the enactment of that legislation, there were very few laws in place to regulate immigration to the United States. In fact, the primary governmental entity that engaged in immigration control was each of the individual states, despite the express assignment of that responsibility to the federal government in the Constitution. Finally, in 1875, the United States Supreme Court handed down a ruling that unequivocally declared that the regulation of immigration was the responsibility of the federal government.

That same year, 1875, Congress passed legislation that barred convicts and prostitutes from immigrating to the United States. Next, Congress passed the Immigration Act of 1882, which specified the various grounds for excluding foreigners from visiting or residing in the United States. The Act also gave the Secretary of the Treasury the authority to contract with state and local governments for the provision of law enforcement services at the nation's ports of entry.[5]

Then, in 1891, the Bureau of Immigration was established in the Treasury Department. This bureau employed immigration inspectors at 24 different inspection stations. The inspectors were responsible for examining the passenger manifests of ships coming into the United States, as well as for questioning the passengers about their eligibility for entering and remaining in the United States. As the years passed, several organizational and mission changes occurred for the Bureau of Immigration. In 1903, the bureau was moved under the newly created U.S. Department of Commerce. In 1906, the added mission of naturalization (i.e., the process of granting American citizenship to immigrants) became part of the bureau's responsibility (The bureau was renamed the Bureau of Immigration and Naturalization). In 1933, it was transferred to the U.S. Department of Labor. At that point, its name was changed to the "Immigration and Naturalization Service." Finally, in 1940, the INS was moved to the Justice Department, where it remained until 2003.[6]

The transfer to the Justice Department coincided with significant growth of the organization. The INS in 1940 employed approximately 4,000 people. These included inspectors and border patrol officers as well as adjudication officers, advocates, and immigration judges. One year later, the agency employed just under 6,900 people. In 1942, the number grew to 8,500 INS employees.[7]

In its annual report to Congress in 1942, the INS declared that it understood its primary mission to include:

- Examination of all seeking entry into the United States to determine their right to enter
- Preventing illegal entry of aliens into the United States
- Enforcing the departure from the United States of illegal aliens
- Locating and tracking all aliens in the United States
- Examination of those seeking citizenship for their eligibility to naturalize.

Because the nation was at war, the foregoing primary mission of the INS was especially important.

The mission of INS articulated in its 1942 report continued essentially unfettered into the 1980s, when additional law-enforcement related duties were assigned to it. In particular, the Immigration Reform Act of 1986 empowered INS criminal investigators to investigate American employers who knowingly (thereby unlawfully) hired illegal ("undocumented") aliens. By that time, the INS had grown to well over 30,000 employees.

Until the reorganization in 2003, the law enforcement apparatus at INS consisted of several different types of positions. Immigration inspectors continued to be the first point of contact for foreigners arriving in the United States. While they did not exercise law enforcement authority (i.e., they did not carry firearms or make arrests), their primary job was to ascertain the legality of a person's entry into the country, and they worked closely with INS law enforcement officers when a foreigner's legal status was suspect.

Immigration agents in the INS did possess law enforcement authority. Their primary mission has been to locate aliens who are in the United States illegally, arrest them, and hold them until deportation proceedings were held. They would also work closely with INS detention enforcement officers to ensure that aliens were escorted to their home countries when deportation was ordered.

Immigration agents are not to be confused with INS special agents. Special agents with the INS were fully empowered criminal investigators whose primary responsibilities were investigating aliens committing crimes in the United States such as human trafficking, alien smuggling, and immigration fraud (such as the classic phony marriage arrangement between a foreigner and an American so that the former may remain in the country), and investigating employer violations of immigration laws. Special agents of the Immigration and Naturalization Service also served on antigang taskforces and joint terrorism task forces (JTTFs). JTTFs exist in every state and most major cities. They are organized and managed by the FBI and are staffed by agents and officers from various federal, state, and local law enforcement agencies. The purpose of the JTTFs is to bring the investigative expertise of agents and officers from across the broad spectrum of law enforcement to bear on the fight against terrorism.

One of the most well-known law enforcement components of what was the Immigration and Naturalization Service is the U.S. Border Patrol. The Border Patrol was established in May of 1924 as a part of the Bureau of Immigration. Border Patrol agents, who are uniformed patrol officers, were assigned predominantly along the southern border of the United States, just as they are today.

In 1925, a total of 450 Border Patrol agents were hired—primarily from the ranks of local and state law enforcement in southern border states. That number nearly doubled 10 years later and by 1941, the Border Patrol employed over 1,500 agents. The number of agents in the Border Patrol remained relatively stable from the 1940s through the 1970s. However, in the late 1970s, the Border Patrol ranks grew to over 2,000 and continued to grow. In 1992, the number of Border Patrol agents was over 4,000. By the year 2000, there were more than 9,000 agents.[8] In 2003, there were over 11,000, and politicians were promising authorization for even more.[9]

The Border Patrol's mission reflects that of the larger INS law enforcement mission—to detect and apprehend illegal aliens, prevent the smuggling of humans or contraband (such as drugs or weapons) into the country, and arrange for the return of illegal aliens to their home countries upon capture. The Border Patrol fulfills this mission, as its name suggests, through patrol work. Agents use automobiles, all-terrain vehicles, horses, boats, and aircraft to patrol America's borders with Mexico and Canada. In total, the Border Patrol is responsible for securing 7,000 miles of land border and 2,000 miles of coastal waters surrounding the Florida peninsula and Puerto Rico.

Although the majority of Border Patrol agents are located on America's southern border, the terror attacks of September 11, 2001, created an impetus for a greater Border Patrol presence on the porous northern border with Canada. For some time, Canada has had relatively liberal and permissive immigration policies vis-à-vis foreign nationals from countries considered hostile to the United States. After 9/11, border security with Canada was tightened out of concern that potential terror suspects would seek to enter the United States from Canada.

While the U.S. Marshals Service serves more arrest warrants than all other federal law enforcement agencies combined, the Border Patrol makes more total arrests, with or without a warrant, than all other law enforcement agencies combined, including the Marshals Service. According to the Department of Homeland Security, the Border Patrol arrested 1.2 illegal aliens and smugglers in Fiscal Year 2005. That year, they also interdicted illegal drugs valued at $1.4 billion.[10]

As a result of the Homeland Security Act of 2002, all law enforcement officers of the Immigration and Naturalization Service were transferred to various bureaus and directorates of the U.S. Department of Homeland Security in 2003. Specifically, INS special agents were transferred to the newly created bureau, U.S. Immigration and Customs Enforcement (ICE), Office of Investigations. The detention and removal officers were also transferred to ICE, under the ICE Office of Detention and Removal.

Immigration inspectors were transferred to the U.S. Bureau of Customs and Border Protection (CBP) within the Department of Homeland Security, as was the U.S. Border Patrol, which remains an organizationally distinct agency.

The duties and authorities of these various officers and agents remain basically the same. More about this transfer and the creation of the Department of Homeland Security—which was the largest reorganization of the federal government since the creation of the Department of Defense in 1947—will be addressed in the last chapter of this book.

DRUG ENFORCEMENT ADMINISTRATION

The Drug Enforcement Administration (DEA) is an agency within the U.S. Department of Justice. However, like many other federal law enforcement agencies, the heritage of the DEA is actually rooted in the U.S. Treasury Department. On December 17, 1914, the Harrison Narcotics Tax Act became the law of the land. That legislation required that all persons who produced, imported, manufactured, dispensed, sold, distributed, or gave away opium or coca leaves, their salts, derivatives, or preparations, had to register with the government. The purpose of the registration was to facilitate a special tax on all transactions involving narcotic substances. In 1914, addiction to cocaine or heroin was seen as a growing problem, but not necessarily a law enforcement issue. It was a tax issue. As such, the enforcement of drug laws such as the Harrison Act was the responsibility of the Treasury Department.[11]

With the passage of the 18th Amendment to the U.S. Constitution in 1919, which prohibited the manufacture, sale, and transportation of intoxicating liquor in the United States, the Treasury Department set up a Prohibition Unit to investigate violations of the Volstead Act, which was the codification of 18th Amendment violations as a federal crime. Responsibility for investigating violations of anti-drug statutes was also given to the Treasury Department's Prohibition Unit. Most enforcement efforts were directed at violations of the Volstead Act. Treasury special agent Elliot Ness of the Prohibition Unit became widely known for his fight against Chicago-area organized crime, which routinely violated the Volstead Act through their speakeasy establishments.

In 1933, the constitutional prohibition of alcohol was repealed by the 21st Amendment. Yet anti-drug laws remained on the books. By this time, heroin and marijuana had been effectively banned in the United States, in 1925 and 1930, respectively. The Prohibition Unit at Treasury was dissolved, but a new federal drug enforcement agency was created. This new agency, the Bureau of Narcotics, remained a part of the Treasury Department until 1968. In 1968, the Bureau of Narcotics was moved to the Department of Justice and combined with the Bureau of Drug Abuse Control, which came from the Department of Health, Education, and Welfare's Food and Drug Administration. The two bureaus merged to form the Justice Department's Bureau of Narcotics and Dangerous Drugs (BNDD). The BNDD, as a Justice Department agency, eventually changed its name to the Drug Enforcement Administration in 1973, absorbing additional drug enforcement personnel from other government agencies in the process. But effectively, the DEA as we know it today began in the form of the Bureau of Narcotics and Dangerous Drugs in 1968.

Drug enforcement as a federal law enforcement function has always been surrounded by some controversy. Most Americans believe that the country should outlaw potentially dangerous drugs. But not all Americans do. A sizable minority in the United States views drug use as a victimless crime—or believe it would be victimless if the criminal enterprises behind drug trafficking no longer had reason to exist. Few Americans have robbed a bank or stolen checks out of the mail. Little sympathy exists for such federal offenders. But according to DEA estimates, 74 million Americans have engaged in illegal drug use at one time or another.[12]

In 1970, the Comprehensive Drug Prevention and Control Act was enacted into law. Title II of this legislation, known as the Controlled Substances Act, went into effect in May of 1971. The Controlled Substances Act became and continues to be the cornerstone of drug enforcement in the United States. The Act replaced over 50 disparate drug laws and consolidated existing prohibitions into a single bill. The Bureau of Narcotics and Dangerous Drugs was pegged as the chief investigative agency for the enforcement of the Controlled Substances Act. In 1973, when the agency's name changed to the Drug Enforcement Administration, the relevant federal laws empowering the BNDD were amended to reflect the agency's new name—but the enforcement authority continued without missing a beat.

The DEA receives its law enforcement authority from Title 21, Section 828. Title 21 is the portion of the United States Code that contains most of America's food and drug laws. Section 828(a) states:

(a) Any officer or employee of the Drug Enforcement Administration or any State or local law enforcement officer designated by the Attorney General may

 (1) carry firearms;
 (2) execute and serve search warrants, arrest warrants, administrative inspection warrants, subpoenas, and summonses issued under the authority of the United States;
 (3) make arrests without warrant (A) for any offense against the United States committed in his presence, or (B) for any felony, cognizable under the laws of the United States, if he has probable cause to believe that the person to be arrested has committed or is committing a felony;
 (4) make seizures of property pursuant to the provisions of this subchapter; and
 (5) perform such other law enforcement duties as the Attorney General may designate.

Interestingly, subsection (a) (5) gives the Attorney General of the United States broad authority to use special agents of the DEA in any way he or she sees fit. Regardless of the merit one assigns to the enforcement of drug laws in the United States, the DEA is an agency that exists for a well-defined purpose—going after federal drug offenders. However, many critics of the growing federal law enforcement community look to the language in subsection (a) (5) and rightfully note that most federal agents can be used in virtually any capacity the Attorney General sees fit. The effect is that, instead of several small federal agencies with narrow missions, there actually exists a single, very large federal law enforcement machine that can be utilized for general federal law enforcement purposes—usually at the expense (say the critics) of civil liberties.

The DEA's ancestor, the federal Bureau of Narcotics, was in fact caught up in a major violation of a citizen's civil rights that eventually produced a landmark Supreme Court case. In the 1971 case of *Bivens v. Six Unknown Narcotics Agents*, the Supreme Court ruled that federal agents who violated the civil rights of citizens would no longer be deemed absolutely immune to civil liability if they acted with gross negligence or intentionality. In this case, the narcotics special agents carelessly served search and arrest warrants at the wrong address, causing injury and property damage. The Justice Department sought to have Bivens' liability suit dismissed due to the immunity of federal agents and the lack of applicability of 42 USC 1983 (which does provide for the liability of state and local law enforcement officers). The Supreme Court in *Bivens* agreed that 42 USC 1983 did not apply to federal agents; on the other hand, the Federal Tort Claims Act did—and the effect on the case was just the same. The actions of narcotics agents in the Bivens case resulted in the elimination of sovereign immunity for federal law enforcement agents (403 US 388 (1971)).

Despite tepid support by some for the federal drug laws of the United States, the DEA has grown over the years—thanks in large part to the so-called "War on Drugs" that began in the 1980s under President Ronald Reagan. During that time, federal penalties for drug violators, including first-time offenders, were greatly enhanced. In fact, prior to the 1980s and the stepped-up effort to fight drug trafficking and drug use, most of the federal prison population was made up of criminals from relatively higher socioeconomic backgrounds, such as those who were engaged in organized crime, mail fraud, defrauding the government, and so forth. By the mid-1990s, after about a decade of the "War on Drugs," approximately 60% of the federal prison inmate population were there for federal drug offenses.[13]

In 1973, the DEA employed 1,470 special agents nationwide and in outposts around the world. Just two years later, the number of special agents rose to 2,135. In 2005, the DEA employed over 5,200 special agents and 5,500 support personnel. The annual budget allocation for the agency exceeds $2 billion.[14]

The Drug Enforcement Administration has identified several priorities as a part of its mission. The priorities are:[15]

- Investigation and preparation for the prosecution of major violators of controlled substance laws operating at interstate and international levels.

- Investigation and preparation for prosecution of criminals and drug gangs who perpetrate violence in our communities and terrorize citizens through fear and intimidation.

- Management of a national drug intelligence program in cooperation with federal, state, local, and foreign officials to collect, analyze, and disseminate strategic and operational drug intelligence information.

- Seizure and forfeiture of assets derived from, traceable to, or intended to be used for illicit drug trafficking.

- Enforcement of the provisions of the Controlled Substances Act as they pertain to the manufacture, distribution, and dispensing of legally produced controlled substances.

- Coordination and cooperation with federal, state and local law enforcement officials on mutual drug enforcement efforts and enhancement of such efforts through exploitation of potential interstate and international investigations beyond local or limited federal jurisdictions and resources.

- Coordination and cooperation with federal, state, and local agencies, and with foreign governments, in programs designed to reduce the availability of illicit abuse-type drugs on the United States market through non-enforcement methods such as crop eradication, crop substitution, and training of foreign officials.

- Responsibility, under the policy guidance of the Secretary of State and U.S. Ambassadors, for all programs associated with drug law enforcement counterparts in foreign countries.

- Liaison with the United Nations, Interpol, and other organizations on matters relating to international drug control programs.

In identifying the organization's investigative priorities, the DEA leadership resisted the temptation to include a call to arms against international terrorism. Many federal agencies have found ways to link their own investigative jurisdiction to the broader cause against terrorism, thus enhancing the value of the investigative programs in the eyes of the White House and Congress, who have shown no reluctance to expend funds in that fight.

The DEA actually could quite legitimately claim a nexus between a segment of its cases and the "War on Terror." The term "narco-terrorism" has existed for many years and generally refers to the campaign of terror that drug cartels and political insurgent groups wage against their own governments (usually in Latin America). The ability to wage these campaigns are funded by the profits from the illegal drug trade. Today, we know that Islamic terror groups such as Al Qaeda have indeed profited from drug trafficking and have funded some of their efforts by trading opium grown in the fields of Afghanistan. It is also true that the DEA has conducted precisely those types of investigations in various other parts of the world, including Latin America, Asia, and elsewhere.

Further, the DEA is neck-deep in the business of intelligence gathering, because it operates the El Paso Intelligence Center (EPIC) in El Paso, Texas. EPIC was established in 1974 and has been a major source of intelligence data for all of federal law enforcement for most of the years since. While DEA runs the center, law enforcement officers from 15 other federal agencies and the Texas Department of Public Safety are also detailed to EPIC. Currently, over 300 special agents, state agents, and intelligence analysts work at the center for the purpose of collecting and analyzing information about drug trafficking and immigration movement patterns. EPIC has also collected data on other criminal enterprises that have an interest in exploiting the border between the United States and Mexico, including terrorist organizations.

Despite this involvement in the antiterrorism effort, and to the agency's credit, the mission statement focuses on DEA's drug interdiction mission. The agency appears to know who it is and what it is all about—and it is content with that knowledge.

U.S. CUSTOMS SERVICE

For its entire 200 year history, until 2003, the U.S. Customs Service and its forerunner organizations had been housed in the U.S. Department of the Treasury. Like the Immigration and Naturalization Service at the Justice Department, the U.S. Customs Service ceased to exist in March 2003. Also like INS, the entirety of law enforcement operations at U.S. Customs was transferred to the Department of Homeland Security as a result of the Homeland Security Act of 2002.

In Chapter 2, it was noted that the Customs Service originated, in part, with the Revenue Cutter Service in the late 18th century (along with the Coast Guard). But like many other federal law enforcement agencies, the U.S. Customs Service—known as the Bureau of Customs for most of its history— began to actually take on the appearance of a bone fide law enforcement organization in the late 19th and early 20th centuries.

For example, in 1870 Congress passed a law that established a "Special Agency Service" within the Customs Division at the Treasury Department. That was the earliest of the forerunners to the modern-day Office of Investigations for U.S. Customs.[16] In 1917, the Bureau of Customs established an investigative arm to deal with smuggling and suspicious documentation of American sailors. In 1918, the Bureau of Customs adopted standard uniforms for all of its employees. The uniforms were not unlike the police uniforms that had been adopted by state and local law enforcement agencies. In the 1920s, Customs employees participated in the Treasury Department's Prohibition Bureau by going after bootleggers and organized crime. At that time, U.S. Customs agents clearly engaged in the investigations as full-fledged federal law enforcement agents. According to Customs historian Anne Saba, more Customs officers lost their lives in the line of duty during Prohibition than at any other time in American history.[17] In 1935, the Bureau of Customs established an academy for its officers and plainclothes agents. The academy instructed the employees on the law, revenue collection, criminal investigation techniques, and firearms use. Certainly by the 1930s, United States Customs was a bone fide federal law enforcement agency that at least some segments of the nation's criminal element would have to reckon with.

The authority of the U.S. Customs continued to expand in the 1940s. In addition to playing a key role in countering espionage and embargo violations during World War II, the Bureau of Customs received statutory authority in 1948 to enforce drug laws and in 1949 to enforce the Export Control Act, which regulated or banned the export of technology and weaponry to various countries.

Throughout the middle and latter part of the 20th century, U.S. Customs built a reputation as tenacious protectors of America's borders. Attempts to smuggle contraband and human beings (human trafficking, espionage, and illegal immigration) were repeatedly thwarted by the efforts of Customs inspectors and criminal investigators.

In the 1960s and 1970s, the Bureau of Customs began to meet the growing challenges of advanced transportation technology. To do so, it established both air and marine interdiction programs, in 1969 and 1973, respectively, to chase down smugglers who were using speedboats and aircraft in their criminal enterprises. Eventually, in 1999, the two programs united into a single Air and Marine Interdiction Division within U.S. Customs.

In 1973, the Bureau of Customs changed its name to the U.S. Customs Service, which persevered until the service's transfer to the Department of Homeland Security in 2003.

According to the Department of Homeland Security, the agency that was the United States Customs Service (and its legacy elements in Homeland Security today) had the following key responsibilities including:[18]

The United States Customs Service ensures that all imports and exports comply with U.S. laws and regulations. The Service collects and protects the revenue, guards against smuggling, and is responsible for the following:

- Assessing and collecting Customs duties, excise taxes, fees and penalties due on imported merchandise.
- Interdicting and seizing contraband, including narcotics and illegal drugs.
- Processing persons, baggage, cargo and mail, and administering certain navigation laws.
- Detecting and apprehending persons engaged in fraudulent practices designed to circumvent Customs and related laws.
- Protecting American business and labor and intellectual property rights by enforcing U.S. laws intended to prevent illegal trade practices, including provisions related to quotas and the marking of imported merchandise; the Anti-Dumping Act; and, by providing Customs Recordations for copyrights, patents and trademarks.
- Protecting the general welfare and security of the United States by enforcing import and export restrictions and prohibitions, including the export of critical technology used to develop weapons of mass destruction, and money laundering.
- Collecting accurate import and export data for compilation of international trade statistics.

These mission statements have been a part of the Customs Service duty list for many years, and some of them have been on that list since Customs' inception. By all accounts, the United States Customs Service became one of the nation's premier federal law enforcement agencies in the 20th century as it fulfilled its mission. The Customs Service developed investigative expertise to combat cybercrime, including child pornography, money laundering, smuggling, technology export and embargo violations, cargo thefts, narcotics violations, terrorism, and other crimes. Customs law enforcement personnel include special agents (criminal investigators), canine enforcement officers, customs inspectors, technical enforcement officers, and customs pilots. Prior to the transfer of functions to the Department of Homeland Security, the U.S. Customs Service was the second largest federal law enforcement agency (the INS was the largest).

By 2003, the Customs Service employed nearly 12,000 sworn law enforcement officers with firearms and arrest authority. In March of 2003, all Customs special agents were transferred to U.S. Immigration and Customs Enforcement (ICE), Office of Investigations. This transfer joined legacy Customs special agents and legacy INS special agents into a single investigative entity. Today, ICE's Office of Investigations is the second largest federal criminal investigative agency (the FBI is the largest). All other Customs law enforcement personnel, including inspectors, agents, and air and marine interdiction officers, were transferred to U.S. Customs and Border Protection. The remnant organizational units within the Department of Homeland Security that were the component parts of the U.S. Customs Service are all expected to continue to grow within the context of their new homes in the U.S. Department of Homeland Security.

BUREAU OF ALCOHOL, TOBACCO, FIREARMS AND EXPLOSIVES

The Bureau of Alcohol, Tobacco, Firearms and Explosives (ATF) is one of the most significant and recognizable law enforcement elements of the Treasury Department's law enforcement history. The special agents of this agency have been intimately involved in many of the nation's most high-profile criminal investigations. ATF special agents played a leading role in quickly breaking open the bombing cases of the World Trade Center in February of 1993 and the Alfred P. Murrah Federal Building in April of 1995, to name just two major cases. ATF special agents, before the agency bore the name "ATF," worked tirelessly during the years of Prohibition and afterward to investigate and arrest "bootleggers," that is, those who illegally manufactured and distributed alcohol. In the context of those cases, which were a predominant share of the ATF's workload during the 1930s–1960s, the nickname "rev'nooers" was often used to identify the agents by those under investigation. It's more likely, though, that "damned rev'nooers" was the phrase used by ATF's targets.

Today, the Bureau of Alcohol, Tobacco, and Firearms is now called the Bureau of Alcohol, Tobacco, Firearms and Explosives. The name change was effective in January of 2003 and is more reflective of the organization's current mission, a significant part of which is the investigation of bombings and other explosives-related violations. Despite the longer name, the acronym officially used by the agency remains "ATF."

In addition to a new name, ATF was given a new home as well. After decades in the U.S. Department of Treasury, the ATF was organizationally transferred to the U.S. Department of Justice, effective

January 2003, as a provision of the Homeland Security Act of 2002. Because so many other agencies were transferred to the Department of Homeland Security, many thought ATF would be placed there as well. However, even with the creation of the Department of Homeland Security, the Federal Bureau of Investigation—a Justice Department agency—retained its role as the lead agency for investigating acts of terrorism, including bombings. In light of the fact that ATF would always share authority with the FBI in such cases, and because of its highly developed and well-respected expertise in bombing cases, it was thought that coordination between the two agencies would be enhanced by their existence within the same cabinet-level department (i.e., the Justice Department).

Some in Congress had even argued for the absorption of ATF into the FBI. Agency officials in both organizations were generally opposed to this idea. Unofficial conventional wisdom in 2002 was that the ATF wanted to protect its turf and its identity as a premier federal law enforcement agency in its own right and that the FBI didn't want to pollute its ranks with less well-trained (from their perspective) Treasury agents who had not "grown up" buying into the FBI culture and mystique. Moving ATF to the Justice Department, on other hand, turned out to be a good compromise. Both organizations would answer to the Attorney General in the chain of command, and yet both organizations' identities and culture would remain intact.

Like other current and former Treasury Department law enforcement agencies, ATF's roots are with the Prohibition Unit within the Bureau of Internal Revenue (which became the Internal Revenue Service in 1952) from the 1920s and 1930s. In July of 1930, the Prohibition Unit was transferred to the Department of Justice. But it returned to the Treasury Department's Bureau of Internal Revenue in March of 1934 and took the name "Alcohol Tax Unit," and then in 1951, the "Alcohol and Tobacco Tax Division" (ATTD). Even with end of national Prohibition, investigators in the ATTD were very busy working moonshine cases. Many states and counties, particularly in the South, remained alcohol free ("dry") through state law and local ordinances. This resulted in a continued incentive for some small-scale companies to manufacture liquor as a side business (without any accounting records), which resulted in failure to pay federal liquor taxes. In fact, during the 1950s and 1960s, ATTD agents were the dominant federal law enforcement presence in the Southern United States.[19]

Although for most of its history, the ATF and its forerunner, the ATTD, enforced alcohol laws, the organization investigated firearms cases as far back as 1941. In 1934, Congress had passed the National

Firearms Act. That statute provided for the registration and taxing of the transfer of certain types of firearms, including machine guns, short-barreled rifles and shotguns, and silencers. Because the taxing authority of the federal government was at the root of the law, ATTD was the logical choice for its enforcement.

However, firearms tax enforcement was not a priority for the agency until the late 1960s and early 1970s. From 1966 through 1968, only 275 arrests had been made for violating the National Firearms Act and other firearms-related legislation. Further, no dealers had been charged under the National Firearms Act until 1968.[20]

However, the 1960s was a period of time characterized by a growth in violent crime, including gun and bomb violence. Congress attempted to address the problem at a national level by passing the Gun Control Act of 1968. That bill amended the National Firearms Act of 1934 by extending coverage and imposing a cost-prohibitive tax on destructive devices such as bombs, hand grenades, and so on. The legislation also imposed new and harsher penalties for those convicted of committing federal crimes with firearms. Further, the Gun Control Act of 1968 tightened up registration requirements and made it a federal crime for convicted felons or mental defectives to possess firearms.

The ATTD, as the lead unit for investigating firearms violations, soon began to step up its investigations in this area. State and local police officers were hired away from their police organizations to become agents with the ATTD. Those officers retained and leveraged their contacts in local law enforcement; worked closely with drug enforcement personnel at the federal, state, and local levels; and developed informant networks. The culture of the ATTD increasingly became primarily law enforcement-oriented rather than tax or regulatory enforcement-minded.[21]

On July 1, 1972, under Treasury Department Order No. 221, the ATTD was transferred out of the Internal Revenue Service and became a stand-alone organization within the U.S. Department of the Treasury. The organization's name changed to the Bureau of Alcohol, Tobacco and Firearms. Since then, Congress has continually passed legislation that has bolstered the agency's authority and recognized the agency's expertise—particularly in the area of firearms and explosives. Notable examples include the Organized Crime Control Act of 1972 and the Anti-Arson Act of 1982.[22]

Since that time, however, the ATF's reputation has not always been high in the eyes of Congress. Several top ATF officials lost their jobs as a result of the 1993 raid on the Branch Davidian compound near Waco,

Texas. The Branch Davidians were a separatist, communal sect of the Seventh Day Adventists that had occupied several buildings and some acreage outside of Waco, Texas. David Koresh, the sect's leader, preached an apocalyptic message of a showdown with government forces. As a result, the sect had made an effort to become well armed. In arming the sect, David Koresh and others violated federal firearms statutes by securing banned weapons—particularly unregistered, fully automatic rifles.

On February 28, 1993, the ATF showed up at the Branch Davidian compound in full force. Over 100 ATF special agents were present to serve the search warrant and execute an arrest warrant for David Koresh. It was hoped that the raid would be as successful as earlier and highly successful large-scale raids that had enhanced the reputation of the ATF among contemporary federal law enforcement agencies. In April of 1985, pursuant to search and arrest warrants, the ATF had executed a large-scale raid of the compound belonging to a white supremacist group called "The Covenant, Sword, and Arm of the Lord" in northern Arkansas. That organization was a Christian Identity group led by minister Jim Ellison. Christian Identity theology blends white supremacy, antigovernment zealotry, and unconventional biblical exegesis. During that raid, the compound was surrounded for three days; the occupants then surrendered and were served the warrants.

That scenario was not repeated on February 28, 1993. Instead of surrender, Branch Davidians opened fire on ATF agents, killing four of them and seriously wounding dozens more with bullets and fragment grenades. The news media was present for the raid. The images on television were shocking. ATF agents, clad in dark, military-style tactical fatigues, appeared as an army, not a police force. The image gave rise to a claim by critics (including some talk-radio hosts, some members of Congress, and the National Rifle Association) that the government, and particularly the ATF, employed "jack-booted thugs" reminiscent of the Nazis, ready and willing to steal away average citizens' rights and liberties, if not their lives. Lost on many critics was the fact that, in retrospect, an army was just about needed against the well-armed and fortified Branch Davidians. Also lost on many critics was the fact that ATF indeed had secured lawful search and arrest warrants and were therefore entitled to enter the compound. No mistake as to who they were or what their authority was could have been made by the Branch Davidians. It was the Davidians and David Koresh who intentionally repelled legitimate law enforcement officers engaged in the scope of their duties.

The greatest controversy from the Branch Davidian incident occurred on April 19, 1993, when the FBI attempted to end the siege with tear gas.

As mentioned in the previous chapter, a fire was started by the Davidians inside the compound and nearly 80 Davidians inside perished, including 19 children. Autopsies would later show that many of the Davidians, including the children, had been shot by other Davidians in an apparent murder-suicide, or possibly a mercy-killing as the fire reached their hiding places. Nonetheless, the FBI received significant criticism from Congress, and the ATF was criticized along with the FBI despite the fact that the ATF had nothing to do with the tragedy of April 19.

The criticism of the ATF notwithstanding, Congress has not moved to disband the agency. The ATF has been in chronic danger of being dissolved entirely. It has always been an agency in a state of insecurity.[23] After Waco, the critics of the ATF had their best opportunity to strike a mortal blow to the agency, but Congress kept it alive and has continued to empower it since. The sheer numbers of guns that exist in the United States appear to be both a blessing and a curse for the ATF. There are over 200 million firearms in circulation in the United States today. Approximately 40% of all American households possess at least one firearm; 25% of households have handguns.[24] Because the majority of Americans who possess weapons do so legally, the ATF faces a tremendous political obstacle when it appears to become too zealous in anti-gun causes. Conversely, there were over 11,000 murders committed with firearms in 2003 in the United States. Further, 343,000 people were victims of other violent crimes involving the use of firearms, including sexual assault, aggravated assault, and robbery.[25] With these numbers, Congress has never been quite willing to take the position that firearms do not pose a special problem in the United States that requires law enforcement specialists who can address the problem somewhat aggressively.

Today, ATF special agents are vested with full federal law enforcement authority under Title 18, Section 3051, which states in part:

(a) Special agents of the Bureau of Alcohol, Tobacco, Firearms and Explosives, as well as any other investigator or officer charged by the Attorney General with the duty of enforcing any of the criminal, seizure, or forfeiture provisions of the laws of the United States, may carry firearms, serve warrants and subpoenas issued under the authority of the United States and make arrests without warrant for any offense against the United States committed in their presence, or for any felony cognizable under the laws of the United States if they have reasonable grounds to believe that the person to be arrested has committed or is committing such felony.

(b) Any special agent of the Bureau of Alcohol, Tobacco, Firearms and Explosives may, in respect to the performance of his or her duties, make seizures of property subject to forfeiture to the United States.

The ATF employs over 2,300 special agents. It has identified three strategic goals that, not surprisingly, correspond to the agency's name. The three strategic goals are:[26]

(1) Prevent violent crime involving firearms;
(2) Resolve and prevent explosives and fire related crimes;
(3) Prevent illegal domestic and international trafficking of alcohol and tobacco products.

Arguably, these strategic goals are not treated with an equal sense of priority by the special agent cadre at ATF. While agents do serve on gang and violent crime taskforces and regularly refer street-crime offenders found possessing a gun to federal prosecutors, much of the firearms enforcement effort is done through the ATF's compliance inspectors and other regulatory (non-sworn) personnel. Similarly, inspectors and tax collectors expend much of their effort on alcohol and tobacco enforcement. Special agents do conduct trafficking investigations—particularly of tobacco—but these cases are of comparatively low importance in relation to other ATF special agent operations.

In the age of an increased threat from domestic and international terrorism, the ATF spends a considerable portion of its time working on explosives and arson cases as well as serving on joint-terrorism and antiterrorism taskforces around the country. By focusing its attention on such matters, and through its new affiliation with the Department of Justice, the modern ATF appears to be well-insulated from its critics. The American people and Congress appreciate the role ATF has played and continues to play in the fight against terrorism—especially against those who would use explosives or other weapons of mass destruction. There is probably no other federal law enforcement function that is more widely supported.

INTERNAL REVENUE SERVICE (CID AND INSPECTION)

As we have seen, many criminal investigative agencies of the federal government has roots in the Internal Revenue Service (IRS), and prior to that, the Bureau of Internal Revenue. But while many units have split off of the Internal Revenue Service or its predecessors, two federal law enforcement agencies remained: the IRS Criminal Investigation Division and the IRS Inspection Service.

The IRS Criminal Investigation Division (IRS-CID) traces its roots back to 1919 when the commissioner of Internal Revenue created the

"Intelligence Unit." The purpose of that unit was to investigate serious occurrences of tax fraud and evasion. The unit's creation was facilitated by the transfer of six United States postal inspectors to the Bureau of Internal Revenue.

Agents within the intelligence unit gained a national reputation for their ability to leverage financial and accounting skills in conducting sophisticated criminal investigations against sophisticated criminal offenders. The most famous arrest and conviction resulting from the investigative prowess of Intelligence Unit agents, on loan to the Prohibition Unit, was that of Al Capone. In June of 1931, Al Capone was indicted by a federal grand jury on 22 counts of tax evasion. On October 17, 1931, Capone was convicted on some of those tax evasion counts. He was sentenced to 11 years in federal prison.

Over the years, the Intelligence Unit at the Bureau of Internal Revenue, and later, the Internal Revenue Service, would expand its investigations so as to target tax violators of all stripes, including ordinary citizens, businesses, government officials, and organized crime.[27] In 1978, the Intelligence Unit changed its name to the Criminal Investigation Division.

Today, the Internal Revenue Service's Criminal Investigation Division employs 2,800 special agents and 1,600 support personnel. The IRS-CID is the only federal criminal investigative agency which requires university-level accounting education for all prospective special agent applicants. Potential IRS-CID agents must possess a minimum of 21 credits of college accounting to be considered for employment.

Special agents in IRS-CID are unique in other ways as well. While many federal agencies have overlapping or concurrent jurisdiction covering a host of federal crimes, only criminal investigators of the Internal Revenue Service have the statutory authority to investigate criminal violations of Title 26, that is, the Internal Revenue Code. Even the Federal Bureau of Investigation must necessarily rely on special agents of the IRS if the investigation involves violations of Title 26, given CID's exclusive jurisdiction.

In Section 7608 of Title 26, IRS special agents are given a broad range of law enforcement authorities, including the power to carry firearms, make arrests, execute search warrants, serve subpoenas, and engage in undercover operations. The investigative range of IRS-CID potentially encompasses all cases involving money or other property of value, where the acquisition of that money or property was not reported for tax purposes. Consequently, investigations involving bribery, insurance fraud, health care fraud, bankruptcy fraud, drug trafficking, embezzlement, organized crime, money laundering banking law violations, and many, many other statutes are part of the IRS' criminal investigative domain.

Organizationally, the IRS-CID breaks violations into three strategic categories:[28] legal source tax crimes (i.e., not paying tax on legal income), illegal source financial crimes (i.e., violations involving money earned through illegal activities), and narcotics-related financial crimes. This last area comprises a significant enough portion of the CID's case load that it warranted its own grouping apart from other illegal activities.

IRS criminal investigations are generally regarded in federal law enforcement as among the most complex cases to work. These cases can take several years to complete. Even so, the IRS has a remarkable track record of opening and closing cases annually. In Fiscal Year 2005, IRS-CID initiated nearly 4,300 criminal investigations. They made nearly 2,900 referrals for prosecution. They secured approximately 2,400 indictments and nearly 2,200 convictions.[29] Despite the image of "white collar" crime being less serious than other types of offenses, over 80% of the offenders convicted in Fiscal 2005 were sentenced to prison. The above case statistics are similar to the figures from fiscal 2003 and 2004.

In addition to the IRS Criminal Investigation Division, there existed for many years a unit with IRS known alternatively as the Inspection Service, or the Internal Security Division. Criminal investigators within this unit, known as "inspectors" rather than "special agents," investigated matters relating to the protection and integrity of the IRS. For examples, cases involving the bribery or assault of IRS employees were handled by Internal Security. In the mid- and late-1990s, Congress began to take a serious look at IRS-CID and other tax enforcement and collection elements of IRS. Members of Congress began to uncover a record of abuses by the IRS in relation to the general public. The organization was also seen as too aggressive where average citizens were concerned. During congressional hearings, members of Congress learned that IRS Inspection investigators had been hamstrung by IRS leadership who provided cover for other elements of the IRS. In other words, the Inspection Service was deemed to be not very effective at policing the IRS.

Consequently, with the passage of the Internal Revenue Service Restructuring and Reform Act of 1998, the Internal Security Division of IRS was removed from the IRS chain of command and became a stand-alone law enforcement agency within the Department of the Treasury. Its name changed with the restructuring. The Inspection Service became the Treasury Inspector General for Tax Administration.[30] Its investigative jurisdiction remained intact. Only now, the agency had the autonomy to police the IRS in an effective, unobstructed way.

Like other Offices of Inspectors General throughout the federal government, TIGTA operates both audit and investigation units. The primary purpose of any Office of Inspector General is to detect and prevent fraud, waste, and abuse, committed against or within the larger organization to which the Inspector General is beholden. In this case, TIGTA serves as the Inspector General's Office for the IRS and is responsible for protecting its operations, funds, and integrity from threats both inside and outside of the IRS.

U.S. SECRET SERVICE

The history of the United States Secret Service was discussed earlier in this book. The Secret Service was perhaps the most famous and respected of Treasury Department law enforcement agencies for much of the 20th century. Today, the Secret Service is no longer a part of the U.S. Treasury Department. As with so many other law enforcement organizations, the Secret Service was relocated under the U.S. Department of Homeland Security in 2003 as a result of the Homeland Security Act of 2002. Unlike most of the other agencies that were transferred to Homeland Security, however, the Secret Service retained its status as an independent, stand-alone agency within the Homeland Security Department.

The United States Secret Service is known for protecting the President of the United States and investigating counterfeiters. However, since acquiring both of those responsibilities, the Secret Service's protection and investigative missions have expanded considerably.

On the protection side, the modern Secret Service is statutorily responsible for the physical security and protection of the following people:[31]

1. The President, the Vice President, the President-elect and Vice President-elect;
2. The immediate families of the above individuals;
3. Former Presidents and their spouses for up to 10 years after leaving office;
4. Children of former presidents until age 16;
5. Visiting heads of foreign states or governments and their spouses traveling with them, other distinguished foreign visitors to the United States, and official representatives of the United States performing special missions abroad;
6. Major Presidential and Vice Presidential candidates, and their spouses within 120 days of a general Presidential election.

The Secret Service has also been assigned the responsibility of serving as the lead security agency for events designated as "national special security events." Large-scale events of national interest receive this designation, such as the Olympics, the Super Bowl, the World Series, or the national conventions of the major political parties.

The investigative mission of the Secret Service has also grown over the years. Today, Secret Service special agents continue to investigate counterfeiting of currency. But they also have statutory jurisdiction to investigate identity theft and fraud, food stamp fraud, credit card fraud, fraud involving electronic transfers, telemarketing fraud, bank fraud, money laundering, computer crimes, and of course, threats and assaults made against persons or events under the Secret Service's protection.

In addition to special agents, the Secret Service also fields a full-service uniformed police department. This unit, known as the Uniformed Division of the U.S. Secret Service, started out as the White House Police Department in 1930. This department was responsible for providing a uniformed police presence on the White House grounds. Although its own entity, it answered to the Chief of the Secret Service. In 1970, the department was renamed the Executive Protection Service and was given the additional responsibility of protecting foreign embassies and consulates (externally) in Washington DC and around the United States. In 1977, the unit's name changed again to the Uniformed Division of the Secret Service.

In addition to protecting the White House, the Vice-President's residence, and foreign missions, the Secret Service Uniformed Division, along with other uniformed federal police agencies, has been given concurrent jurisdiction in certain Washington DC neighborhoods to assist and back up the DC Metro Police in basic municipal police functions.

Today, over 4,200 special agents and police officers work for the United States Secret Service. Over its history, the agency's law enforcement authority has never receded—it has done nothing but expand. In 1984, credit card fraud became a federal crime. The Secret Service was given primary jurisdiction to investigate credit card fraud, as well as fraud occurring as a result of computer transactions and crimes involving fraudulent identification documents. In 1998, federal legislation was enacted that made federal crimes of engaging in telemarketing fraud and in identity theft. The Secret Service was given primary jurisdiction for both offenses. In 2000, the Secret Service was given statutory authority to serve as the lead agency for national special security events. Further, the Secret Service is the agency that designates which events qualify as national special security events.

Because the Secret Service has moved to the Department of Homeland Security and still retains its independent status, there appears little doubt that it will continue to expand its jurisdiction, personnel, influence, and prestige within the federal law enforcement community for many years to come.

CHAPTER 6

The Inspectors General (And the Battle Against Fraud, Waste, and Abuse)

One of the most interesting developments in federal law enforcement during the 20th century was the creation and rise of the Offices of Inspector General (OIG or IG). Every federal executive branch cabinet-level department, as well as dozens of smaller, independent agencies, has an OIG. In fact, there are 58 OIGs in federal service today (see Appendix C) with nearly 3,000 special agents whose primary function is to conduct criminal investigations.

The Offices of Inspector General are not exclusively law enforcement agencies. Each OIG possesses within its organization a criminal investigative unit. OIGs have both an Office of Audit and an Office of Investigation. The mission of the OIG is then pursued through audits of the various programs, funds, contractors, and expenditures of the parent agency and the conduct of criminal investigations.

The mission and structure of the federal OIG offices are declared in the Inspector General Act of 1978. The Act states in part:

Sec. 2. Purpose and establishment of Offices of Inspector General; departments and agencies involved

In order to create independent and objective units—

(1) to conduct and supervise audits and investigations relating to the programs and operations of the establishments listed in Section 11(2);
(2) to provide leadership and coordination and recommend policies for activities designed
   (A) to promote economy, efficiency, and effectiveness in the administration of, and
   (B) to prevent and detect fraud and abuse in, such programs and operations; and
(3) to provide a means for keeping the head of the establishment and the Congress fully and currently informed about problems and deficiencies relating to the administration of such programs and operations and the necessity for and progress of corrective action;

The statute then went on to create Offices of Inspector General in 12 federal agencies: the Departments of Agriculture, Commerce, Housing and Urban Development, Interior, Labor, Transportation, the Community Services Administration, the General Services Administration, the Small Business Administration, the Veterans Administration, the National Aeronautics and Space Administration, and the Environmental Protection Agency. In addition to these 12, the Department of Health, Education, and Welfare and the Department of Energy already possessed OIGs of their own that had been statutorily established in 1976 and 1977, respectively.

The excerpt from the statute that was just presented reveals a great deal about the nature, organization, and mission of federal OIGs. The cabinet-level and independent agencies named in the Inspector General Act of 1978 were tasked with establishing Offices of Inspector General. First and foremost, it is clear that the Offices of Inspector General were to be independent. In other words, through organizational autonomy, they would be free to "call it like they see it." This is an important feature of any OIG or inspection unit. As noted in the previous chapter, the Inspection unit for the Internal Revenue Service was justifiably criticized for its inability to plainly and accurately critique the IRS' operations and actions. The IRS Inspection Service was thus converted into an independent OIG, answering only to the Secretary of the Treasury.

The newly created OIGs were also required to possess both audit and investigations units. The goals of auditors and investigators within the OIGs are broadly the same and are outlined in Sec. 2 (2) of the statute.

Within the OIGs, the audit function has traditionally been best suited to tackle the promotion of economy, efficiency, and effectiveness within the department and in the administration of its programs. OIG criminal investigators, on the other hand, have traditionally addressed the matter of fraud and abuse within government programs. Hence, OIG special agents then and now are primarily known as fraud investigators specializing in a variety of white-collar crimes where the United States Government has been victimized.

THE HISTORY OF THE OFFICES OF INSPECTOR GENERAL

The concept of an independent inspector general in place to review government operations for efficiency and effectiveness has been around for hundreds of years. George Washington appointed Frederick William Augustus von Steuben as the U.S. Army's Inspector General in 1778. His mission as the Army's IG was to review the troops, ensure that soldiers were properly and uniformly trained, ensure that discipline was observed within the ranks, and determine that Army commanders were treating soldiers justly. General von Steuben is widely seen today as the father of the military inspector general system in the United States.[1]

It wasn't until much more recent times, however, that the perceived need for Inspectors General in the civilian federal government arena became acute. In 1962, the U.S. Secretary of Agriculture Orville Freeman created within the Department of Agriculture what is widely seen today as the first modern Office of Inspector General.[2] The Agriculture OIG was created not by statute, as would happen later through the Inspector General Act of 1978, but by administrative order of the Secretary of Agriculture. The U.S. Department of Agriculture (USDA) Office of Inspector General was created in the wake of the Billy Sol Estes scandal.

Billy Sol Estes was a wealthy Texas businessman who sold irrigation equipment and fertilizer to cotton farmers in Texas during the 1950s. When business began to slump due to USDA regulating the production of cotton, Estes schemed with individuals inside and outside of the USDA to fraudulently secure agricultural subsidies. In April of 1962, Estes was indicted on dozens of counts of fraud. He was convicted in 1963 and sentenced to eight years in prison. Congressional investigations ensued following the scandal and Washington DC appeared to be thirsty for government reform initiatives. As an immediate "stop-gap" measure to shore up poor internal audit mechanisms at the USDA, Secretary Freeman created the USDA OIG with a dual track structure (audit and investigation units) that would serve as a model for the statutory OIGs created by the Inspector General Act in 1978.[3]

In the early and mid-1970s, politicians and the public had seen many stories relating to government corruption and ineptness. As Genevieve Nowlinski reminds us, the 1970s saw the tragic shooting deaths by National Guardsmen of anti-war protesters at Kent State University in Ohio, the environmental catastrophes of Three Mile Island and Love Canal, and of course the resignation of the President of the United States and the prosecution of many of his staff due to corruption. It was also learned that the Medicaid Program administered by the Department of Health, Education, and Welfare (HEW) was replete with fraud and waste.[4] According to one congressional investigation, the Medicaid Program cost the federal government $1.8 billion in kickbacks, fraudulent billing, overcharges, and unnecessary care.[5]

Paul Light recollected the findings of a University of Michigan study concerning the devolving American public perception of government in his book, *Monitoring Government: Inspectors General and the Search for Accountability.* The findings show that public agreement with the statement "quite a few people running the government are a little crooked" increased from 24% of Americans in 1958 to 42% in 1976. The percentage of Americans who said that they "could not trust the government to do right most of the time" increased from 23% in 1958 to 63% in 1976. The percentage of Americans that believed "government is run by a few big interests looking out for themselves" went from 29% in 1964 to 66% in 1976. Finally, the percentage of Americans who believed that "people in government waste a lot of money we pay in taxes" rose from 43% in 1958 to 74% in 1976. Without doubt, growing congressional interest in doing something about the perceived and actual ineptness and corruption in government had peaked by 1976.[6]

The HEW Inspector General Act of 1976 established the first statutory OIG within the civilian federal government. The HEW OIG was very similar in structure to the USDA's administratively established OIG. However, the HEW Inspector General would be a presidential appointee and not necessarily the choice of the HEW Secretary. The HEW OIG would be independent, could be removed only by the President of the United States, and would keep Congress informed of the OIG's findings and recommendations, pursuant to Congress' responsibilities for oversight of the federal executive bureaucracy.

In 1977, similar legislation passed creating a statutory OIG at the Department of Energy. It was clear, however, that creating OIGs piecemeal for each government agency presenting an evident need for it was itself an inefficient way for Congress to address inefficiency in government. So, the following year, after considerable debate over the concern of the growth of federal law enforcement, among other things, Congress passed the Inspector General Act of 1978, which established a total of 14 presidentially appointed federal Inspectors General.

Under the Act, OIG criminal investigators were granted the authority to investigate criminal offenses relating to their parent organizations. Typically, this meant they investigated program fraud and public corruption, such as bribery or embezzlement involving federal employees. OIG special agents also were granted the authority to serve administrative subpoenas (i.e., subpoenas issued from the OIG they work for, not court-issued subpoenas). Interestingly, the Act did not bestow law enforcement powers on OIG special agents. The statute was silent on that issue. OIG special agents, although conducting criminal investigations, did not yet possess the statutory power to make arrests and carry firearms. Further, the Federal Bureau of Investigation was expressly given the right of first refusal to investigate offenses falling under the purview of the OIGs.

In 1988, the Inspector General Act of 1978 was amended. In the decade between 1978 and 1988, many federal agencies not designated in the original Act had created their own Offices of Inspector General, much as USDA had done in 1962. In addition to clarifying reporting requirements, the 1988 amendment to the Act statutorily established 28 additional Offices of Inspector General. Once again, however, Congress intentionally skirted the opportunity to grant OIG special agents full (or even limited) federal law enforcement powers.

INSPECTOR GENERAL LAW ENFORCEMENT AUTHORITY

The debate over just what law enforcement powers OIG special agents should have was rooted in the general concern about the growing federal law enforcement presence. Many members of Congress were reluctant to arm and empower a whole new class of federal agents who may not be savvy enough to wisely use those powers—despite the fact that OIG agents were trained through the Basic Criminal Investigator School of the Federal Law Enforcement Training Center (FLETC). FLETC, until its transfer to the Department of Homeland Security in 2003, was operated by the Treasury Department. The training at the Basic Criminal Investigator School was the same as the training for special agents from more well-known federal law enforcement agencies, including the Secret Service, U.S. Customs, the Bureau of Alcohol, Tobacco and Firearms, the Internal Revenue Service, and others.

By the early 1990s, only three OIGs possessed statutory law enforcement authority for their special agents. U.S. Department of Agriculture special agents received firearms, search warrant, and arrest authority under Title 7, Section 2207. The special agents of the Defense Criminal Investigative Service (DCIS), which is the investigative branch of the civilian Defense Department OIG, received those powers under Title 10, Section 1585. Finally, OIG special agents of the General Services Administration received their police powers under Title 40, Section 318d—the same statute that empowered "non-uniformed special policemen" of the Federal Protective Service. The rest of the OIG criminal investigative community could be deputized by the U.S. Marshals Service on an agent-by-agent, case-by-case basis.[7]

The deputation process was cumbersome. It could take weeks for the Marshals Service to process the deputation request of special agents, and by the time the authority was granted (authority was granted only for a specific case), the need for the authority often no longer existed. The opportunity to serve a warrant had passed, or another federal agency or local department may have been called upon to make an arrest.[8]

During the 1980s and 1990s, the Inspectors General compiled statistics demonstrating the need for law enforcement authority.[9] They produced examples for Congress' consideration of how the absence of law enforcement authority jeopardized investigations due to delays and often endangered special agents. Many assaults of badge-carrying but unarmed special agents occurred during that period of time. Congress, however, remained reluctant to grant to the OIGs the law enforcement powers of carrying firearms, executing warrants, and making arrests that it had granted to so many other agencies.

By 1995, the U.S. Marshals Service was growing weary of deputizing OIG agents on a case-by-case basis. Many OIG agents possessed a genuine, ongoing need for law enforcement authority. For example, special agents with the Department of Housing and Urban Development spent considerable time conducting investigations in or near dangerous public housing projects in urban centers. Without deputation, they did so unarmed—despite presenting themselves as law enforcement officers. Similarly, special agents of the Department of Interior's OIG regularly conducted investigations on Indian reservations with histories of marked hostility and even violence against federal law enforcement officers due to a general resentment toward the federal government.

In 1995, the Marshals Service began to grant blanket one-year deputation to most OIG offices. In other words, OIG agents no longer
needed to demonstrate a case-by-case need for the authority. They were
simply declared special deputy U.S. marshals. By 2001, the Marshals
Service began to grant blanket deputation on a three-year basis.[10]

Also in 1995, Congress passed legislation that removed the Social
Security Administration (SSA) from the Department of Health and
Human Services and made it an independent agency of the federal
government. Embedded in that legislation was the creation of the SSA
Office of Inspector General. Special agents with the SSA OIG were
given statutory law enforcement authority. Later, Congress would add
new agencies to the Inspector General community, including the U.S.
Postal Service Office of Inspector General in 1996 and the Treasury
Inspector General for Tax Administration (TIGTA) in 1998. The criminal investigators for these two agencies were also granted full federal
authority by Congress. By the end of the 1990s, six OIGs possessed
statutory law enforcement authority. The lack of statutory authority
for the remaining OIGs continued to be a source of irritation for them
and had a negative effect on morale and retention in those OIGs.

In 2000, the U.S. Department of Justice agreed that OIGs should possess statutory law enforcement authority. Legislation to grant firearms,
search warrant, and arrest authority to OIG agents was proposed in
Congress. However, officials at the Federal Bureau of Investigation
opposed the legislation. With the FBI against it, even while the Attorney
General was for it, the support in Congress for the new OIG authorities
subsided and the bill died.[11] The FBI had always expressed disapproval
of statutory law enforcement authority for OIGs. It was a classic turf
battle. Any enhancement of OIG law enforcement authority was seen
by FBI leadership as a diminishing of FBI influence in government
fraud and corruption cases. For the FBI, law enforcement authority was
a zero-sum game.

The Offices of Inspector General eventually received their statutory
law enforcement authority in the aftermath of the terror attacks of
September 11, 2001. After those attacks, no one on Capitol Hill was
prepared to be stingy about granting federal law enforcement authority. After all, federal agents from all agencies assisted with the response
to those attacks. Virtually every federal law enforcement agency with
firearms and arrest authority donated agents to the Transportation
Security Administration in order to temporarily serve as air marshals
until sufficient numbers of permanent air marshals could be hired.
Further, Congress believed that after 9/11 the FBI would be busier

than ever with its mission of preventing terrorism and would have precious few resources to devote toward government fraud and corruption. It was generally felt that the OIGs were no longer a turf threat to the FBI because of its clear direction and urgent priorities following the terrorist attacks on 9/11. On October 4, 2002, FBI Director Robert Mueller wrote a letter to Congress expressing the FBI's support for OIG's acquiring statutory law enforcement authority.[12]

The Homeland Security Act of 2002 contained many provisions that changed federal law enforcement. Among the provisions was Section 812 of the Act, which amended the Inspector General Act of 1978 to include statutory law enforcement authority for 25 specified Offices of Inspector General. The Act states in part:

SEC. 812. LAW ENFORCEMENT POWERS OF INSPECTOR GENERAL AGENTS. (a) IN GENERAL – Section 6 of the Inspector General Act of 1978 (5 U.S.C. App.) is amended by adding at the end the following:

(a) (1) In addition to the authority otherwise provided by this Act, each Inspector General appointed under Section 3, any Assistant Inspector General for Investigations under such an Inspector General, and any special agent supervised by such an Assistant Inspector General may be authorized by the Attorney General to—

   (A) carry a firearm while engaged in official duties as authorized under this Act or other statute, or as expressly authorized by the Attorney General;

   (B) make an arrest without a warrant while engaged in official duties as authorized under this Act or other statute, or as expressly authorized by the Attorney General, for any offense against the United States committed in the presence of such Inspector General, Assistant Inspector General, or agent, or for any felony cognizable under the laws of the United States if such Inspector General, Assistant Inspector General, or agent has reasonable grounds to believe that the person to be arrested has committed or is committing such felony; and

   (C) seek and execute warrants for arrest, search of a premises, or seizure of evidence issued under the authority of the United States upon probable cause to believe that a violation has been committed.

(2) The Attorney General may authorize exercise of the powers under this subsection only upon an initial determination that—

   (A) the affected Office of Inspector General is significantly hampered in the performance of responsibilities established by this Act as a result of the lack of such powers;

(B) available assistance from other law enforcement agencies is insufficient to meet the need for such powers; and

(C) adequate internal safeguards and management procedures exist to ensure proper exercise of such powers.

(3) The Inspector General offices of the Department of Commerce, Department of Education, Department of Energy, Department of Health and Human Services, Department of Homeland Security, Department of Housing and Urban Development, Department of the Interior, Department of Justice, Department of Labor, Department of State, Department of Transportation, Department of the Treasury, Department of Veterans Affairs, Agency for International Development, Environmental Protection Agency, Federal Deposit Insurance Corporation, Federal Emergency Management Agency, General Services Administration, National Aeronautics and Space Administration, Nuclear Regulatory Commission, Office of Personnel Management, Railroad Retirement Board, Small Business Administration, Social Security Administration, and the Tennessee Valley Authority are exempt from the requirement of paragraph (2) of an initial determination of eligibility by the Attorney General.

The statute did not specifically include the USDA OIG, the DCIS, the TIGTA, or the Postal Service OIG, because their pre-existing statutory authority was sufficient. The OIGs belonging to GSA and the SSA were included by name in the Homeland Security Act because that legislation was seen as expanding upon their previously granted authorities. The statute also grants the Attorney General the power to delegate full law enforcement authority to any other OIG not listed in the Act but deemed to have a need for those powers.

Today, criminal investigators are regularly called upon to investigate a broad array of federal criminal offenses. In addition to the traditional mission of detecting government program fraud, OIG special agents frequently participate in various task forces, including the FBI's Joint Terrorism Task Forces, which may require those agents to investigate matters beyond their normal programmatic boundaries. Additionally, OIG special agents in many organizations are responsible for providing dignitary protection to high-ranking officials within their own parent agencies. Usually, protective services are provided for officials at the department Secretary and Undersecretary level—especially while they travel. Some OIGs, such as those at USDA and at Health and Human Services, have permanently staffed Secretary protection units. Special agents assigned to such units receive specialized training in personal and physical security—often from the Secret Service or the State Department's Bureau of Diplomatic Security.

As a segment of the federal law enforcement community, the nation's 3,000 OIG special agents have contributed significantly to the federal government's criminal enforcement efforts, and they continue to do so. In Fiscal Year 2004, OIG audit and investigations resulted in $18 billion of cost savings to the federal government. Additionally, OIG criminal investigations resulted in 6,500 criminal prosecutions. An additional 5,000 individuals or businesses were suspended or debarred from conducting business with the federal government. There were also 2,500 civil and personnel actions taken as a result of OIG audits and investigations.[13]

A LOOK AT SPECIFIC OFFICES OF INSPECTOR GENERAL

Although the mission of the OIGs can be summed up as combating fraud, waste, and abuse, the criminal investigations conducted by OIG agents are as varied as there are programs administered by the many federal agencies. In the sections that follow, selected specific OIGs are described. The discussion of each of these OIGs will serve to demonstrate the wide variety of activities embodied in the larger mission of OIGs.

U.S. Central Intelligence Agency, Office of Inspector General

The Central Intelligence Agency (CIA) is often mistaken for a federal law enforcement agency, but by and large, it is not. The CIA is prohibited by federal law from permitting its agents (operatives) from conducting clandestine intelligence-gathering duties inside the United States. That responsibility is reserved for the Federal Bureau of Investigation. Further, intelligence gathered by the CIA is generally not intended for use in the criminal justice system. The information collected and analyzed by "the Agency" (as it is sometimes called) is for political consumption. The information is used by government leaders in power who rely upon the information in making decisions with geopolitical consequences.

The unit within the CIA that comes closest to that of a federal law enforcement agency is the OIG. It is worth noting that the CIA's OIG was not among those OIGs that were granted statutory law enforcement authority. Nevertheless, CIA OIG criminal investigators may obtain law enforcement authority from the Attorney General if the need presents itself.

CIA OIG investigators do conduct criminal investigations. But they do not relate to spying—they relate to operational and misconduct issues within the agency. For example, the mishandling of classified material or the leaking of classified information is a federal crime. This type of offense would fall under the jurisdiction of the CIA's OIG investigators. They also investigate fraud within the agency and fraud committed against the agency along with employee misconduct. Serious criminal offenses that affect national security would be worked jointly with agents of the FBI and other federal agencies.

U.S. Department of Agriculture, Office of Inspector General

The USDA OIG was among the first OIGs to receive statutory law enforcement authority for its criminal investigators. The rationale for granting the law enforcement authority was rooted in the investigation of fraud within the USDA's food stamp program. Prior to the mid-1990s, all food stamps came in the form of paper coupons. Today, food stamp benefits are issued to recipients using an electronic transfer card (much like a debit card). Food stamp recipients receive varying amounts of food stamp allotments each month depending on the number of dependents for whom they need to purchase food. When USDA OIG received its law enforcement authority, a significant number of OIG's criminal investigations related to food stamp trafficking. Food stamp trafficking is the exchange of food stamps for cash or some other commodity of value, or for contraband, rather than for eligible grocery items.

In the past, food stamp coupons were treated like currency. Today, recipients wishing to perpetrate this fraud must take their food stamp debit card to an unscrupulous grocer who will give cash for the stamps. The typical exchange rate has been and still is 50 cents on the dollar. The recipient would receive $150 cash for the $300 in food stamps, and the store would receive 100% profit when redeeming the food stamp benefits with the federal government, as if it had sold $300 worth of groceries.

When food stamps came in the form of printed coupons, they were easy to exchange for drugs, sex, and other contraband in street transactions. USDA-OIG special agents were involved in several shooting incidents over the years when trying to arrest a trafficker or when undercover agents attempting to sell food stamps were the targets of robbers.

While food stamp investigations tend to be set in urban environments, the investigation of fraud in the various USDA farm programs takes OIG agents into rural America. Commonly investigated fraud schemes relate to converting property secured by the USDA, false crop insurance claims, and illegal planting and harvesting on land enrolled in conservation programs.

OIG agents also investigate bribery and allegations of threats or assaults committed against USDA personnel. This latter occurrence is particularly common when the USDA takes action to foreclose on farmers who are in default on USDA loans. OIG special agents also investigate felony violations of food adulteration and meat inspection laws. While the USDA employs meat inspectors to ensure the health and safety of the consuming public, OIG special agents will assert investigative jurisdiction when meat inspectors believe that meat packing plants and slaughterhouses are going to criminal lengths to circumvent or clear the inspection process.

Defense Criminal Investigative Service

The Defense Criminal Investigative Service (DCIS) is the investigations unit of the Department of Defense (DOD), Office of Inspector General. The DCIS is comprised of entirely civilian criminal investigators. The DCIS works closely with the criminal investigative branches of the armed forces. In fact, the DCIS has oversight authority over all military criminal investigations and may assert its jurisdiction on a case affecting the operations of any DOD department or unit.

Special agents of the DCIS spend most of their time conducting criminal investigations of contract fraud and embezzlement of DOD funds. They work closely with the fraud units of the Army Criminal Investigation Division, the Air Force Office of Special Investigations, and the Naval Criminal Investigative Service. Contract fraud is viewed as an especially serious offense by DOD officials, because substandard or deficient products can put military personnel in jeopardy while in the field of battle.

DCIS special agents are also frequently called upon to investigate allegations of misconduct among civilian DOD and military personnel. The DCIS was the lead agency in the investigation of the Navy's infamous Tailhook scandal in 1991. That investigation centered on allegations that sexual assaults of dozens of women and men took place during a convention of Naval aviators in Las Vegas, Nevada, and on allegations that the Naval aviators were the perpetrators. The DCIS has been called upon to investigate several other high-profile sexual misconduct charges against military personnel.

Finally, DCIS agents play a critical role in counterterrorism. They work closely with the FBI and military investigative agencies to detect and defeat attempted espionage and sabotage. The DCIS plays the lead role at the DOD for investigating cybercrimes, including the intentional hacking of DOD computers for the purpose of causing damage or obtaining information.

U.S. Department of Homeland Security, Office of Inspector General

The U.S. Department of Homeland Security (DHS) Office of Inspector General is the newest member of the OIG community. It was established by the Homeland Security Act of 2002, which created the Department of Homeland Security.

Although the DHS-OIG is relatively new, its personnel and investigative purview is not. The Department of Homeland Security was created by transferring 22 disparate agencies from across the federal government into the DHS. When this occurred, proportional elements of the legacy Offices of Inspector General also were transferred to the new DHS OIG. For example, the entire Federal Emergency Management Agency (FEMA) was absorbed by Homeland Security. Consequently, all FEMA OIG agents were transferred to the DHS OIG. However, only some organizational elements of the Department of Transportation came over to DHS; as a result, a proportional number of Transportation OIG agents were transferred to DHS.

DHS-OIG special agents investigate fraud and corruption within the wide realm of DHS programs. When disasters strike, FEMA responds by providing disaster relief. Given the hectic environment in the immediate aftermath of disasters, the disaster relief funds are especially vulnerable to fraudulent schemes. DHS-OIG agents spend a great deal of time confronting those types of offenses. In fact, after Hurricane Katrina devastated New Orleans in 2005, the DHS-OIG transferred agents from all around the country to the Gulf Coast region for two-year temporary assignments just to work on fraud resulting from that disaster.

Another significant area of investigation for the DHS-OIG is criminal levels of employee misconduct—particularly by those occupying key sensitive positions or positions of trust. Each year, several Border Patrol agents and border inspectors are arrested by OIG for offenses that include bribery, conspiracy to smuggle drugs or illegal aliens, and murder. Drug cartels in Mexico frequently attempt to secure protection from DHS law enforcement officials stationed on the border. This cooperation and protection is usually secured through extortion or bribery. These types of public integrity cases are a very high priority for the DHS-OIG.

U.S. Department of Housing and Urban Development, Office of Inspector General

OIG special agents with Housing and Urban Development (HUD) work an interesting mix of mundane white-collar fraud cases and cases involving serious violent crime. As a counter-fraud agency, HUD OIG investigated fraud committed within the many individual and public housing programs, including the Section 8 housing program, which provides subsidies to landlords who provide housing for poor tenants.

However, in recent years, HUD OIG has also investigated other (often violent) offenses. The investigative jurisdiction to do so is rooted in federal rules that bar violent crimes and drug crimes from taking place in public housing. Consequently, when such violations do occur, HUD OIG has a nexus to get involved. Commonly, HUD special agents partner with local law enforcement agencies to rid public housing of those who commit violent offenses and criminal drug offenses (often they are gang members). HUD agents serve on gang and fugitive task forces. From October 2004 through March of 2005, HUD special agents made nearly 1,800 arrests nationwide.[14] Most of these arrests were related to HUD initiatives to root out those who commit violent offenses and criminal drug offenses in public housing.

U.S. Department of Labor, Office of Inspector General

The U. S. Department of Labor's (DOL) Office of Inspector General has two broad investigative responsibilities. First, DOL special agents perform duties similar to other OIGs. They investigate allegations of fraud and abuse within DOL programs. There are dozens of DOL programs that are particularly vulnerable to fraud. These include workers' compensation, employee disability insurance, and pension and welfare programs. OIG agents also investigate criminal violations of worker health and safety laws.

The second broad area of investigative jurisdiction for DOL OIG is the area of labor racketeering. The Department of Labor's OIG is unique in that it possesses investigative jurisdiction in an area that is external to DOL funds and programs. Essentially, the DOL OIG, through its Labor and Racketeering Unit, shares concurrent jurisdiction with the FBI to detect and confront organized crime's attempted and actual influence over labor unions. Such cases investigated by the DOL OIG include the embezzlement of funds from union pension plans and dues, loan-sharking, money laundering, extortion, and violence committed against union members. These cases tend to be very complex and can result in severe criminal sanctions under the federal Racketeer Influenced and Corrupt Organizations (RICO) Act. Such cases often also include violations of tax laws. As a result, DOL OIG special agents working on labor racketeering investigations often do so jointly with both the FBI and the IRS.

Social Security Administration, Office of Inspector General

Social Security Administration (SSA) OIG special agents have primary jurisdiction for investigation of all crimes that affect or involve Social Security programs. Generally, SSA special agents confront a variety of common fraud schemes, including the fraudulent receipt of Social Security benefit payments, the fraudulent billing by doctors or other eligible service providers for reimbursement under Social Security insurance programs, and the fraudulent use of Social Security numbers.

SSA special agents are liaisons for the Social Security Administration to the larger law enforcement community. Social Security information, including Social Security numbers, is private and protected data. Law enforcement officers are generally required to work with SSA special agents when Social Security information is needed for their non-Social Security investigations. Commonly, violations of criminal laws relating to Social Security programs occur incidentally to other violations of law. For example, identity theft or the creation of new identities by criminal offenders, including terrorists, often involves the theft of existing Social Security numbers or creation of new ones for a fabricated identity. Further, Social Security cards are frequently counterfeited and sold to illegal aliens and others to be used as fraudulent identification.

Because of the connection of Social Security information and programs to so many other criminal schemes and enterprises, SSA special agents are frequently invited to work jointly with other criminal investigative agencies. SSA special agents also work on various task forces, including Joint Terrorism and Anti-Terrorism task forces, as well as fugitive apprehension task forces (because it is a federal crime in its own right to collect Social Security benefits, or most other federal benefits, while being a fugitive from justice).

THE FUTURE OF THE INSPECTORS GENERAL

The federal Offices of Inspector General have grown in number and influence at a tremendous pace in the past few decades. In 1962, there was one modern Office of Inspector General, which was administratively created at the Department of Agriculture. By the end of 1978, there were 14 statutory Inspectors General. Today, there are 58 OIGs scattered about the federal government landscape. Some are housed in prominent parent agencies. Others are located in more obscure contexts.

Presently, Congress appears content to have so many distinct OIGs operating at once throughout the federal government. However, an argument can be made for consolidating the OIGs in to a single civilian Inspector General whose responsibility would be—for the entire federal government—what the responsibilities of the various currently existing OIGs are to their respective departments today. Consolidation would not result in a monstrous new federal police agency, however. After all, there are no more than 3,000 special agents among all of the OIGs nationwide. A consolidated OIG would merely rival in number, not surpass, existing law enforcement agencies such as the ATF, ICE, the IRS, and the Secret Service. Further, consolidation creates an economy of scale that might result in the need for fewer OIG special agents nationwide. Smaller government agencies and programs that must employ idle criminal investigators until work comes in could instead be assigned criminal investigators from a consolidated OIG as needed.

While Congress is uninterested in the consolidation concept, the collection of Inspectors General around the country finds the concept to be a positively horrible idea. Although OIGs have frequently complained about the FBI's reluctance to give up or even share investigative turf, there is little evidence that OIGs themselves would ever do anything that would harm their own interests—including the irreversible, axiomatic, and chief desire of any bureaucratic organization—to simply exist.

CHAPTER 7

And Then There Were 100 (The Rest of the Federal Law Enforcement Community)

When Americans generally, and even when law enforcement professionals in particular, think about federal law enforcement, typical agencies come to mind. Famous federal law enforcement organizations include the Federal Bureau of Investigation; the U.S. Marshals Service; the Bureau of Alcohol, Tobacco, Firearms and Explosives; the Secret Service; and the Drug Enforcement Administration. Additionally, the U.S. Immigration and Customs Enforcement, Office of Investigations, has garnered significant attention, visibility, and praise as a result of some very high-profile human-trafficking and sexual-predator investigations in the agency's relatively short life.

However, those agencies and the many Offices of Inspector General discussed in the previous chapter, constitute only a partial list of federal law enforcement organizations. The federal government has over 100 federal law enforcement organizations and units across the entire federal domain. This chapter provides a brief look at some of these other agencies—who they are and what their law enforcement jurisdiction is. It is likely that most Americans and perhaps even most criminal justice professionals are unaware that some of these agencies even exist much less what they do.

U.S. DEPARTMENT OF AGRICULTURE

U.S. Forest Service

The United States Forest Service is responsible for 155 national forests covering 191.6 million acres throughout the continental United States. Each year, the national forests are visited by 1 billion people. The U.S. Forest Service provides law enforcement protection for the forests and for forest visitors through its Division of Law Enforcement. Currently, there are approximately 590 law enforcement officers with the U.S. Forest Service, including uniformed law enforcement rangers (known as LEOs) who serve as a patrol force and approximately 100 Forest Service special agents who conduct criminal investigations inside the forests.[1]

The responsibilities of U.S. Forest Service law enforcement officers and agents in the national forests include the investigation of thefts and assaults, the protection of archeological artifacts, detection and prevention of timber theft, enforcement of fish and wildlife laws and regulations, investigation and apprehension of arsonists, and investigation of drug manufacturing and possession violations. In fact, one of the more common criminal investigative responsibilities of Forest Service special agents is the investigation of drug crimes.

According to the U.S. Forest Service, violations of the Controlled Substance Act of 1970 and subsequent amendments are a high priority for its criminal investigators. Forest Service law enforcement officers have statutory authority to investigate narcotics violations under the National Forest System Drug Control Act of 1986. Given the vast and remote nature of many of the national forests, they have become ideal locations for marijuana grow operations and portable clandestine methamphetamine labs. During the years 1996–1999, the Forest Service eradicated over 3.2 million pounds of marijuana growing in the forests as a result of drug traffickers' grow operations.[2]

Forest Service uniformed LEOs and special agents have full law enforcement authority on in the national forests, as well as outside of the forests when performing their official duties.

U.S. DEPARTMENT OF COMMERCE

Bureau of Industry and Security, Office of Export Enforcement

The Office of Export Enforcement (OEE) in the Bureau of Industry and Security is a criminal investigative unit within the U.S. Commerce

Department. Export Enforcement special agents possess full statutory law enforcement authority, including the power to carry firearms, execute search warrants, and make arrests.

The mission of Export Enforcement is to prevent or detect the export of sensitive goods and technology to foreign countries whose receipt of the goods and technology is prohibited by law. While the mission of Customs agents primarily relates to products coming into the United States, the mission of Export Enforcement is to prevent certain products from leaving the United States, or at least leaving the United States without governmental authorization.

During the Cold War, the Office of Export Enforcement played a key role in defending the nation's national security interests by preventing advanced technology from being transferred to Soviet bloc countries. Today, with the heightened concern over international terrorism, OEE special agents' highest priority is preventing the transfer of weapons and technology to nations or groups that are known to sponsor terrorism, such as Iran and Syria.

NOAA, Fisheries Office of Law Enforcement

The Fisheries Office of Law Enforcement, a division within the Department of Commerce's National Oceanic and Atmospheric Administration (NOAA), is responsible for the enforcement of dozens of marine wildlife and natural resource conservation laws. Formally known as the National Marine Fisheries Service, the NOAA Fisheries Office of Law Enforcement is staffed by criminal investigators (special agents) and uniformed marine patrol officers. Special agents and officers have the authority to carry firearms, make arrests, and secure and execute search warrants on vessels or on land.

The primary federal statutes enforced by the NOAA Fisheries Office of Law Enforcement include the Magnuson-Stevens Fishery Conservation and Management Act, the Marine Mammal Protection Act of 1972, the Endangered Species Act of 1973, the Lacey Act and Amendments of 1981, and the Marine Protection, Research and Sanctuaries Act. Additionally, elements of various international treaties, such as the Convention of International Trade and Endangered Species of Wild Fauna and Flora and the Convention on the Conservation of Antarctic Marine Living Resources, are enforced by NOAA Fisheries Office of Law Enforcement in international waters.

Fisheries patrol officers conduct their patrols of designated marine sanctuaries with both watercraft and aircraft. The patrol areas of the

NOAA Fisheries Office of Law Enforcement cover 3.36 million square miles. In addition to patrol work and providing protection and assistance to visitors of the sanctuaries, fisheries patrol officers frequently board fishing vessels to ensure compliance with laws relating to the protection of marine life. These laws deal with the protection of particular species as well as the regulation of fishing methods in order to ensure that protected wildlife is not inadvertently threatened by otherwise legitimate commercial activities. NOAA fisheries patrol officers work closely with state marine enforcement officers and game wardens, the U.S. Coast Guard, and other law enforcement agencies.

NOAA Fisheries special agents conduct criminal and civil investigations of violations of the same laws and treaties just mentioned. Most criminal investigations tend to focus on illegal fishing practices and catches. Special agents also get involved with investigations relating to smuggling contraband (particularly endangered species) into and out of the United States. As a result, NOAA Fisheries special agents work closely with special agents of U.S. Immigration and Customs Enforcement, the Coast Guard, the U.S. Fish and Wildlife Service, the Department of Commerce's Office of Export Enforcement, and other law enforcement agencies. Although a small organization with less than 50 special agents, the NOAA Fisheries Office of Law Enforcement spent nearly 103,000 hours investigating marine fisheries violations in Fiscal Year 2003.[3]

U.S. DEPARTMENT OF DEFENSE

Army Criminal Investigation Division

The United States Army's Criminal Investigation Division (CID) is the detective bureau for the Army. The CID traces its origins to the creation of a criminal investigative division within the Military Police Corps to investigate crimes committed by American soldiers in France toward the end of World War I. The primary mission of Army CID is to investigate any and all serious crimes in which the Army has an interest. This includes the investigation of all major crimes on Army installations in the United States and around the world, including in combat zones. CID also investigates major criminal offenses involving Army personnel (as victims or as offenders) wherever the crimes may occur, particularly if there is a connection to the U.S. Army's mission or operations.

Offenses and occurrences commonly investigated by the U.S. Army CID include robberies, rape, death investigations, major accidents, burglaries, espionage, and major fraud committed against the U.S. Army. Criminal offenses committed by military personnel are not generally prosecuted under Title 18 (i.e., the federal criminal code). These offenses are prosecuted under the Uniform Code of Military Justice (UCMJ), which is rooted in Title 10. Additionally, CID special agents provide force protection support to Army troops in the field and perform dignitary protection duties for high-ranking military and Department of Defense officials.

Currently, approximately 2,000 civilian and military personnel work for Army CID full-time, including 900 special agents.[4] Army CID employs both military and civilian special agents. Military CID agents include both enlisted and warrant officer ranks, with the latter group fulfilling supervisory special agent functions. There are no CID special agents holding a commissioned officer rank (i.e., 2nd Lieutenant and higher). Instead, officers in CID's chain of command are a part of the Military Police Branch of the United States Army and do not possess the same statutory investigative powers of the subordinate special agents. In addition to active-duty CID agents, there are also hundreds of Army Reserve and National Guard CID special agents who are routinely called up to active duty. Most of these agents are also employed in some law enforcement capacity in their civilian jobs.

In addition to the military personnel serving as Army CID special agents (active duty and reserves), there are also civilian federal criminal investigators employed as CID special agents. These special agents have similar training requirements, pay, and career paths as other civilian federal law enforcement agents. Civilian CID special agents work primarily on major fraud cases, leaving the general crime, including violent crime, to be investigated by the military CID agents.

Special agents of the Army CID have full law enforcement authority over military personnel while on military installations. Enlisted CID agents are more limited than the warrant officer agents in that enlisted personnel do not possess the authority to arrest civilians on military installations. Civilian special agents with CID have broader law enforcement authority than their military counterparts in that they may execute warrants and make arrests relating to violations of not only the UCMJ, but also crimes under Title 18, and they may do so on and off military installations. Their authority to do so is defined in Title 10, Section 4027. Non-civilian criminal investigators are not permitted to investigate Title 18 criminal offenses, because the Posse Comitatus Act prohibits military personnel from engaging in civilian law enforcement activities. However, military CID agents frequently work on cases jointly with civilian law enforcement agencies because many federal and state offenses are outlawed under both Title 18 (and state criminal laws) as well as the UCMJ. All CID special agents may carry their firearms on and off military installations in the performance of their official duties.

Naval Criminal Investigative Service

Just as the Criminal Investigative Division is the Army's detective bureau, the Naval Criminal Investigative Service (NCIS) is likewise the criminal investigative arm of the United States Navy and the United States Marine Corps. In many ways, it is similar to Army CID in that NCIS has both military and civilian special agents in the organization. Additionally, the military agents include both active-duty and reserve personnel. However, unlike Army CID, there is no confinement to fraud investigations for the civilian agents. In fact, most of the general crime investigations are conducted by civilian NCIS special agents, both in the United States and abroad. Currently, there are approximately 2,300 employees working for the NCIS. About one-half of that number consists of civilian special agents. Most of the remainder work in support positions as forensic analysts, physical security specialists, and crime analysts.[5]

The NCIS began as a unit within the Office of Naval Intelligence during World War I. By 1966, the criminal investigative function housed in the Office of Naval Intelligence was moved into its own office—the Naval Investigative Service (NIS). The name changed to the Naval Criminal Investigative Service in 1992.[6]

The NCIS is responsible for all criminal investigations of offenses of interest or relating to the U.S. Navy and the U.S. Marine Corps. Civilian special agents of the NCIS have the authority to carry firearms and make arrests on and off military reservations and installations under Title 10, Section 7480. This includes general crimes such as murder, rape, robbery, assaults, thefts, and espionage. The NCIS also investigates major fraud committed against the U.S. Navy and the U.S. Marine Corps—primarily procurement fraud. Unless perpetrated by civilians, these offenses are prosecuted under the Uniform Code of Military Justice.

The NCIS also has significant statutory responsibilities in other areas besides criminal investigation. Most notable is its role in counterintelligence. The NCIS works closely with other intelligence and counterintelligence agencies, including the Federal Bureau of Investigation, the Central Intelligence Agency, the National Security Agency, the Defense Intelligence Agency, and others to defeat intelligence efforts directed against American military operations and status.

Special agents with the NCIS, as with agents from other military investigative organizations, have unique opportunities to draw assignments overseas. The NCIS has jurisdiction over all Navy and Marine Corps personnel stationed abroad. Further, criminal investigators with the NCIS may be asked to serve in the "Agent Afloat" program. In that program, civilian special agents are assigned to a deployed aircraft carrier for several months at a time. Those agents are then responsible for investigating all crimes committed on any of the ships in the carrier group. An agent may find himself or herself being flown off the deck of an aircraft carrier in a helicopter and deposited on a destroyer or cruiser to investigate a serious assault or the sale of drugs, for example. The "Agent Afloat" program is unique among all civilian federal law enforcement agencies.

Air Force Office of Special Investigations

The United States Air Force's criminal investigative arm is the Office of Special Investigations (OSI). The Air Force OSI was created in 1948 and is the youngest of all military investigative agencies. This is not surprising, because the Air Force is the youngest of the military branches, created in 1947 through separation of the Army Air Corps from the Army. According to the Air Force, the OSI's top four priorities are: detecting threats to Air Force operations, installations, and personnel worldwide; investigating and resolving crimes that impact the readiness, good order, and discipline of Air Force personnel; detecting and combating threats against Air Force information systems and technology; and detecting and prosecuting contract/procurement fraud relating to Air Force weapons systems.

Over 2,500 people work for Air Force OSI, 1,900 of which are special agents. Special agents include active duty and reserve military special agents as well as a cadre of civilian special agents. Among the military agents, over 360 are active-duty Air Force officers, nearly 800 are active-duty enlisted personnel, nearly 380 are reservists, and over 400 are civilian special agents. As with the Army CID and NCIS, special agents in the reserve can be called up to active duty to serve full-time as special agents to augment the active-duty and civilian force when needed.[7]

Air Force special agents, like NCIS and Army CID agents, possess law enforcement authorities, including the ability to carry firearms, make arrests, and execute search warrants on military installations.

Additionally, civilian special agents have full federal law enforcement authority off military reservations under Title 10, Section 9027. OSI agents investigate general crimes involving Air Force personnel or on Air Force installations, including homicide, rape, robbery, assault, and drug violations. They also investigate economic crimes such as contract fraud, fraud perpetrated via computers, bribery, and embezzlement. Further, OSI special agents work closely with other federal agencies to investigate and deter acts of terrorism, cyberterrorism, and sabotage against Air Force equipment. As with the Army CID and NCIS, special agents with Air Force OSI also engage in dignitary protection duties for high-ranking Air Force and Department of Defense officials.

U.S. ENVIRONMENTAL PROTECTION AGENCY

Criminal Investigation Division

The Environmental Protection Agency's Criminal Investigation Division (EPA-CID) began in 1982 with the mission of fighting environmental crime. In 1988, the U.S. Congress passed legislation granting criminal investigators with EPA-CID full federal law enforcement authority. The jurisdiction of EPA-CID special agents was expanded even further by the Pollution Prosecution Act of 1990. Additionally, this legislation required that the EPA employ no fewer than 50 civil compliance investigators by 1991 and no fewer than 200 criminal investigators by 1995.[8]

Special agents with EPA-CID possess full federal law enforcement authority, which they receive under Title 18, Section 3063. This statutes states:

(a) Upon designation by the Administrator of the Environmental Protection Agency, any law enforcement officer of the Environmental Protection Agency with responsibility for the investigation of criminal violations of a law administered by the Environmental Protection Agency, may

   (1) carry firearms;

   (2) execute and serve any warrant or other processes issued under the authority of the United States; and

   (3) make arrests without warrant for

      (A) any offense against the United States committed in such officer's presence; or

      (B) any felony offense against the United States if such officer has probable cause to believe that the person to be arrested has committed or is committing that felony offense.

(b) The powers granted under subsection (a) of this section shall be exercised in accordance with guidelines approved by the Attorney General.

Special agents with the EPA investigate a wide range of criminal statutes intended to protect the environment. Environmental crimes include the illegal dumping of hazardous wastes, polluting the air with illegal emissions, the submission of false environmental data by businesses to the EPA, the illegal dumping of waste into the ocean, causing oil spills due to negligence, the improper removal and disposal of asbestos, and the misuse of various chemicals and pesticides. Commonly investigated federal statutes under the investigative jurisdiction of EPA-CID include the Clean Water Act, the Resource Conservation and Recovery Act, and the Clean Air Act.

The Environmental Protection Agency's CID has also ventured into the realm of counterterrorism. With the prospect of the deployment of weapons of mass destruction by terrorists in the United States, especially weapons involving the use of noxious or toxic chemicals, the EPA-CID created counterterrorism response teams and counterterrorism evidence teams around the country. The EPA notes that these teams are charged with the responsibility of detecting and evaluating terrorist activities, investigating terrorism involving the use of chemicals and other hazardous substances, collecting and processing hazardous materials evidence, responding to weapons of mass destruction attacks, and serving as a technical resource for other law enforcement agencies involved in such investigations. EPA special agents also serve on Joint Terrorism Task Forces (JTTFs) around the country.

U.S. DEPARTMENT OF HEALTH AND HUMAN SERVICES

U.S. Food and Drug Administration, Office of Criminal Investigations

The Office of Criminal Investigations (OCI) at the U.S. Food and Drug Administration (FDA) is a subunit of the FDA's Office of Regulatory Affairs. The Food and Drug Administration is a branch of the U.S. Department of Health and Human Services. The FDA's self-identified mission is to:[9]

"...protect[t] the public health by assuring the safety, efficacy, and security of human and veterinary drugs, biological products, medical devices, our nation's food supply, cosmetics, and products that emit radiation...[and to] advance[e] the public health by helping to speed innovations that make medicines and foods more effective, safer, and more affordable; and helping the public get the accurate, science-based information they need to use medicines and foods to improve their health..."

The FDA-OCI serves as the agency's criminal investigative arm and possesses full law enforcement authority under Title 21. FDA special agents are not to be confused with FDA inspectors who ensure compliance with food and drug laws through inspection activities but are not law enforcement officers.

FDA-OCI special agents primarily investigate criminal violations of the Food, Drug, and Cosmetic Act, the Federal Anti-Tampering Act, the Prescription Drug Marketing Act, the Safe Medical Device Act, and other relevant criminal violations falling under Title 18, including conspiracy, bribery, and embezzlement. Typical investigations relate to food or drug product tampering and the counterfeiting of food and drug products.

Special agents with the FDA Office of Criminal Investigation work closely with other federal law enforcement agencies, including the Federal Bureau of Investigation, the Drug Enforcement Agency, and the Offices of Inspector General for the Department of Health and Human Services and the Department of Agriculture.

U.S. DEPARTMENT OF HOMELAND SECURITY

Federal Protective Service

The U.S. Department of Homeland Security absorbed several well-known federal law enforcement agencies when it was created in 2002. These agencies include the U.S. Customs Service, the Immigration and Naturalization Service, and the Secret Service. However, the Department of Homeland Security was created by combining not just those three agencies but a total of 22 separate agencies or organizational units. One of these agencies was the Federal Protective Service (FPS).

The Federal Protective Service was a part of the U.S. General Services Administration prior to its move to the Department of Homeland Security. The General Services Administration, among other things, is the property manager of the civilian federal government. Most federal buildings and courthouses are owned and operated by the General Services Administration. Title 42, Section 318 gave the General Services Administration the authority to field police officers and criminal investigators (described in the statute as "non-uniformed special policemen") to provide law enforcement services on federal property.

With the passage of the Homeland Security Act of 2002, the FPS was removed from the General Services Administration and placed under the Bureau of Immigration and Customs Enforcement (ICE) in the Department of Homeland Security. Now, its law enforcement authority is found under Title 40, Section 1315, which states in part:

Officers and Agents—

(1) Designation – The Secretary may designate employees of the Department of Homeland Security, including employees transferred to the Department from the Office of the Federal Protective Service of the General Services Administration pursuant to the Homeland Security Act of 2002, as officers and agents for duty in connection with the protection of property owned or occupied by the Federal Government and persons on the property, including duty in areas outside the property to the extent necessary to protect the property and persons on the property.

(2) Powers – While engaged in the performance of official duties, an officer or agent designated under this subsection may—

    (A) enforce Federal laws and regulations for the protection of persons and property;

    (B) carry firearms;

    (C) make arrests without a warrant for any offense against the United States committed in the presence of the officer or agent or for any felony cognizable under the laws of the United States if the officer or agent has reasonable grounds to believe that the person to be arrested has committed or is committing a felony;

    (D) serve warrants and subpoenas issued under the authority of the United States;

    (E) conduct investigations, on and off the property in question, of offenses that may have been committed against property owned or occupied by the Federal Government or persons on the property; and

    (F) carry out such other activities for the promotion of homeland security as the Secretary may prescribe.

The language granting law enforcement authority to the Federal Protective Service is stronger than it had been under 40 USC 318 when FPS was a part of the General Services Administration. Under the present language, FPS has full law enforcement authority on and off of federal property while in the performance of its responsibilities—particularly the prevention and investigation of crime that takes place on federal property.

Interestingly, the final provision of the FPS' authority in subsection (2) (F) of the statute is for the FPS to be used in any additional capacity as the Secretary of Homeland Security sees fit. Indeed, this specific piece of the authority language has been relied upon to significantly broaden the police powers and responsibilities of FPS.

Three types of law enforcement officers are employed by the Federal Protective Service: police officers, law enforcement security officers (LESOs), and criminal investigators (special agents). FPS police officers perform general patrol duties on and around federal property. They conduct their patrols primarily on foot and in squad cars, although in some areas horses and motorcycles are also utilized. In Washington DC, where so many federal buildings are located, the FPS police officers are a visible presence and, like the Uniformed Division of the Secret Service, possess the authority to assist other federal and local law enforcement agencies within the District of Columbia. Law enforcement security officers may work either in uniform or in plain clothes. They have full enforcement authority and do engage in patrol and investigative work. However, anywhere from half to most of a LESO's time is spent conducting physical security assessments for federal facilities. Finally, FPS criminal investigators are the investigative arm of the agency. These special agents conduct investigations of assaults, thefts, robberies, rapes, burglaries, and other serious crimes that occur on or around federal property. FPS special agents also serve on various law enforcement taskforces, including the Joint Terrorism Task Forces in various major cities across the country.

FPS also enforces the applicable state laws on federal property when no relevant federal law exists. This is done through the Assimilated Crimes Act, codified in Title 18, Section 13. This statute states in part:

Whoever within or upon any of the places now existing or hereafter reserved or acquired as provided in Section 7 of this title, or on, above, or below any portion of the territorial sea of the United States not within the jurisdiction of any State, Commonwealth, territory, possession, or district is guilty of any act or omission which, although not made punishable by any enactment of Congress, would be punishable if committed or omitted within the jurisdiction of the State, Territory, Possession, or District in which such place is situated, by the laws thereof in force at the time of such act or omission, shall be guilty of a like offense and subject to a like punishment.

The Assimilated Crimes Act is a significant tool for any federal law enforcement agency given the responsibility to provide general policing services on federal property. Through this statute, what is illegal in the areas surrounding a federal building or reservation is also illegal within that federal building or reservation, regardless of whether or not Congress thought to outlaw particular conduct federally.

The Federal Protective Service's jurisdiction is rather broad in light of its employing fewer than 500 law enforcement officers. Each year, the FPS responds to over 50,000 calls for service, provides a law enforcement presence at over 2,000 protest demonstrations, and makes over 3,000 arrests.[10] In addition to providing police services to the 8,800 federal buildings around the country, they also provide police protection for Federal Emergency Management Agency officials deployed to disaster sites, assist in providing police protection for national special security events, and maintain rapid response teams for WMD incidents and other major emergencies.

Federal Air Marshal Service

The Federal Air Marshal Service (FAMS) is a unit within the Transportation Security Administration (TSA) of the U.S. Department of Homeland Security. Federal air marshals are primarily responsible for detecting and defeating would-be hijackers of commercial airliners while in flight. The Federal Air Marshal Service was created in the aftermath of the terrorist hijackings of four American commercial airliners on September 11, 2001, and the subsequent destruction of the World Trade Center and the damage to the Pentagon by three of the hijacked planes. Prior to the creation of the FAMS under the Aviation and Transportation Security Act of 2001, the only in-flight security for commercial airliners (other than the occasional armed federal agent flying from one destination to another on business) was provided by the U.S. Department of Transportation's - Federal Aviation Administration (FAA). Before the existence of the FAMS, the FAA deployed civil aviation security specialists. These employees possessed a dual responsibility. In the United States, they conducted administrative inspections of airport and aviation security. In that capacity, they served as regulatory officers and possessed no law enforcement authority. However, they also served as armed security officers on designated international flights to or from the United States. It was through the performance of this duty that they began to be informally dubbed "air marshals." Their authority was limited to the confines of the aircraft on which they were traveling and only during the flight. Once on the ground, the appropriate local or federal law enforcement agencies for that airport had jurisdiction for anything that had happened on the plane. The need for armed security on international flights arose in the wake of several hijackings of American airliners by Cuban nationals in the 1960s and 1970s.

The cadre of civil aviation security specialists was very small. Leading up to the events of September 11, 2001, there were less than 40 civil aviation security specialists nationwide. Today, although the exact number is classified, there are easily over 2,000 federal air marshals in service, with the majority of them flying on domestic commercial flights within the United States.

Unlike their predecessors at the FAA, the federal air marshals of today as officers of the U.S. Department of Homeland Security possess full law enforcement authority on or off aircraft. Title 49, Section 114 states in part:

Law Enforcement Powers—

(1) In general – The Under Secretary may designate an employee of the Transportation Security Administration to serve as a law enforcement officer.

(2) Powers – While engaged in official duties of the Administration as required to fulfill the responsibilities under this section, a law enforcement officer designated under paragraph (1) may—

(A) carry a firearm;

(B) make an arrest without a warrant for any offense against the United States committed in the presence of the officer, or for any felony cognizable under the laws of the United States if the officer has probable cause to believe that the person to be arrested has committed or is committing the felony; and

(C) seek and execute warrants for arrest or seizure of evidence issued under the authority of the United States upon probable cause that a violation has been committed.

The Aviation and Transportation Security Act of 2001 didn't just grant the powers just presented in the Title 49 excerpt to law enforcement officers within the Transportation Security Administration— particularly federal air marshals. The law also required the Transportation Security Administration to provide for in-flight armed security for any and all civil aviation commercial flights within the United States. The TSA immediately set out to hire thousands of federal air marshals from the ranks of other federal law enforcement agencies (the U.S. Border Patrol lost hundreds of agents to the FAMS), from state and local law enforcement entities, and from the military.

Today, federal air marshals perform a variety of law enforcement duties pursuant to their mission of securing the commercial aviation industry, including criminal investigations, background checks, interviews, making arrests, and executing warrants. Additionally, the TSA has begun to deploy air marshals to other public transportation venues, including passenger rail and maritime carriers, in order to provide in-travel security in those contexts. Congress has also begun to consider legislation requiring the presence of air marshals on cargo flights that pose a high risk of being commandeered by terrorists.

United States Coast Guard Investigative Service

As noted earlier in this text, the United States Coast Guard has its historical roots in the Revenue Cutter Service. Throughout its history, the Coast Guard has been in the unique position of possessing both military and civilian responsibilities. In times of war, elements of the U.S. Coast Guard are transferred to the command of the United States Navy. Under the Navy, the Coast Guard is primarily responsible for providing port security at home and abroad. When not at war, the Coast Guard is a law enforcement and emergency services agency. In that capacity, the Coast Guard over its history has been an agency of the U.S. Treasury Department, the U.S. Transportation Department, and now the U.S. Homeland Security Department.

In addition to the law enforcement efforts performed by uniformed enlisted and officer personnel, the Coast Guard also fields a criminal investigative unit staffed by both civilian and military special agents. This unit is known as the Coast Guard Investigative Service (CGIS) and is very similar in its mission and structure to the Army CID, NCIS, and the Air Force OSI. However, the CGIS is not a Department of Defense agency. Like the rest of the Coast Guard, it was transferred to the Department of Homeland Security in March of 2003.

The CGIS conducts criminal investigations relating to maritime law and the broader Coast Guard law enforcement mission. Criminal investigations may relate to environmental or conservation crimes, the smuggling of illegal immigrants, drugs or other contraband on the high seas and in U.S. waters, and even piracy. The CGIS also investigates violations of the Uniform Code of Military Justice committed by Coast Guard personnel. Further, like the other military investigative agencies, the CGIS also performs dignitary protection duties for high-ranking government officials.

The CGIS has its roots in Coast Guard Intelligence, which was established in 1915. During the years of Prohibition, Coast Guard Intelligence employed as many as 45 criminal investigators.[11] During World War II, investigators with Coast Guard Intelligence primarily performed counterterrorism and security clearance investigations relating to Coast Guard operations. After the war, the responsibilities of this unit included the conduct of all criminal and personnel security investigations relating to the Coast Guard. In 1996, all criminal investigative, counterintelligence, and protective service functions of the Coast Guard were organized under the Coast Guard Investigative Service.[12]

U.S. DEPARTMENT OF THE INTERIOR

Bureau of Land Management, Office of Law Enforcement and Security

The Bureau of Land Management (BLM) controls approximately 264 million acres of public lands in the western United States. The BLM Office of Law Enforcement and Security polices that land along with state and local law enforcement. BLM Law Enforcement consists of approximately 200 uniformed rangers and 60 special agents.[13] In addition to performing general law enforcement duties on the BLM lands, such as patrolling, traffic enforcement, accident investigation, BLM Law Enforcement officers prevent and investigate major crimes that occur on BLM land, such as rape, homicide, assaults, robberies, and drug violations. Further there are several criminal statutes designed to protect BLM land and resources that are enforced by BLM Law Enforcement. These include the Archeological Resources Protection Act, the Wild Free-Roaming Horse and Burro Act of 1971, the Sikes Act, the Antiquities Act, the Resource Conservation and Recovery Act.[14]

While different components of the Department of the Interior have possessed law enforcement authority for many decades, the BLM was first given law enforcement authority in 1976 with the passage of the Federal Land Policy and Management Act. This law enforcement authority, which includes the ability to carry firearms, make arrests, and execute search warrants, is extended to both uniformed rangers and special agents of the BLM.

Rangers spend most of their time patrolling BLM lands. The land any particular ranger is responsible for is incredibly vast. Some rangers are individually responsible for as much as 1.8 million acres of land.

Rangers patrol their assigned areas via four-wheel drive vehicles, aircraft, ATVs, watercraft, and horseback. Rangers tend to patrol those areas that are most widely used by campers and other recreation seekers. The BLM serves more than 3 million campers and issues over 32,000 special use permits annually.[15]

BLM special agents conduct criminal investigations of BLM-related violations, such as the theft of artifacts, using BLM lands to manufacture drugs or grow marijuana, the theft of wild horses, arson, and violent crimes that occur on BLM lands. Special agents received many investigative leads from BLM rangers patrolling in the field. They also work closely with other federal law enforcement agents, including those from the Forest Service, the National Park Service, and state and local investigators.

Bureau of Indian Affairs Law Enforcement Services

The Department of the Interior's Bureau of Indian Affairs (BIA) is responsible for managing 56 million acres of federal land held in trust for various federally recognized Native American tribes.[16] Most who work for the BIA are Native Americans themselves. The BIA is the lone federal agency permitted to apply a racial preference in its hiring practices. To be employed at the BIA, one must generally be able to document that one is at least one-eighth Indian.

While much of the BIA is dedicated to providing human services to the Indian communities, such as health care and education, the BIA also operates a law enforcement division known as Law Enforcement Services. BIA Law Enforcement is responsible for providing police services to Indian lands where tribes have not established tribal police departments of their own. BIA employs both uniformed police officers who patrol Indian territory and criminal investigators (special agents) who act as detectives on Indian lands.

BIA police officers perform police duties in the same way patrol officers in municipal or county government do. They are assigned a patrol area (generally, an Indian reservation) and respond to calls for service, including accidents, minor offenses, thefts, domestic assaults, burglaries, drug violations, robberies, aggravated assaults, and homicides.

BIA special agents, operating under the authority of the Indian General Crimes Act (18 USC 1152) and the Indian Major Crimes Act (18 USC 1153), perform as local detectives would by investigating serious crimes, responding to crime scenes, collecting evidence, interviewing suspects and witnesses, preparing reports, and testifying in court.

BIA agents work closely with the Federal Bureau of Investigation, which has concurrent jurisdiction on Indian land and tends to involve itself with serious cases such as homicides, child sexual abuse, other sexual assaults, and major drug cases.[17]

National Park Service

The National Park Service (NPS) has a long tradition of federal law enforcement responsibilities. The NPS itself was created in 1916 for the purpose of managing and preserving the natural and historic resources of the national park system (totaling 84 million acres) in the United States for the enjoyment and education of its visitors, which number in the millions each year.[18]

To ensure the safety of the visitors to the national parks, the NPS employs both uniformed park rangers and criminal investigators. Under Title 16, Sections 1a-6 and 1b, both park rangers and NPS special agents possess law enforcement authority, including the right to carry firearms, make arrests, and execute search warrants.

As with their counterparts at the Bureau of Land Management and the Forest Service in their respective jurisdictions, NPS rangers and special agents provide general policing services to visitors of the parks and conduct investigations of criminal offenses committed against the National Park Service or inside the national parks. These offenses include various property and violent crimes, arson, and drug violations under Title 21. Law enforcement officers with the National Park Service are cross-designated with the BLM and the Forest Service (as are the law enforcement agents of those organizations) so that coordination among land management law enforcement agencies can occur without jurisdictional impediments.[19]

In addition to the law enforcement rangers and special agents, the United States Park Police is also a part of the National Park Service. Today, the United States Park Police is a full-service police organization that provides traditional police protection for designated National Park areas—which are primarily located in Washington DC. Other significant contingents of the U.S. Park Police are located in San Francisco, California, and New York City. The Park Police conducts its patrols primarily with squad cars. But it also utilizes horses, motorcycles, helicopters, watercraft, and bicycles.

The U.S. Park Police also employs detectives (not special agents) who advance through the ranks as detectives typically must do in other traditional police agencies at the local level. Park Police detectives investigate crimes that occur on lands under the police protection of the Park Police, including national monuments, forested preserves, and large vehicular parkways.

Fish and Wildlife Service, Office of Law Enforcement

The U.S. Fish and Wildlife Service (FWS) of the Department of the Interior serves as the primary conservation agency for the federal government. The Office of Law Enforcement is responsible for the criminal enforcement piece of the FWS conservation mission. Special agents of the FWS investigate a wide range of criminal offenses, including the smuggling of protected animals to or from the United States, illegal hunting or fishing on federally protected lands, violating game limits imposed by federal migratory bird protection laws on any lands, and violations of treaty provisions relating to the shipment of wildlife across international borders.

In Fiscal Year 2004, the 231 special agents of the Fish and Wildlife Service carried a caseload of over 10,500 cases.[20] Approximately half of these cases related to violations of the Endangered Species Act. The next largest category of cases (over 2,500) related to violations of laws and treaties concerning migratory birds. That year, FWS cases resulted in over 9,600 prosecutions and in fines totaling nearly $3 million. An addition $916,000 in civil penalties was also assessed.[21]

National Railroad Passenger Corporation (Amtrak)

Amtrak is the nation's publicly subsidized passenger rail service. It was created by Congress in 1970 to replace passenger rail services provided by freight railroad companies. Amtrak operates over 22,000 route miles and 500 stations. Each day in the United States, approximately 68,000 people travel on Amtrak trains. This figure does not include 850,000 daily commuters riding Amtrak trains where it has contracted with localities to provide commuter rail service. [22]

The Amtrak Police and Security Department provides police protection on Amtrak trains as well as at Amtrak stations. Amtrak police officers are primarily uniformed law enforcement officers who perform duties similar to regional or municipal transit police officers in various communities around the country. The Amtrak Police and Security Department employs approximately 340 sworn police officers.[23] In 1992, the Amtrak Police and Security Department became the first federal law enforcement agency to secure accreditation by the Commission on Accreditation of Law Enforcement Agencies (CALEA). Accreditation by CALEA is difficult to achieve and is generally seen as a hallmark of professionalism and achievement for an American law enforcement organization.[24]

In addition to patrolling the rail cars and train stations on foot, Amtrak police officers use vehicles to patrol rail lines and facilities. Amtrak police officers also utilize canines to detect narcotics and potential explosive devices among the passengers or stored in Amtrak-controlled spaces. Despite Amtrak's being a quasi-for-profit corporation, Amtrak police officers and detectives, who conduct investigations of crimes occurring on the trains or in Amtrak facilities, are granted their law enforcement authority from the federal government. This authority includes the power to carry firearms, make arrests, and execute search warrants.

U.S. DEPARTMENT OF STATE

Bureau of Diplomatic Security

The Bureau of Diplomatic Security (formally the Diplomatic Security Service), is the chief law enforcement arm of the U.S. State Department. The responsibilities of the Bureau of Diplomatic Security (DS) are broadly twofold:[25]

(1) To conduct criminal investigations of matters directly relating to the State Department mission, including the investigation of visa fraud, passport fraud, and acts of terrorism or planned acts of terrorism; and

(2) To provide for the physical security of State Department facilities and missions abroad, as well as for American diplomats, their staff, and their families while abroad, and foreign dignitaries visiting the United States.

The importance of the criminal investigative mission of DS cannot be overstated. Visa and passport fraud are federal felonies that commonly occur in conjunction with other more serious federal offenses. For example, would-be terrorists or drug traffickers attempting to gain access into the United States would use fraudulently obtained passports and visas to gain entry for themselves or their operatives. As a result, DS special agents work closely with other federal criminal investigators, as well as law enforcement agencies from around the world, and with INTERPOL.

The protective mission of the Bureau of Diplomatic Security includes duties overseas and in the United States. In addition to protecting 157

American missions around the world, the State Department also requires DS security services for over 100 State Department facilities domestically.[26]

Title 22, Section 2709 of the United States Code bestows upon special agents of the Bureau of Diplomatic Security the ability to exercise law enforcement authority. That statute states in part:

Under such regulations as the Secretary of State may prescribe, special agents of the Department of State and the Foreign Service may—

(1) conduct investigations concerning illegal passport or visa issuance or use;

(2) for the purpose of conducting such investigations—

    (A) obtain and execute search and arrest warrants

    (B) make arrests without warrant for any offense concerning passport or visa issuance or use if the special agent has reasonable grounds to believe that the person has committed or is committing such offense, and

    (C) obtain and serve subpoenas and summonses issued under the authority of the United States.

(3) protect and perform protective functions directly related to maintaining the security and safety of—

    (A) heads of a foreign state, official representatives of a foreign government, and other distinguished visitors to the United States, while in the United States;

    (B) the Secretary of State, Deputy Secretary of State, and official representatives of the United States Government, in the United States or abroad;

    (C) members of the immediate family of persons described in subparagraph (A) or (B);

    (D) foreign missions…and international organizations…within the United States;

    (E) a departing Secretary of State for a period of up to 180 days after the date of termination of that individual's incumbency as Secretary of State, on the basis of a threat assessment; and

    (F) an individual who has been designated by the President to serve as Secretary of State, prior to that individual's appointment.

(4) if designated by the Secretary and qualified, under regulations approved by the Attorney General, for the use of firearms, carry firearms for the purpose of performing the duties authorized by this section; and

    (5) arrest without warrant any person for a violation of Sections 111, 112, 351, 970, or 1028 of Title 18—

        (A) in the case of a felony violation, if the special agent has reasonable grounds to believe that such person—

            (i) has committed or is committing such violation; and

            (ii) is in or is fleeing from the immediate area of such violation; and

        (B) in the case of a felony or misdemeanor violation, if the violation is committed in the presence of the special agent.

In 2004, the Bureau of Diplomatic Security had nearly 600 special agents worldwide. Approximately 480 of those special agents were serving overseas at American missions.[27] The need for vigilant protections of United States embassies and consulates was made extremely plain in 1998 when suicide bombers simultaneously detonated truck bombs the American embassies in the African countries of Tanzania and Kenya, killing hundreds of people. Prior to those bombings, there had been interest by some in the State Department and in the Clinton Administration in reducing the number of DS special agents and to deemphasizing the law enforcement role of the State Department. The bombings in Africa proved, however, to be an object lesson about the need for an aggressive security posture.

TENNESSEE VALLEY AUTHORITY

Tennessee Valley Authority Police

The Tennessee Valley Authority (TVA) was established during the "New Deal" expansionist federal program years of the Franklin Roosevelt administration. The TVA is a federally owned corporation that provides electrical power to government and private sector consumers inside the Tennessee Valley, which covers 80,000 square miles and is located in parts of Tennessee, Mississippi, Alabama, Georgia, North Carolina, Virginia, and Kentucky.[28] The mission of the TVA is to provide affordable power to the region, to foster economic development throughout the region, and to protect the natural resources of the Tennessee Valley.[29]

In support of the TVA's overall mission, the TVA Police Department provides uniformed law enforcement services to recreation seekers and other visitors to TVA land as well as protection for TVA employees and facilities. To generate energy in the Tennessee Valley, the TVA operates 3 nuclear plants, 11 fossil plants, 29 hydro-electric plants, 6 combustion turbine plants, and several solar and wind energy facilities. TVA also manages over 100 recreational areas.[30] All of these sites are policed by officers of the TVA Police.

The TVA Police is a full-service law enforcement agency and provides both uniformed patrol services and criminal investigative services through its detective division. Detectives of the TVA work closely with other local, state, and federal law enforcement agencies to investigate crimes that occur on TVA land or in TVA facilities. TVA police officers and detectives receive their law enforcement authority from Title 16, Section 831c-3, which states in part:

The Board may designate employees of the corporation to act as law enforcement agents in the area of jurisdiction described in subsection (c) of this section.

(b) Duties and Powers

    (1) Duties
      A law enforcement agent designated under subsection (a) of this section shall maintain law and order and protect persons and property in the area of jurisdiction described in subsection (c) of this section and protect property and officials and employees of the corporation outside that area.

    (2) Powers
      In the performance of duties described in paragraph (1), a law enforcement agent designated under subsection (a) of this section may—

      (A) make arrests without warrant for any offense against the United States committed in the agent's presence, or for any felony cogizable under the laws of the United States if the agent has probable cause to believe that the person to be arrested has committed or is committing such a felony;

      (B) execute any warrant or other process issued by a court or officer of competent jurisdiction for the enforcement of any Federal law or regulation issued pursuant to law in connection with the investigation of an offense described in subparagraph (A);

      (C) conduct an investigation of an offense described in subparagraph (A) in the absence of investigation of the offense by any Federal law enforcement agency having investigative jurisdiction over the offense or with the concurrence of that agency; and

      (D) carry firearms in carrying out any activity described in subparagraph (A), (B), or (C).

(c) Area of Jurisdiction

A law enforcement agent designated under subsection (a) of this section shall be authorized to exercise the law enforcement duties and powers described in subsection (b) of this section—

(1) on any lands or facilities owned or leased by the corporation or within such adjoining areas in the vicinities of such lands or facilities as may be determined by the board under subsection (e) of this section; and

(2) on other lands or facilities—

(A) when the person to be arrested is in the process of fleeing from such lands, facilities, or adjoining areas to avoid arrest;

(B) in conjunction with the protection of property or officials or employees of the corporation on or within lands or facilities other than those owned or leased by the corporation; or

(C) in cooperation with other Federal, State, or local law enforcement agencies.

Interestingly, in the case of TVA police officials, their authority has some limitations. According to the authorizing statute, their law enforcement powers are generally restricted to TVA lands and facilities. Further, they do not have general criminal investigative jurisdiction for crimes involving the TVA if other federal law enforcement agencies with relevant jurisdiction should choose to investigate the matter in question themselves. This status of inferiority to other federal agencies has posed some problems for morale in the TVA police department over the years. However, the relationships that have been fostered between the TVA police and state and local law enforcement agencies has softened the negative effects of the statute on the TVA Police. Through the TVA Police's cooperative efforts with state and local law enforcement, the TVA has been able to effectively involve itself in virtually any cases it wishes where there are state criminal offenses implicated, regardless of other federal agency interests.

UNITED STATES POSTAL SERVICE

Postal Inspection Service

In an earlier chapter, this text briefly addressed the early beginnings of the Postal Inspection Service. By all accounts, it is certainly one of the oldest federal law enforcement agencies in the United States. But more noteworthy is the agency's present reputation. The Postal Inspection

Service is widely considered one the federal government's premier federal law enforcement agencies today.

The Postal Inspection Service employs approximately 2,000 criminal investigators nationwide.[31] The working title for these investigators is not "special agent," but rather "postal inspector." Postal inspectors have full federal law enforcement authority under Title 18, Section 3061, which grants them the power to make warrantless arrests based upon probable cause, carry firearms, execute search warrants, and seize property. Postal inspectors investigate a wide range of federal offenses. These include homicides, assaults, robberies, letter bombs, burglary of postal facilities, using the mail for child exploitation and pornography, drug violations on postal property and through the mail, fraud perpetrated through the mail, embezzlement, extortion (where demands are communicated through the mail), theft of mail, identity theft, and many other criminal offenses.

Unlike the Federal Bureau of Investigation and the Drug Enforcement Administration, which train at the FBI Academy in Quantico, Virginia, and unlike most other federal law enforcement agencies, which train at the Federal Law Enforcement Training Center in Glynco, Georgia, the Postal Inspection Service operates its own academy for the exclusive use of postal inspectors. The Postal Inspection Service also operates one of several federal law enforcement forensic laboratories. Postal inspectors routinely work with other federal law enforcement agencies, including the FBI, DEA, ATF, and special agents from the various Inspector General offices.

The Postal Inspection Service also maintains a uniformed police force of over 1,000 officers who patrol postal facilities at key locations around the country.[32] These officers provide physical security for these postal facilities inside and outside of the buildings, ensure the safety of postal customers and employees in such facilities by acting as first responders in an emergency, and provide escorts for high-value or sensitive shipments.

STILL OTHER AGENCIES

The agencies described in this and the preceding chapters represent just a sampling of federal organizations possessing law enforcement authority. Others not addressed here but worth mentioning include the police departments of the U.S. Department of Veterans Affairs, the U.S. Mint, the U.S. Bureau of Engraving and Printing, the U.S. Capitol Police, and the U.S. Supreme Court Police. All of these agencies exercise federal police power in the provision of law enforcement services to their respective parent organization.

The fact is that federal law enforcement power has remained, in most cases, narrowly tailored. The framers of the Constitution and most American political sentiment of the past rejected the idea of a national police agency with broad, sweeping powers. Historically, American politicians intentionally missed every opportunity that presented itself to grant broader police power to the military or to consolidate all of civilian federal law enforcement under a single roof. Instead, federal law enforcement organizations have been created as the need has arisen for specific agencies and inside of specific jurisdictional boundaries.

However, as the federal government at large has grown, so has the number of police agencies under the federal mantle. Instead of simply expanding the powers of a single or a few law enforcement agencies to change with the times and expanding those agencies resources to keep up with broadening missions, the United States government has seen fit to simply create new police agencies to address new challenges and operate in new enforcement environments. Therefore, while most federal law enforcement agencies are narrow in their scope, they are plentiful in number—some would say to a unreasonable degree—and protective of their own turf and allocated resources. The turf mindset, critics point out, often comes at the expense of efficient, cooperative, and effective police work.

In the next chapter, this text will explore how critical events tend to drive public policy and how one recent historical event in particular—the September 11, 2001 terrorist attacks—drove Congress, the President, and the American people to reassess the value of disparate, isolated federal law enforcement agencies operating independently of each other.

CHAPTER 8

Public Policy, Homeland Security, and the Future of Federal Law Enforcement

A theme throughout this text has been to explore the narrow nature of federal law enforcement. The federal government of the United States is limited in its exercise of law enforcement authority; that much is known. What has been grappled with over the decades and even centuries is where those lines of boundaries are drawn. It seems fairly evident that over time, within the context of American history, the lines have been moving. But why have they moved? And how is it that one generation's understanding of the scope and reach of appropriate federal police power is found to be completely obsolete one or two generations later?

In attempting to answer these questions, one will not find significant guidance in the Constitution. After all, there have only been a couple of dozen amendments added to the Constitution over the nation's 200-plus years, and only a few of those amendments resulted in expanded federal police power—and only for narrowly defined kinds of cases. The amendments do not explain the enormous growth of the federal criminal code, which now contains thousands of federal criminal statutes, the violation of which could result in criminal prosecution and imprisonment upon conviction. Nor do the relatively few changes to the

Constitution explain the growth in number of federal law enforcement agencies. Appendix C of this book identifies a little over 90 federal law enforcement agencies, and that is not an all-inclusive list.

For answers to the questions relating to how the scope and reach of federal police power has changed over time (rightly or wrongly depending on one's perspective), one must look to the public policy process. Federal law enforcement is inherently a public policy issue and has been so from the very start. Political scientists today study public policy processes and have developed various models explaining how laws and policies are developed and implemented. But even before the discipline of political science existed per se, and before models explaining the policy process could be conceived and consulted, the axioms of public policy-making have always been at work, and the ingredients necessary for the shifting of public policy have always been present.

THE PUBLIC POLICY PROCESS

Political scientist Thomas Dye defines public policy, in its simplest sense, as whatever governments choose to do or not to do.[1] Governments may or may not pass particular laws; they may or may not spend money on particular types of programs or potential initiatives; they may or may not make the enforcement of some existing laws a priority over others.

Of course, when a government does nothing concerning a particular issue, it is often perceived by the public as not caring about that issue. The government having no concern about an issue is certainly one possible explanation. Indeed, the government conveys to the public what it thinks is important through its public policies. When government codifies public policy decisions into criminal law for example, it sends a message to the public that certain behavior is not to be tolerated, that certain behavior warrants punishment in response, and that the government is concerned enough about an issue to bother legislating the matter in the first place.[2] Often, the most important objective achieved through the public process is the latter—that is, conveying the message that government cares. Symbolism is as important as and sometimes more important than substantive results.

However, other explanations for government inaction are also possible. The government may care about an issue but care about another issue or issues even more. Therefore, in doing nothing about the first issue, it has actually done something: it has chosen to spend its resources elsewhere. Another explanation might be that the government is simply unaware of problems associated with an issue. It is not that it doesn't care but rather that it is simply ignorant.

So how does government become aware of those areas needing public policy attention? And how does government determine the priorities among many different but legitimate public policy goals when resources are limited, or when the goals contain mutually exclusive elements (such as the need for greater safety balanced against the need for protecting civil liberties)? The answers lie in how the public policy agenda for government is set.

The "agenda" for government are those issues on the government's radar screen that it has determined need attending to. Agendas are set by way of different processes, some of which are gradual and some of which are acute. John Kingdon, a well-known scholar in the field of public policy, identified three processes that shape the government's agenda: policy concept development, politics, and problems.[3] The first process is the gradual accumulation of knowledge gained by experts in a particular policy area. Over time, successive generations of policy proposals may gain enough support to become matters government chooses to address. Kingdon's second process refers to how political machinations affect the agenda. As he notes, swings in the national mood, ambiguity in public opinion, changes in the presidency and turnover in Congress all impact the policy agenda. Third, problems shape the agenda—especially acute or critical problems that emerge suddenly and appear to have severe implications if unattended to. A classic example is that of the Japanese attack on Pearl Harbor on December 7, 1941. While prior to that date, politics and policy experts may have been slowly moving the United States toward a war footing because of the conflict already raging around the world at that time against countries generally regarded as friends, the impetus for making drastic changes in policies, laws, and procurement (of weaponry) came in the form of the attack. That was a critical incident that demanded immediate government attention. One day later, Congress declared war, not only against Japan but also against Germany and Italy. Dangers posed by other countries were now the most pressing agenda matter and the battle was immediately joined.

Another clear example, and one that has profound implications for federal law enforcement, is that of the terrorist attacks on September 11, 2001. Government policy makers immediately mobilized and took up the critical agenda item of the nation's vulnerability to terrorist attacks. The vulnerabilities identified had long existed, as had terrorism. But now, with the World Trade Center destroyed on national television and thousands of Americans dead, all of the agenda setters and policy makers quickly began working on how to deal with America's latest security crisis.

The players in setting the agenda and ensuring a serious government response included many people and institutions inside and outside the federal government. To be sure, the players included the President of the United States and his advisors, and they included Congress. But others also played a key role in shaping the agenda. Noteworthy mentions include the media, the federal bureaucracy, the courts, state and local government officials, and interest groups.

The influence that the President of the United States has on setting the agenda is obvious. Presidents have the bully pulpit. They can make their appeals directly to the American people when Congress is less interested in initiatives the President seeks to implement. In the hours and days after the September 11 attacks, President Bush made several appearances on national television. The purpose was in part to reassure the public. But the President also began to prepare and persuade the public, and by extension, the public's representatives in Congress, that America must enter into a long and difficult war against terrorism.

Members of Congress also helped shape the agenda. Immediately after 9/11, it was difficult to distinguish most Republicans from Democrats. Everyone appeared to be in agreement. Most in Congress reinforced the messages coming from the White House. And virtually all members in both of houses of Congress voted to authorize the President to go war in Afghanistan, to revamp national security laws in the United States, and to reorganized elements of the United States government in order to more ably respond to the threat of terrorism. The power of Congress to shape the agenda was particularly demonstrated in the creation of the Department of Homeland Security. The President initially resisted the idea, preferring instead to appoint a homeland security coordinator within the Office of the White House. A homeland security "czar" in the White House was to work with existing law enforcement, intelligence, and military agencies to ensure the sharing of information and a coordinated response to threats. Members of Congress in both parties, however, went on the Sunday morning news shows and pushed the need for creating a new government department. This approach gained support and the President, seeing the writing on the wall, wisely did not tarry too long before adopting it and making it his own.

The President (and his staff) and members of Congress effectively persuaded the American public to embrace the war on terror and thus shaped the public policy agenda. But they weren't alone. Government officials can do little to win public support on an issue without the help of the media. Further, government officials frequently receive their cues about what is important among the American populace from the media. The media does several things that directly impact the policy agenda. News outlets, including those on television and radio, in print, and on the Internet serve as vehicles of communication among those in the policy community. The media also amplifies ideas that began in some segment of government or in some part of the country and quickly turns them into national matters needing immediate attention. In covering some ideas or news stories over others, the media helps the public, politicians, and bureaucrats deduce what is important and what is not important—the latter having received little or no media attention.

The media also can shape public opinion by the way news is covered. News items that garner extended commentary from one side or another, or policy proposals that are defended or attacked by political players, give the media ample choices as to which statements—for or against to run as well as how much of each. A public who sees 4 out of 5 media commentators and policy wonks oppose a particular law or policy will likely start to embrace the notion that there are more reasons to oppose the measure than there are to support it. The many sharp arguments against the policy on one side are set against a few feeble arguments on the other; the unsuspecting public may tend to believe that all has been said that could be said about the matter. If members of the public themselves had notions to the contrary, many of them will lose confidence in their own initial understanding of the issue, because their views are not being reinforced by the "experts" on TV. It should also be noted that the influence of the media on the public at large in this way is less effective today than it used to be. This is because there are so many different alternatives for receiving one's news. Cable television has opened up several news source alternatives apart from the traditional network broadcasts by ABC, NBC, and CBS. Further, the Internet has created significantly less reliance on the major daily newspapers for those who do not get their news from the television.[4]

Over the years, the federal government has responded to many crises, or perceived crises, by adjusting its law enforcement reach. When drug use was perceived as a national epidemic, a "war on drugs" was declared, new federal drug laws were passed, and federal drug agents became among the most active and busy members of the federal law enforcement community. When President Reagan, his press secretary James Brady, a Secret Service agent, and a DC Metro police officer were all shot in 1981 by John Hinckley with a small handgun, Congress went on to pass the Brady Bill, which restricted the possession of such weapons. When Hinckley was found not guilty of the shooting by reason of insanity, Congress passed legislation reforming the insanity defense so that federal criminals could be found "guilty but insane."

When 3,000 people lost their lives on September 11, 2001, President Bush and Congress went to work. While many legislative and executive initiatives emerged in the wake of 9/11 and continue to emerge, two major pieces of legislation changed the way federal law enforcement conducted its business in the United States. One was the United and Strengthening America by Providing Appropriate Tools Required to Intercept and Obstruct Terrorism (USA PATRIOT) Act of 2001. The other was the Homeland Security Act of 2002.

USA PATRIOT ACT OF 2001

After 9/11, the American public demanded to know how those events could have happened. After all, 19 or more hijackers from foreign countries had been involved. Some of the hijackers had taken flight training in the United States. In fact, would-be hijacker Zacarias Moussaoui had been arrested for immigration violations after raising the suspicions of flight instructors. Moussaoui had expressed a specific interest in learning how to fly a plane but not land one. Americans and American politicians began to wonder out loud how it was that federal law enforcement and intelligence services, which had snippets of information relating to the hijackers here and there, had not "connected the dots." It was in this context that the USA PATRIOT Act was born.

Prior to 9/11, America was not without laws in place that empowered federal law enforcement and intelligence agencies to thwart acts of terror. But with the empowerment also came significant impediments, and the impediments had become more difficult to surmount over the years because of changing times and technology. It was the removal of some of those impediments that was the objective of the USA PATRIOT Act.

In 1978, Congress passed the Foreign Intelligence Surveillance Act (FISA). That legislation created a distinct federal court that would be responsible for authorizing federal law enforcement activities related to top-secret national security investigations. Through FISA court orders, federal agents were given the ability to more readily secure taps on telephones and other electronic communications, obtain search and surveillance warrants for which no immediate notification had to be made to the target of an investigation, and gain greater access to sensitive financial records.

It was required that the targets of FISA investigations were agents of foreign powers. In other words, FISA court orders could only be used in cases of espionage. Purveyors of child pornography, even if citizens of a foreign country, could not be investigated under FISA, for example. Instead, they would be subject to the normal criminal investigative process under normal rules of criminal procedure. Two excellent benefits of FISA for law enforcement were that the investigative processes were automatically secret (i.e., no special effort had to be made to seal court documents) and no specific criminal plot had to be shown (i.e., simply being a foreign intelligence agent warranted one's investigation). To obtain a FISA search or surveillance warrant, federal agents had to demonstrate to the court that the target was indeed an agent of a foreign power; how the surveillance would take place; certification from an intelligence official that the information sought by federal agents is foreign intelligence information; and the reasons why the information could not be obtained through normal investigative processes.[5]

Even with the passage of FISA, however, there remained in place a wall between federal law enforcement (namely, the FBI) and intelligence agencies such as the Central Intelligence Agency (CIA) and the National Security Agency (NSA). This wall, which precluded the sharing of intelligence information with law enforcement, was established through executive order and legislation as a result of the findings of the Church Committee in 1976. The Church Committee was a Senate committee headed by Senator Frank Church of Idaho. His committee found numerous examples of intelligence agencies sharing information gathered through intelligence operations with domestic federal law enforcement agencies such as the FBI, Secret Service, the Drug Enforcement Administration, and others. The agencies would then proceed to use the information to further their criminal investigation and prosecute criminal offenders. The net effect was that law enforcement agencies were routinely using intelligence agencies to gather information for them so as to circumvent the Fourth Amendment requirement of securing a search warrant to seize evidence or the requirements under Title III of the Omnibus Crime Act of 1968 for a wiretap, which include a court order and permission from the United States Attorney General. The Church Commission report was very critical of this practice. Intelligence agencies have been severely restricted from sharing information with the FBI and other law enforcement agencies ever since.

During the 1980s and 1990s, numerous acts of terrorism were perpetrated against Americans—particularly overseas. However, one act—the World Trade Center bombing in 1993, demonstrated that terrorists could operate inside America's borders. In response to the demonstrable threat of terrorism, Congress passed the Anti-Terrorism and Effective Death Penalty Act of 1996. This legislation made certain acts of terrorism a capital offense—a punishment unavailable for terrorists convicted in the 1993 World Trade Center bombing. The Act also made it a federal felony to provide material support, assistance, and resources to foreign terrorist organizations. Further, the law made it easier for the federal government to prevent from entering the country or to deport individuals believed to have ties to terrorism. Finally, the law allowed federal law enforcement to open investigations based upon facts that included activities protected by the First Amendment—namely, speech, assembly, and religion. The bans against opening investigations on the basis of volatile speech and demonstrations had been holdovers from the Church Commission, which had also criticized the FBI for attending meetings, demonstrations, and religious services in order to rummage for reasons to open investigations.

One thing the 1996 Act did not do, however, was tear down the wall inhibiting the communication from intelligence agencies to law enforcement. In fact, keeping that wall in place was a high priority for the Justice Department under President Clinton, who went to even greater lengths than the law required to keep law enforcement criminal investigations uncontaminated by intelligence information. In a 1995 Justice Department memorandum that outlined the prohibition against interagency information sharing, then Deputy Attorney General Jamie Gorelick wrote in part:

Although the counterintelligence investigation may result in the incidental collection of information relevant to possible future criminal prosecutions, the primary purpose of the counterintelligence investigation will be to collect foreign counterintelligence information. Because the counterintelligence investigation will involve the use of surveillance techniques authorized under the Foreign Intelligence Surveillance Ace (FISA) against targets that, in some instances, had been subject to surveillance under Title III, and because it will involve some of the same sources and targets as the criminal investigation, we believe that it is prudent to establish a set of instructions that will clearly separate the counterintelligence investigation from the more limited, but continued, criminal investigations.

These procedures, which go beyond what is legally required, will prevent any risk of creating an unwarranted appearance that FISA is being used to avoid procedural safeguards which would apply in a criminal investigation.

Immediately after 9/11, Congress and the White House worked together to quickly craft legislation that would improve federal law enforcement's ability to detect and defeat acts of terrorism in the United States. On October 12, 2001, a mere month after the 9/11 hijackings, Congress passed the USA Act. That legislation permitted federal agents to investigate, under FISA, terrorists who were not agents of a foreign power. In other words, a target with ties to terrorism need not be working on behalf of a foreign power. Terrorists acting alone or as a member of a small or informal group could now be investigated under FISA. This authorization was reaffirmed later with the passage of the Intelligence Reform and Terrorism Prevention Act of 2004.

On October 17, 2001, Congress passed the Financial Anti-Terrorism Act. That law gave expanded powers to federal law enforcement to investigate the financial supporters of terrorism and to seize financial assets. Both the USA Act and the Financial Anti-Terrorism Act were precursors of larger bill that would follow only a few days later: the USA PATRIOT Act. In fact, both the USA Act and the Financial Anti-Terrorism Act were rolled into the USA PATRIOT Act.

The USA PATRIOT Act was signed into law on October 26, 2001. A variety of laws were amended as a result of this legislation, including those relating to money laundering, banking, financial privacy, immigration, and FISA, as well as the provision of additional federal funds for law enforcement and intelligence operations. The breadth of the legislation was remarkable in view of the fact that only a month and a half had elapsed since the 9/11 terrorist attacks (see Appendix D).

The USA PATRIOT Act was a widely supported bipartisan piece of legislation when it became law. The House of Representatives passed the law by a vote of 357 to 66. The Senate was even more unified in its support, with 98 senators voting for the law and only one senator voting against it (one senator was not present for the vote). However, since its passage, the USA PATRIOT Act has become aggressively criticized by politicians and special interest groups such as the American Civil Liberties Union and the American Library Association.[6]

The primary purpose of the Act was to make a number of technical corrections to existing laws so that law enforcement could effectively conduct counterterrorism and foreign intelligence investigations in a way that recognizes changing technology and changing times. For example, law enforcement had long been permitted to secure a court order for a wiretap (i.e., interception and eavesdropping) of electronic communications. However, wiretaps were not only person-specific, but phone specific. This posed a difficult problem for investigators attempting to monitor suspects' communications in an age when cell phones are disposable and can readily be replaced. The USA PATRIOT Act recognized the nature of modern electronic communications and granted law enforcement the authority to obtain "roving wiretaps." The justification for the wiretap must still be demonstrated to the FISA court by federal agents, but agents no longer need to receive a new court order each time the target individual or individuals change the means of communication. In other words, wiretaps obtained under the USA PATRIOT Act are target-specific, not phone- or computer-specific.

Another element of the USA PATRIOT Act is that federal agents were given greater power to obtain "sneak and peak" search warrants for FISA investigative targets. Under normal criminal investigative circumstances, the Federal Rules of Criminal Procedure require that law enforcement officers notify subjects of a search warrant about the existence of the warrant, the items the agents are searching for, and the items that were in fact seized at the conclusion of serving the warrant. With a "sneak and peak" warrant, agents can enter a target's business or home and look around while the person is away. Although targets are still entitled to notification, the court can authorize an indefinite delay of notification. In fact, notification that agents were searching a person's home and opening his or her mail might not come until the subject is arrested or exonerated, in some cases, months later.

The Act also made more efficient law enforcement's use of pen registers and trap and trace devices. Pen registers record the phone numbers being dialed out from a particular phone. Trap and trace devices record the phone numbers of callers dialing into a particular phone. Pen registers and trap and traces have long been tools for local, state, and federal law enforcement investigating all types of criminal cases. They are relatively easy to obtain from a court because they do not involve eavesdropping. They merely record outgoing and incoming phone numbers. The USA PATRIOT Act empowers federal law enforcement to obtain pen registers and trap and trace device authorization for anywhere in the country. Agents no longer must to go to each jurisdiction and receive separate court orders when, for example, a target takes his cell phone across state lines into a different federal judicial district. Additionally, the Act permits the equivalent of pen registers and trap and trace devices for e-mail communication. While the content of e-mail cannot be read under such authorization, the destination or origin of e-mail may be recorded and used in the investigation. If agents have reason to read e-mail contents, they can go to the FISA court for a subpoena to be served on Internet and e-mail service providers for actual e-mail transmissions. Prior to the USA PATRIOT Act, the FISA court was only empowered to issue subpoenas for computerized financial and business records.

One of most controversial elements of the USA PATRIOT Act is the provision in Section 215 that allows federal agents to obtain a FISA warrant for library and bookstore records relating to anyone suspected of being connected to international terrorism or espionage. Section 215 of the USA PATRIOT Act amends Title V of the Foreign Intelligence Surveillance Act of 1978, Section 501, by stating in part:

(a) (1) The Director of the Federal Bureau of Investigation or a designee of the Director (whose rank shall be no lower than Assistant Special Agent in Charge) may make an application for an order requiring the production of any tangible things (including books, records, papers, documents, and other items) for an investigation to protect against international terrorism or clandestine intelligence activities, provided that such investigation of a United States person is not conducted solely upon the basis of activities protected by the first amendment to the Constitution....

(b) No person shall disclose to any other person (other than those persons necessary to produce the tangible things under this section) that the Federal Bureau of Investigation has sought or obtained tangible things under this section.

Federal agents had always been able to obtain such records with a valid court order. However, under the USA PATRIOT Act, librarians, bookstore employees, and others are barred from disclosing that the information has been sought and obtained from the FBI. Given that there is still the requirement of judicial review, proponents of the USA PATRIOT Act find the non-disclosure requirement placed on libraries and bookstores to be extremely reasonable given the nature and gravity of the investigations covered by this provision. If the FBI determines that a terror suspect wants to fabricate a bomb, this provision enables agents to determine, without the suspect's knowledge, whether the suspect has obtained books or other publications which would aid the suspect in constructing the device.

Section 215 of the USA PATRIOT Act and many other provisions in the Act were subject to a "sunset." That is to say, Section 215 and other provisions were set to expire on December 31, 2005. In addition to the provision permitting access to library and bookstore records, other provisions subject to expiration included those permitting greater sharing of certain kinds of criminal investigative information between agencies, roving wiretap authority, nationwide search warrants for electronic evidence, the enhancements to pen register and trap and trace device authorizations, the ability to conduct FISA investigations against "lone wolves" (i.e., terrorists not acting on behalf of a foreign power), and several other provisions. As of this writing, Congress has extended the life of these provisions (to keep them from expiring) but has not yet made them permanent.

Since the USA PATRIOT Act's passage, there have been many other anti-terror and related pieces of legislation that have become law. The federal government has passed legislation requiring the hiring of thousands of new border patrols agents and hundreds of Immigration and Customs Enforcement special agents. Congress has required the Transportation Security Administration, along with the Coast Guard, to step up security efforts in the non-aviation commercial transportation sector. There have been additional provisions allowing for greater cooperation between federal and local law enforcement concerning anti-terror and immigration matters. Even so, the USA PATRIOT Act itself remains the focal point of ire for many civil liberties and human rights organizations, along with many members of Congress—most of whom voted for the Act in the first place.

HOMELAND SECURITY ACT OF 2002

The other significant—perhaps the single most significant—legislation to come about as a result of the terrorist attacks of 9/11 was the Homeland Security Act of 2002. Through this law, the U.S. Department of Homeland Security (DHS) was created. Today, DHS employs more federal law enforcement officers than any other federal department. In all, more than 170,000 federal employees work for DHS throughout the United States and around the world.

After the attacks on 9/11, considerable analysis of American interior security, border security, immigration enforcement, and the federal law enforcement system in general took place. One of the prevailing themes to emerge from that national, open-air critique of the state of affairs in the United States was that law enforcement and border security efforts needed to be better coordinated overall.

On October 8, 2001, President George Bush issued an executive order establishing the Office of Homeland Security within the Executive Office of the President. President Bush named former Pennsylvania governor Tom Ridge to head that office as the Assistant to the President for Homeland Security. Sections 2 and 3 of the executive order defined the mission and functions of the new office. The new post was to be responsible for bringing together federal, state, and local law enforcement and emergency management agencies to combat terrorism, mitigate threats of disaster, and provide for the recovery of affected parts of America after any such events. With regard to law enforcement functions, the executive order stated in part:

Sec. 2. Mission. The mission of the Office shall be to develop and coordinate the implementation of a comprehensive national strategy to secure the United States from terrorist threats or attacks. The Office shall perform the functions necessary to carry out this mission, including the functions specified in Section 3 of this order.

Sec. 3. Functions. The functions of the Office shall be to coordinate the executive branch's efforts to detect, prepare for, prevent, protect against, respond to, and recover from terrorist attacks within the United States.

  (a) National Strategy. The Office shall work with executive departments and agencies, State and local governments, and private entities to ensure the adequacy of the national strategy for detecting, preparing for, preventing, protecting against, responding to, and recovering from terrorist threats or attacks within the United States and shall periodically review and coordinate revisions to that strategy as necessary.

  (b) Detection. The Office shall identify priorities and coordinate efforts for collection and analysis of information within the United States regarding threats of terrorism against the United States and activities of terrorists or terrorist groups within the United States. The Office also shall identify, in coordination with the Assistant to the President for National Security Affairs, priorities for collection of intelligence outside the United States regarding threats of terrorism within the United States.

  (c) Prevention. The Office shall coordinate efforts to prevent terrorist attacks within the United States. In performing this function, the Office shall work with Federal, State, and local agencies, and private entities, as appropriate, to:

     (i) facilitate the exchange of information among such agencies relating to immigration and visa matters and shipments of cargo; and, working with the Assistant to the President for National Security Affairs, ensure coordination among such agencies to prevent the entry of terrorists and terrorist materials and supplies into the

United States and facilitate removal of such terrorists from the United States, when appropriate;

(ii) coordinate efforts to investigate terrorist threats and attacks within the United States; and

(iii) coordinate efforts to improve the security of United States borders, territorial waters, and airspace in order to prevent acts of terrorism within the United States, working with the Assistant to the President for National Security Affairs, when appropriate.

(d) Protection. The Office shall coordinate efforts to protect the United States and its critical infrastructure from the consequences of terrorist attacks.

Many new responsibilities were outlined in the executive order for the new office. The Assistant to the President for Homeland Security, with a small staff, was expected to somehow coordinate a myriad of anti-terrorism and border security efforts across dozens of federal agencies (that were protective of their own turf) and countless law enforcement, fire, EMS, and other agencies at the state and local level. The head of this office was given no budget authority or line authority over the agencies to be coordinated. Thus, it became quickly clear to politicians, bureaucrats, and Tom Ridge himself that the new White House Office of Homeland Security would be muted in its effectiveness, at best. Discussions just as quickly turned to the possibility of creating a "Department of Homeland Security" that would be mandated to fulfill the various laudable responsibilities outlined in the executive order and that would contain within it all the necessary governmental entities to do so.

Critics of creating a cabinet-level agency to deal with matters of homeland security—primarily Republicans—worried that this would be just another opportunity for the federal government to expand in size and monetary consumption without really being any more effective than the component parts had been. After all, President Bush and many Republicans in Congress had been elected in part on the platform of reducing the size, scope, and cost of the federal government. Creating a new cabinet agency would be a march in the other direction from that platform plank.

Yet the idea of a new department devoted to homeland security and defense was more popular than unpopular on Capitol Hill. Many arguments were put forth for the new department. The variety of these arguments was captured in the testimony of Brookings Institute scholar Paul Light in his testimony before Congress as to why creation of a Department of Homeland Security was a good idea. He provided five overarching reasons for its creation that most members of Congress found compelling (Light 2003):[7]

(1) Creating a cabinet-level department can give a particular issue such as homeland security a higher priority inside the federal establishment. That is certainly what Congress intended when it elevated the Veterans Administration to cabinet status in 1988. Although the bill did not originate in this Committee, its members eventually concluded that veterans policy merited the heightened visibility and importance that would come with a statutory seat at the cabinet table, and the perquisites that come with it.

(2) Creating a cabinet-level department can also integrate, coordinate, or otherwise rationalize existing policy by bringing lower-level organizations together under a single head. That is clearly what Congress intended in creating the Department of Energy in 1977. Congress and the president both agreed that the nation would be better served with a single entity in charge of energy policy than a tangled web of diffuse, often competing agencies. That is also what Congress tried to accomplish in establishing the Department of Defense in 1947, and the National Aeronautics and Space Administration in 1958. It is useful to note that all three of these examples were in response to perceived threats: the Cold War and communism in 1947, fears of losing the space race in 1958, and the moral equivalent of war for energy independence in 1977.

(3) Creating a cabinet-level department can provide a platform for a new or rapidly expanding governmental activity. That is what drove Congress to create the Department of Housing and Urban Development in 1965. Although the federal government was involved in housing long before HUD, the new department was built as a base for what was anticipated to be a rapid rise in federal involvement. However, Congress did not place all housing programs within the new department.

(4) Creating a cabinet-level department can help forge a strategic vision for governing. That is what Congress expected in creating the Department of Transportation in 1966. The federal government had been involved in building roads and bridges for almost two hundred years when Congress created the department, but needed to coordinate its highway programs with its airports, airways, rail, and coastal programs. By pulling all modes of transportation under the same organization, Congress improved the odds that national transportation planning would be better served. Congress expected the same in not disapproving the reorganization plan that created the Environmental Protection Agency in 1970.

(5) Finally, creating a cabinet-level department can increase accountability to Congress, the president, and the public by making its budget and personnel clearer to all, its presidential appointees subject to Senate

confirmation, its spending subject to integrated oversight by Congress and its Office of Inspector General, and its vision plain to see. Although it is tempting to believe that such accountability is only a spreadsheet away, cabinet-status conveys a megaphone that little else in Washington does. One should never discount the impact of perquisites in the political island called Washington, D.C. That is certainly what Congress intended to convey in not disapproving the reorganization plan that created the Department of Health, Education, and Welfare in 1953. It is also what it intended twenty-five years later when it split the Department of Education from that entity.

While Light's third and fourth reasons imply some operational benefits through coordination and providing a logistical framework, or "platform," the primary theme that emerges from his reasons is that creating an organization with cabinet-level status would demonstrate that the United States is serious about homeland security. The arguments were good enough for Congress, and on November 25, 2002, the President signed the Homeland Security Act of 2002—the largest reshuffling of government agencies since the Defense Department was created in 1947.

A total of 22 federal agencies collectively possessing thousands of statutory responsibilities were transferred to The Department of Homeland Security (DHS). The legislation gave the new department until March of 2003 to implement the reorganization plan. The agencies transferring to DHS were organized under four major directorates within the department. The directorates corresponded broadly to the new statutory responsibilities of DHS. The 22 federal agencies transferred to DHS and their respective directorates were:[8]

Border and Transportation Security Directorate
U.S. Customs Service (Treasury)
Immigration and Naturalization Service (part) (Justice)
Federal Protective Service (GSA)
Transportation Security Administration (Transportation)
Federal Law Enforcement Training Center (Treasury)
Animal and Plant Health Inspection Service (part)(Agriculture)
Office for Domestic Preparedness (Justice)

The Emergency Preparedness and Response Directorate
Federal Emergency Management Agency (FEMA)
Strategic National Stockpile and the National Disaster Medical System (HHS)
Nuclear Incident Response Team (Energy)

Domestic Emergency Support Teams (Justice)
National Domestic Preparedness Office (FBI)

The Science and Technology Directorate
CBRN Countermeasures Programs (Energy)
Environmental Measurements Laboratory (Energy)
National BW Defense Analysis Center (Defense)
Plum Island Animal Disease Center (Agriculture)

The Information Analysis and Infrastructure Protection Directorate
Federal Computer Incident Response Center (GSA)
National Communications System (Defense)
National Infrastructure Protection Center (FBI)
Energy Security and Assurance Program (Energy)

Independent Agencies Not Falling Under a Directorate
U.S. Secret Service
U.S. Coast Guard

Today, the various agencies within DHS continue to find their footing in their new home. Many of the agencies found that merging together with other agencies carried with it certain growing pains. For example, when U.S. Customs special agents were joined together with U.S. Immigration and Naturalization special agents under ICE, considerable grumbling could be heard by agents on both sides. Customs agents were upset that ICE as an organization seemed more interested in immigration enforcement than customs enforcement. Early in the ICE's existence, ICE leadership set out to establish itself as the other great federal criminal investigative agency, side by side with the FBI. In this effort, ICE established a number of program initiatives that would catch the public's eye and bring the agency some welcome media attention. One of the most noteworthy initiatives was Operation Predator, which targeted legal and illegal aliens in the country wanted for child abuse and sexual assault. At about the same time, responsibility for Operation Greenquest, which had been a longstanding and successful Customs initiative targeting terror-related financial networks, was ceded to the FBI by ICE. Customs agents were bemoaning their career descent into "mere immigration agents."

Meanwhile, the legacy INS special agents had gripes of their own. For example, they did not feel sufficiently respected by their new colleagues from Customs. This perception was probably accurate. Prior to the merger, INS agents did not have to complete the same degree of criminal investigative training as Customs agents had been required to, and many INS special agents did not possess a four-year college degree. Nor were INS cases typically perceived as complex as those at Customs.

Thus, there was a current of sentiment among Customs special agents that their new partners from INS were substandard criminal investigators (or at least insufficiently trained). Additionally, the agents from INS were paid less than their Customs counterparts. Customs journey-grade agents were paid approximately $13,000–$15,000 more than journey-grade INS agents, because the journey grades in federal law enforcement are not uniform among agencies. The journey grade at INS had historically been one grade less on the federal pay scale than the journey grade at Customs. This discrepancy was eventually rectified in 2004, but not before considerable resentment was bred.

While the Homeland Security Act of 2002 may have brought some disparate agencies together in the hope that communication would be enhanced, one cannot help but notice the conspicuous absence from DHS of the primary agency responsible for defending the homeland— the FBI. In fact, turf battles between the FBI and other agencies continue despite creation of DHS. And why wouldn't they continue? The FBI is a part of the Justice Department. The animus and frustration directed toward the FBI is reflected in the quote of one ICE agent who sounded off on an Internet law enforcement bulletin board:[9]

The FBI did what they always do and that was to kill something they [do not] have. Operation GreenQuest…has ceased to exist as we know it. And in yet another power grab, the FBI has sunk its teeth into Project Shield America….What's next you ask? Whatever the heck they want I suppose!!!

Another ICE agent posted on the same discussion board:

We do more terrorist crap than any FBI agent within 400 miles, and we are 30 miles away from one of the largest concentrations of Muslim radicals in North America and the FBI has shown up ONCE to help…even though we call every time. But [then] some dork calls from the Hoover Building wanting everything we have and you never hear from them again.

THE PROBLEM OF CULTURAL DISCONNECTS IN FEDERAL LAW ENFORCEMENT

Many in Congress, the Executive Branch, the media, and the public at large are at a loss for why it is so difficult to get federal agencies to work together. It is certainly true that turf battles are a part of the problem, however petty they may seem to the American people who are watching from the outside. Perhaps turf battles could be mitigated by clearly defining each agency's jurisdiction and reassuring each agency that its budget is not necessarily going to suffer if another agency performs a particular task and receives funding for it. Of course, to convey such reassurance would require that the conveyance was in fact true, and in today's budget climate, that is simply not the case.

But there is another factor that explains in part the breakdown of communication among federal agencies and the tendency to not cooperate with each other. Federal agencies possess different organizational cultures. From the standpoint of the American people and even members of Congress, this is puzzling. Is it not the case that federal law enforcement agencies are empowered under principally the same Constitutional authority and pursue generally the same ends—namely the protection of the American people and the dispensing of justice? The fact is that an organizational culture's impact on organizational effectiveness cannot be overstated. Further, federal law enforcement does not seem to benefit from a unifying culture; this is true even within DHS.

Although Americans have been told that the federal government has consolidated its law enforcement forces to fight terrorism and other significant threats against the United States, there has been no incentive or opportunity to create a common federal law enforcement culture. This reality fosters persistent suspicion, jealousy, non-communication, and resentment across large segments of the federal law enforcement community.

Noted organizational scholar Edgar Schein, in his classic work, *Organizational Culture and Leadership*, identifies three levels of organizational culture.[10] The first level is that of "artifacts." The artifacts level of culture is that which is visible. When one walks into the lobby of a government agency's office, he or she may see a picture of the President, along with a picture of the head of that agency. Perhaps one might see a motto framed nicely on the wall. The artifacts are the most visible pieces of an organization's culture and are readily identified at the surface.

The next level is that of "values." Another noted organization theorist, Chris Argyris, refers to this as "espoused values." This level of culture reflects that which people within the organization will say. If asked, federal agents in all agencies will certainly confirm that it is their desire to execute justice and defeat the various domestic and international threats to the safety and security of Americans. Agency heads will certainly convey that message, along with the message of magnanimous cooperation, to Congressional members and White House officials. And they will do so with sincerity. They are not lying. Agencies and their agents do intend to work with each other for the good of the United States.

But it is at the third level of culture—the deepest level—that the crucial problem exists. The third level of organizational culture is the "basic assumptions" level. Similarly identified by Chris Argyris as "theories in use," this level of culture is where the agencies and agents are actually mentally and emotionally "living" day to day. It is the taken-for-granted thinking subscribed to by an organization's members. It is not conscious; it is pre-conscious. The instincts of agencies and their agents are found at this level. And federal law enforcement agencies operate, like any other organization, according to instincts and what has always worked.

The various federal law enforcement agencies may indeed present common artifacts appropriate for their federal criminal justice mission. These agencies will likely even espouse similar values. They will all convey sincerely that they value civil rights, diversity in the organization, upholding the rule of law, pursuing justice, defeating criminals, helping and defending the American people, and so forth. But reorganization of portions of the federal law enforcement community under the Homeland Security Act and relaxation of interagency communication restrictions has not resulted in common basic assumptions among the agencies. In fact, federal law enforcement organizations are often the subjects of each other's basic assumptions, with each believing inferiority or recalcitrance in the others—and so they behave accordingly.

There are possibilities to consider for the future that might modify the basic assumptions of law enforcement organizations over time. One option could be to further consolidate agencies. Perhaps each Office of the Inspector General could be brought into one organization, as could all Department of Defense agencies, all land management law enforcement agencies, and all general purpose and national security agencies, either under the Justice Department or under Homeland Security. The result would be considerably fewer (but larger) federal law enforcement agencies poised to embrace a common culture with new generations of special agents and officers. Another possibility is to carve out from federal law enforcement—probably from the FBI—an aggressive national security/counterintelligence agency, much like the British MI-5, and then return the rest of federal law enforcement to a more narrow interpretation of the Interstate Commerce Clause and inferred federal police power. This reform would result in fewer and more heavily restricted federal police agencies that would probably be focused almost entirely on national security and border protection.

This book ends with the note that it began on. Federal law enforcement, like all of American law enforcement, is decentralized—even fragmented. Some would say happily so; others would say hopelessly so. But to be sure, it is so. Changes in the scope and reach of federal law enforcement are almost always controversial. Recent history has demonstrated that after changes resulting from major crises—such as the 9/11 terrorist attacks and the subsequent declared war against terrorism—the urgency of any further needed change that is perceived eventually recedes as politicians, pundits, and the public seek to acclimate to the changes already made. Given the dramatic changes that have taken place in the realm of federal criminal justice during America's short history, and given how significant events occurring in history seem to always drive political action, only time's passage will afford an accurate depiction of what the shape, scope, and power of federal law enforcement will be in the years and decades to come.

APPENDIX A

Chapters of the Federal Criminal Code

TITLE 18 – PART I (CRIMES)
INDEX OF CHAPTERS

Majority and Dissenting Opinions Containing Principle Arguments for and Against Broad Federal Police Power from the Landmark Case of *U.S. v. Lopez* (1995)

U.S. SUPREME COURT

United States, Petitioner *v.* Alfonso Lopez, jr. Certiorari to the United States Court of Appeals for the Fifth Circuit No. 93–1260.

Argued November 8, 1994 Decided April 26, 1995

After respondent, then a 12th-grade student, carried a concealed handgun into his high school, he was charged with violating the Gun-Free School Zones Act of 1990, which forbids "any individual knowingly to possess a firearm at a place that [he] knows...is a school zone," 18 U.S.C. 922(q)(1)(A). The District Court denied his motion to dismiss the indictment, concluding that 922(q) is a constitutional exercise of Congress' power to regulate activities in and affecting commerce. In reversing, the Court of Appeals held that, in light of what it characterized as insufficient congressional findings and legislative history, 922(q) is invalid as beyond Congress' power under the Commerce Clause.

Held

The Act exceeds Congress' Commerce Clause authority. First, although this Court has upheld a wide variety of congressional Acts regulating intrastate economic activity that substantially affected interstate commerce, the possession of a gun in a local school zone is in no sense an economic activity that might, through repetition elsewhere, have such a substantial effect on interstate commerce. Section 922(q) is a criminal statute that by its terms has nothing to do with "commerce" or any sort of economic enterprise, however broadly those terms are defined. Nor is it an essential part of a larger regulation of economic activity, in which the regulatory scheme could be undercut unless the intrastate activity were regulated. It cannot, therefore, be sustained under the Court's cases upholding regulations of activities that arise out of or are connected with a commercial transaction, which viewed in the aggregate, substantially affects interstate commerce. Second, 922(q) contains no jurisdictional element which would ensure, through case-by-case inquiry, that the firearms possession in question has the requisite Page II nexus with interstate commerce. Respondent was a local student at a local school; there is no indication that he had recently moved in interstate commerce, and there is no requirement that his possession of the firearm have any concrete tie to interstate commerce. To uphold the Government's contention that 922(q) is justified because firearms possession in a local school zone does indeed substantially affect interstate commerce would require this Court to pile inference upon inference in a manner that would bid fair to convert congressional Commerce Clause authority to a general police power of the sort held only by the States. Pp. 2–19.

   2 F.3d 1342, affirmed.

   REHNQUIST, C. J., delivered the opinion of the Court, in which O'CONNOR, SCALIA, KENNEDY, and THOMAS, JJ., joined. KENNEDY, J., filed a concurring opinion, in which O'CONNOR, J., joined. THOMAS, J., filed a concurring opinion. STEVENS, J., and SOUTER, J., filed dissenting opinions. BREYER, J., filed a dissenting opinion, in which STEVENS, SOUTER, and GINSBURG, JJ., joined.

CHIEF JUSTICE REHNQUIST delivered the opinion of the Court.

In the Gun-Free School Zones Act of 1990, Congress made it a federal offense "for any individual knowingly to possess a firearm at a place that the individual knows, or has reasonable cause to believe, is a school zone." 18 U.S.C. 922(q)(1)(A) (1988 ed., Supp. V). The Act neither regulates a commercial activity nor contains a requirement that the possession be connected in any way to interstate commerce. We hold that the Act exceeds the authority of Congress "[t]o regulate Commerce...among the several States..." U.S. Const., Art. I, 8, cl. 3.

On March 10, 1992, respondent, who was then a 12th-grade student, arrived at Edison High School in San Antonio, Texas, carrying a concealed .38 caliber handgun and five bullets. Acting upon an anonymous tip, school authorities confronted respondent, who admitted that he was carrying the weapon. He was arrested and charged under Texas law with firearm possession on school premises. See Tex. Penal Code Ann. 46.03(a)(1) (Supp. 1994). The next day, the state charges were dismissed after federal agents charged respondent by complaint with violating the Gun-Free School Zones Act of 1990. 18 U.S.C. 922(q)(1)(A) (1988 ed., Supp. V).[1]

A federal grand jury indicted respondent on one count of knowing possession of a firearm at a school zone, in violation of 922(q). Respondent moved to dismiss his federal indictment on the ground that 922(q) "is unconstitutional as it is beyond the power of Congress to legislate control over our public schools." The District Court denied the motion, concluding that 922(q) "is a constitutional exercise of Congress' well-defined power to regulate activities in and affecting commerce, and the 'business' of elementary, middle and high schools...affects interstate commerce." App. to Pet. for Cert. 55a. Respondent waived his right to a jury trial. The District Court conducted a bench trial, found him guilty of violating 922(q), and sentenced him to six months' imprisonment and two years' supervised release.

On appeal, respondent challenged his conviction based on his claim that 922(q) exceeded Congress' power to legislate under the Commerce Clause. The Court of Appeals for the Fifth Circuit agreed and reversed respondent's conviction. It held that, in light of what it characterized as insufficient congressional findings and legislative history, "Section 922(q), in the full reach of its terms, is invalid as beyond the power of Congress under the Commerce Clause." 2 F.3d 1342, 1367–1368 (1993). Because of the importance of the issue, we granted certiorari, 511 U.S. (1994), and we now affirm.

We start with first principles. The Constitution creates a Federal Government of enumerated powers. See U.S. Const., Art. I, 8. As James Madison wrote, "[t]he powers delegated by the proposed Constitution to the federal government are few and defined. Those which are to remain in the State governments are numerous and indefinite." The Federalist No. 45, pp. 292–293 (C. Rossiter ed. 1961). This constitutionally mandated division of authority "was adopted by the Framers to ensure protection of our fundamental liberties." *Gregory v. Ashcroft*, 501 U.S. 452, 458(1991) (internal quotation marks omitted). "Just as the separation and independence of the coordinate branches of the Federal Government serves to prevent the accumulation of excessive power in any one branch, a healthy balance of power between the States and the Federal Government will reduce the risk of tyranny and abuse from either front." Ibid.

The Constitution delegates to Congress the power "[t]o regulate Commerce with foreign Nations, and among the several States, and with the Indian Tribes." U.S. Const., Art. I, 8, cl. 3. The Court, through Chief Justice Marshall, first defined the nature of Congress' commerce power in *Gibbons v. Ogden,* 9 Wheat. 1, 189–190 (1824):

> "Commerce, undoubtedly, is traffic, but it is something more: it is intercourse. It describes the commercial intercourse between nations, and parts of nations, in all its branches, and is regulated by prescribing rules for carrying on that intercourse."

The commerce power "is the power to regulate; that is, to prescribe the rule by which commerce is to be governed. This power, like all others vested in Congress, is complete in itself, may be exercised to its utmost extent, and acknowledges no limitations, other than are prescribed in the constitution." Id., at 196. The Gibbons Court, however, acknowledged that limitations on the commerce power are inherent in the very language of the Commerce Clause.

> "It is not intended to say that these words comprehend that commerce, which is completely internal, which is carried on between man and man in a State, or between different parts of the same State, and which does not extend to or affect other States. Such a power would be inconvenient, and is certainly unnecessary. "Comprehensive as the word 'among' is, it may very properly be restricted to that commerce which concerns more States than one...The enumeration presupposes something not enumerated; and that something, if we regard the language or the subject of the sentence, must be the exclusively internal commerce of a State." Id., at 194–195.

For nearly a century thereafter, the Court's Commerce Clause decisions dealt but rarely with the extent of Congress' power, and almost entirely with the Commerce Clause as a limit on state legislation that discriminated against interstate commerce. See, e.g., *Veazie v. Moor*, 14 How. 568, 573–575 (1853) (upholding a state-created steamboat monopoly because it involved regulation of wholly internal commerce); *Kidd v. Pearson*, 128 U.S. 1, 17, 20–22 (1888) (upholding a state prohibition on the manufacture of intoxicating liquor because the commerce power "does not comprehend the purely domestic commerce of a State which is carried on between man and man within a State or between different parts of the same State"); see also L. Tribe, American Constitutional Law 306 (2d ed. 1988). Under this line of precedent, the Court held that certain categories of activity such as "production," "manufacturing," and "mining" were within the province of state governments, and thus were beyond the power of Congress under the Commerce Clause. See *Wickard v. Filburn*, 317 U.S. 111, 121(1942) (describing development of Commerce Clause jurisprudence).

In 1887, Congress enacted the Interstate Commerce Act, 24 Stat. 379, and in 1890, Congress enacted the Sherman Antitrust Act, 26 Stat. 209, as amended, 15 U.S.C. 1 et seq. These laws ushered in a new era of federal regulation under the commerce power. When cases involving these laws first reached this Court, we imported from our negative Commerce Clause cases the approach that Congress could not regulate activities such as "production," "manufacturing," and "mining." See, e.g., *United States v. E. C. Knight Co.*, 156 U.S. 1, 12 (1895) ("Commerce succeeds to manufacture, and is not part of it"); *Carter v. Carter Coal Co.*, 298 U.S. 238, 304 (1936) ("Mining brings the subject matter of commerce into existence. Commerce disposes of it"). Simultaneously, however, the Court held that, where the interstate and intrastate aspects of commerce were so mingled together that full regulation of interstate commerce required incidental regulation of intrastate commerce, the Commerce Clause authorized such regulation. See, e.g., *Houston, E. & W. T. R. Co. v. United States*, 234 U.S. 342 (1914) (Shreveport Rate Cases).

In *A. L. A. Schecter Poultry Corp. v. United States*, 295 U.S. 495, 550 (1935), the Court struck down regulations that fixed the hours and wages of individuals employed by an intrastate business because the activity being regulated related to interstate commerce only indirectly. In doing so, the Court characterized the distinction between direct and indirect effects of intrastate transactions upon interstate commerce as "a fundamental one, essential to the maintenance of our constitutional system." Id., at 548. Activities that affected interstate commerce directly were within Congress' power; activities that affected interstate commerce indirectly were beyond Congress' reach. Id., at 546. The justification for this formal distinction was rooted in the fear that otherwise "there would be virtually no limit to the federal power and for all practical purposes we should have a completely centralized government." Id., at 548.

Two years later, in the watershed case of *NLRB v. Jones & Laughlin Steel Corp.*, 301 U.S. 1(1937), the Court upheld the National Labor Relations Act against a Commerce Clause challenge, and in the process, departed from the distinction between "direct" and "indirect" effects on interstate commerce. Id., at 36–38 ("The question [of the scope of Congress' power] is necessarily one of degree"). The Court held that intrastate activities that "have such a close and substantial relation to interstate commerce that their control is essential or appropriate to protect that commerce from burdens and obstructions" are within Congress' power to regulate. Id., at 37.

In *United States v. Darby*, 312 U.S. 100 (1941), the Court upheld the Fair Labor Standards Act, stating:

> "The power of Congress over interstate commerce is not confined to the regulation of commerce among the states. It extends to those activities intrastate which so affect interstate commerce or the exercise of the power of Congress over it as to make regulation of them appropriate means to the attainment of a legitimate end, the exercise of the granted power of Congress to regulate interstate commerce." Id., at 118.

See also *United States v. Wrightwood Dairy Co.*, 315 U.S. 110, 119 (1942) (the commerce power "extends to those intrastate activities which in a substantial way interfere with or obstruct the exercise of the granted power").

In *Wickard v. Filburn*, the Court upheld the application of amendments to the Agricultural Adjustment Act of 1938 to the production and consumption of home-grown wheat. 317 U.S., at 128–129. The Wickard Court explicitly rejected earlier distinctions between direct and indirect effects on interstate commerce, stating:

> "[E]ven if appellee's activity be local and though it may not be regarded as commerce, it may still, whatever its nature, be reached by Congress if it exerts a substantial economic effect on interstate commerce, and this irrespective of whether such effect is what might at some earlier time have been defined as 'direct' or 'indirect.'" Id., at 125.

The Wickard Court emphasized that although Filburn's own contribution to the demand for wheat may have been trivial by itself, that was not "enough to remove him from the scope of federal regulation where, as here, his contribution, taken together with that of many others similarly situated, is far from trivial." Id., at 127–128.

Jones & Laughlin Steel, Darby, and Wickard ushered in an era of Commerce Clause jurisprudence that greatly expanded the previously defined authority of Congress under that Clause. In part, this was a recognition of the great changes that had occurred in the way business was carried on in this country. Enterprises that had once been local or at most regional in nature had become national in scope. But the doctrinal change also reflected a view that earlier Commerce Clause cases artificially had constrained the authority of Congress to regulate interstate commerce.

But even these modern-era precedents which have expanded congressional power under the Commerce Clause confirm that this power is subject to outer limits. In Jones & Laughlin Steel, the Court warned that the scope of the interstate commerce power "must be considered in the light of our dual system of government and may not be extended so as to embrace effects upon interstate commerce so indirect and remote that to embrace them, in view of our complex society, would effectually obliterate the distinction between what is national and what is local and create a completely centralized government." 301 U.S., at 37; see also Darby, supra, at 119–120 (Congress may regulate intrastate activity that has a "substantial effect" on interstate commerce); Wickard, supra, at 125 (Congress may regulate activity that "exerts a substantial economic effect on interstate commerce"). Since that time, the Court has heeded that warning and undertaken to decide whether a rational basis existed for concluding that a regulated activity sufficiently affected interstate commerce. See, e.g., *Hodel v. Virginia Surface Mining & Reclamation Assn., Inc.*, 452 U.S. 264, 276–280 (1981); Perez v. United States, 402 U.S. 146, 155–156 (1971); Katzenbach v. McClung, 379 U.S. 294, 299–301 (1964); Heart of Atlanta Motel, Inc. v. United States, 379 U.S. 241, 252–253 (1964).[2]

Similarly, in *Maryland v. Wirtz*, 392 U.S. 183 (1968), the Court reaffirmed that "the power to regulate commerce, though broad indeed, has limits" that "[t]he Court has ample power" to enforce. Id., at 196, overruled on other grounds, *National League of Cities v. Usery*, 426 U.S. 833 (1976), overruled by *Garcia v. San Antonio Metropolitan Transit Authority*, 469 U.S. 528(1985). In response to the dissent's warnings that the Court was powerless to enforce the limitations on Congress' commerce powers because "[a]ll activities affecting commerce, even in the minutest degree, [Wickard], may be regulated and controlled by Congress," 392 U.S., at 204 (Douglas, J., dissenting), the Wirtz Court replied that the dissent had misread precedent as "[n]either here nor in Wickard has the Court declared that Congress may use a relatively trivial impact on commerce as an excuse for broad general regulation of state or private activities," id., at 197, n. 27. Rather, "[t]he Court has said only that where a general regulatory statute bears a substantial relation to commerce, the de minimis character of individual instances arising under that statute is of no consequence." Ibid. (first emphasis added).

Consistent with this structure, we have identified three broad categories of activity that Congress may regulate under its commerce power. *Perez v. United States*, supra, at 150; see also *Hodel v. Virginia Surface Mining & Reclamation Assn.*, supra, at 276–277. First, Congress may regulate the use of the channels of interstate commerce. See, e.g., Darby, 312 U.S., at 114; Heart of Atlanta Motel, supra, at 256 ("'[T]he authority of Congress to keep the channels of interstate commerce free from immoral and injurious uses has been frequently sustained, and is no longer open to question.'" (quoting *Caminetti v. United States*, 242 U.S. 470, 491 (1917)). Second, Congress is empowered to regulate and protect the instrumentalities of interstate commerce, or persons or things in interstate commerce, even though the threat may come only from intrastate activities. See, e.g., Shreveport Rate Cases, 234 U.S. 342 (1914); *Southern R. Co. v. United States*, 222 U.S. 20 (1911) (upholding amendments to Safety Appliance Act as applied to vehicles used in intrastate commerce); Perez, supra, at 150 ("[F]or example, the destruction of an aircraft (18 U.S.C. 32), or…thefts from interstate shipments (18 U.S.C. 659)"). Finally, Congress' commerce authority includes the power to regulate those activities having a substantial relation to interstate commerce, Jones & Laughlin Steel, 301 U.S., at 37, i.e., those activities that substantially affect interstate commerce. Wirtz, supra, at 196, n. 27.

Within this final category, admittedly, our case law has not been clear whether an activity must "affect" or "substantially affect" interstate commerce in order to be within Congress' power to regulate it under the Commerce Clause. Compare *Preseault* v. ICC, 494 U.S. 1, 17 (1990), with *Wirtz*, supra, at 196, n. 27 (the Court has never declared that "Congress may use a relatively trivial impact on commerce as an excuse for broad general regulation of state or private activities"). We conclude, consistent with the great weight of our case law, that the proper test requires an analysis of whether the regulated activity "substantially affects" interstate commerce.

We now turn to consider the power of Congress, in the light of this framework, to enact 922(q). The first two categories of authority may be quickly disposed of: 922(q) is not a regulation of the use of the channels of interstate commerce, nor is it an attempt to prohibit the interstate transportation of a commodity through the channels of commerce; nor can 922(q) be justified as a regulation by which Congress has sought to protect an instrumentality of interstate commerce or a thing in interstate commerce. Thus, if 922(q) is to be sustained, it must be under the third category as a regulation of an activity that substantially affects interstate commerce.

First, we have upheld a wide variety of congressional Acts regulating intrastate economic activity where we have concluded that the activity substantially affected interstate commerce. Examples include the regulation of intrastate coal mining; Hodel, supra, intrastate extortionate credit transactions, Perez, supra, restaurants utilizing substantial interstate supplies, McClung, supra, inns and hotels catering to interstate guests, Heart of Atlanta Motel, supra, and production and consumption of home-grown wheat, *Wickard v. Filburn*, 317 U.S. 111 (1942). These examples are by no means exhaustive, but the pattern is clear. Where economic activity substantially affects interstate commerce, legislation regulating that activity will be sustained.

Even Wickard, which is perhaps the most far reaching example of Commerce Clause authority over intrastate activity, involved economic activity in a way that the possession of a gun in a school zone does not. Roscoe Filburn operated a small farm in Ohio, on which, in the year involved, he raised 23 acres of wheat. It was his practice to sow winter wheat in the fall, and after harvesting it in July to sell a portion of the crop, to feed part of it to poultry and livestock on the farm, to use some in making flour for home consumption, and to keep the remainder for seeding future crops. The Secretary of Agriculture assessed a penalty against him under the Agricultural Adjustment Act of 1938 because he harvested about 12 acres more wheat than his allotment under the Act permitted. The Act was designed to regulate the volume of wheat moving in interstate and foreign commerce in order to avoid surpluses and shortages, and concomitant fluctuation in wheat prices, which had previously obtained. The Court said, in an opinion sustaining the application of the Act to Filburn's activity:

"One of the primary purposes of the Act in question was to increase the market price of wheat and to that end to limit the volume thereof that could affect the market. It can hardly be denied that a factor of such volume and variability as home-consumed wheat would have a substantial influence on price and market conditions. This may arise because being in marketable condition such wheat overhangs the market and, if induced by rising prices, tends to flow into the market and check price increases. But if we assume that it is never marketed, it supplies a need of the man who grew it which would otherwise be reflected by purchases in the open market. Home-grown wheat in this sense competes with wheat in commerce." 317 U.S., at 128.

Section 922(q) is a criminal statute that by its terms has nothing to do with "commerce" or any sort of economic enterprise, however broadly one might define those terms.[3] Section 922(q) is not an essential part of a larger regulation of economic activity, in which the regulatory scheme could be undercut unless the intrastate activity were regulated. It cannot, therefore, be sustained under our cases upholding regulations of activities that arise out of or are connected with a commercial transaction, which viewed in the aggregate, substantially affects interstate commerce.

Second, 922(q) contains no jurisdictional element which would ensure, through case-by-case inquiry, that the firearm possession in question affects interstate commerce. For example, in *United States v. Bass*, 404 U.S. 336(1971), the Court interpreted former 18 U.S.C. 1202(a), which made it a crime for a felon to "receiv[e], posses[s], or transpor[t] in commerce or affecting commerce…any firearm." 404 U.S., at 337. The Court interpreted the possession component of 1202(a) to require an additional nexus to interstate commerce both because the statute was ambiguous and because "unless Congress conveys its purpose clearly, it will not be deemed to have significantly changed the federal-state balance." Id., at 349. The Bass Court set aside the conviction because although the Government had demonstrated that Bass had possessed a firearm, it had failed "to show the requisite nexus with interstate commerce." Id., at 347. The Court thus interpreted the statute to reserve the constitutional question whether Congress could regulate, without more, the "mere possession" of firearms. See id., at 339, n. 4; see also *United States v. Five Gambling Devices*, 346 U.S. 441, 448 (1953) (plurality opinion) ("The principle is old and deeply imbedded in our jurisprudence that this Court will construe a statute in a manner that requires decision of serious constitutional questions only if the statutory language leaves no reasonable alternative"). Unlike the statute in Bass, 922(q) has no express jurisdictional element which might limit its reach to a discrete set of firearm possessions that additionally have an explicit connection with or effect on interstate commerce.

Although as part of our independent evaluation of constitutionality under the Commerce Clause we of course consider legislative findings, and indeed even congressional committee findings, regarding effect on interstate commerce, see, e.g., *Preseault v. ICC*, 494 U.S. 1, 17 (1990), the Government concedes that "[n]either the statute nor its legislative history contain[s] express congressional findings regarding the effects upon interstate commerce of gun possession in a school zone." Brief for United States 5–6. We agree with the Government that Congress normally is not required to make formal findings as to the substantial burdens that an activity has on interstate commerce. See McClung, 379 U.S., at 304; see also Perez, 402 U.S., at 156 ("Congress need [not] make particularized findings in order to legislate"). But to the extent that congressional findings would enable us to evaluate the legislative judgment that the activity in question substantially affected interstate commerce, even though no such substantial effect was visible to the naked eye, they are lacking here.[4]

The Government argues that Congress has accumulated institutional expertise regarding the regulation of firearms through previous enactments. *Cf. Fullilove v. Klutznick*, 448 U.S. 448, 503 (1980) (Powell, J., concurring). We agree, however, with the Fifth Circuit that importation of previous findings to justify 922(q) is especially inappropriate here because the "prior federal enactments or Congressional findings [do not] speak to the subject matter of Section 922(q) or its relationship to interstate commerce. Indeed, Section 922(q) plows thoroughly new ground and represents a sharp break with the long-standing pattern of federal firearms legislation." 2 F.3d, at 1366.

The Government's essential contention, in fine, is that we may determine here that 922(q) is valid because possession of a firearm in a local school zone does indeed substantially affect interstate commerce. Brief for United States 17. The Government argues that possession of a firearm in a school zone may result in violent crime and that violent crime can be expected to affect the functioning of the national economy in two ways. First, the costs of violent crime are substantial, and, through the mechanism of insurance, those costs are spread throughout the population. See *United States v. Evans*, 928 F.2d 858, 862 (CA9 1991). Second, violent crime reduces the willingness of individuals to travel to areas within the country that are perceived to be unsafe. Cf. Heart of Atlanta Motel, 379 U.S., at 253. The Government also argues that the presence of guns in schools poses a substantial threat to the educational process by threatening the learning environment. A handicapped educational process, in turn, will result in a less productive citizenry. That, in turn, would have an adverse effect on the Nation's economic well-being. As a result, the

Government argues that Congress could rationally have concluded that 922(q) substantially affects interstate commerce.

We pause to consider the implications of the Government's arguments. The Government admits, under its "costs of crime" reasoning, that Congress could regulate not only all violent crime, but all activities that might lead to violent crime, regardless of how tenuously they relate to interstate commerce. See Tr. of Oral Arg. 8–9. Similarly, under the Government's "national productivity" reasoning, Congress could regulate any activity that it found was related to the economic productivity of individual citizens: family law (including marriage, divorce, and child custody), for example. Under the theories that the Government presents in support of 922(q), it is difficult to perceive any limitation on federal power, even in areas such as criminal law enforcement or education where States historically have been sovereign. Thus, if we were to accept the Government's arguments, we are hard-pressed to posit any activity by an individual that Congress is without power to regulate.

Although JUSTICE BREYER argues that acceptance of the Government's rationales would not authorize a general federal police power, he is unable to identify any activity that the States may regulate but Congress may not. JUSTICE BREYER posits that there might be some limitations on Congress' commerce power such as family law or certain aspects of education. Post, at 10–11. These suggested limitations, when viewed in light of the dissent's expansive analysis, are devoid of substance.

JUSTICE BREYER focuses, for the most part, on the threat that firearm possession in and near schools poses to the educational process and the potential economic consequences flowing from that threat. Post, at 5–9. Specifically, the dissent reasons that (1) gun-related violence is a serious problem; (2) that problem, in turn, has an adverse effect on classroom learning; and (3) that adverse effect on classroom learning, in turn, represents a substantial threat to trade and commerce. Post, at 9. This analysis would be equally applicable, if not more so, to subjects such as family law and direct regulation of education.

For instance, if Congress can, pursuant to its Commerce Clause power, regulate activities that adversely affect the learning environment, then, a fortiori, it also can regulate the educational process directly. Congress could determine that a school's curriculum has a "significant" effect on the extent of classroom learning. As a result, Congress could mandate a federal curriculum for local elementary and secondary schools because what is taught in local schools has a significant "effect on classroom learning," cf. post, at 9, and that, in turn, has a substantial effect on interstate commerce.

JUSTICE BREYER rejects our reading of precedent and argues that "Congress...could rationally conclude that schools fall on the commercial side of the line." Post, at 16. Again, JUSTICE BREYER'S rationale lacks any real limits because, depending on the level of generality, any activity can be looked upon as commercial. Under the dissent's rationale, Congress could just as easily look at child rearing as "fall[ing] on the commercial side of the line" because it provides a "valuable service – namely, to equip [children] with the skills they need to survive in life and, more specifically, in the workplace." Ibid. We do not doubt that Congress has authority under the Commerce Clause to regulate numerous commercial activities that substantially affect interstate commerce and also affect the educational process. That authority, though broad, does not include the authority to regulate each and every aspect of local schools.

Admittedly, a determination whether an intrastate activity is commercial or noncommercial may in some cases result in legal uncertainty. But, so long as Congress' authority is limited to those powers enumerated in the Constitution, and so long as those enumerated powers are interpreted as having judicially enforceable outer limits, congressional legislation under the Commerce Clause always will engender "legal uncertainty." Post, at 17. As Chief Justice Marshall stated in *McCulloch v. Maryland*, 4 Wheat. 316 (1819):

"The [federal] government is acknowledged by all to be one of enumerated powers. The principle, that it can exercise only the powers granted to it...is now universally admitted. But the question respecting the extent of the powers actually granted, is perpetually arising, and will probably continue to arise, as long as our system shall exist." Id., at 405.

See also *Gibbons v. Ogden*, 9 Wheat., at 195 ("The enumeration presupposes something not enumerated"). The Constitution mandates this uncertainty by withholding from Congress a plenary police power that would authorize enactment of every type of legislation. See U.S. Const., Art. I, 8. Congress has operated within this framework of legal uncertainty ever since this Court determined that it was the judiciary's duty "to say what the law is." *Marbury v. Madison*, 1 Cranch. 137, 177 (1803) (Marshall, C. J.). Any possible benefit from eliminating this "legal uncertainty" would be at the expense of the Constitution's system of enumerated powers.

In Jones & Laughlin Steel, 301 U.S., at 37, we held that the question of congressional power under the Commerce Clause "is necessarily one of degree." To the same effect is the concurring opinion of Justice Cardozo in Schecter Poultry:

> "There is a view of causation that would obliterate the distinction of what is national and what is local in the activities of commerce. Motion at the outer rim is communicated perceptibly, though minutely, to recording instruments at the center. A society such as ours 'is an elastic medium which transmits all tremors throughout its territory; the only question is of their size.'" 295 U.S., at 554 (quoting *United States v. A.L.A. Schecter Poultry Corp.*, 76 F.2d 617, 624 (CA2 1935) (L. Hand, J., concurring)).

These are not precise formulations, and in the nature of things they cannot be. But we think they point the way to a correct decision of this case. The possession of a gun in a local school zone is in no sense an economic activity that might, through repetition elsewhere, substantially affect any sort of interstate commerce. Respondent was a local student at a local school; there is no indication that he had recently moved in interstate commerce, and there is no requirement that his possession of the firearm have any concrete tie to interstate commerce.

To uphold the Government's contentions here, we would have to pile inference upon inference in a manner that would bid fair to convert congressional authority under the Commerce Clause to a general police power of the sort retained by the States. Admittedly, some of our prior cases have taken long steps down that road, giving great deference to congressional action. See supra, at 8. The broad language in these opinions has suggested the possibility of additional expansion, but we decline here to proceed any further. To do so would require us to conclude that the Constitution's enumeration of powers does not presuppose something not enumerated, cf. *Gibbons v. Ogden*, supra, at 195, and that there never will be a distinction between what is truly national and what is truly local, cf. Jones & Laughlin Steel, supra, at 30. This we are unwilling to do.

For the foregoing reasons the judgment of the Court of Appeals is Affirmed.

JUSTICE BREYER, with whom JUSTICE STEVENS, JUSTICE SOUTER, and JUSTICE GINSBURG join, dissenting.

The issue in this case is whether the Commerce Clause authorizes Congress to enact a statute that makes it a crime to possess a gun in, or near, a school. 18 U.S.C. 922(q)(1)(A) (1988 ed., Supp. V). In my view, the statute falls well within the scope of the commerce power as this Court has understood that power over the last half-century.

I

In reaching this conclusion, I apply three basic principles of Commerce Clause interpretation. First, the power to "regulate Commerce ...among the several States," U.S. Const., Art. I, 8, cl. 3, encompasses the power to regulate local activities insofar as they significantly affect interstate commerce. See, e.g., *Gibbons v. Ogden*, 9 Wheat. 1, 194–195 (1824) (Marshall, C. J.); *Wickard v. Filburn*, 317 U.S. 111, 125 (1942). As the majority points out, ante, at 10, the Court, in describing how much of an effect the Clause requires, sometimes has used the word "substantial" and sometimes has not. Compare, e.g., *Wickard*, supra, at 125 ("substantial economic effect"), with *Hodel v. Virginia Surface Mining and Reclamation Assn., Inc.*, 452 U.S. 264, 276 (1981) ("affects interstate commerce"); see also *Maryland v. Wirtz*, 392 U.S. 183, 196, n. 27 (1968) (cumulative effect must not be "trivial"); *NLRB v. Jones & Laughlin Steel Corp.*, 301 U.S. 1, 37 (1937) (speaking of "close and substantial relation" between activity and commerce, not of "substantial effect") (emphasis added); *Gibbons*, supra, at 194 (words of Commerce Clause do not "comprehend ... commerce, which is completely internal ... and which does not ... affect other States"). And, as the majority also recognizes in quoting Justice Cardozo, the question of degree (how much effect) requires an estimate of the "size" of the effect that no verbal formulation can capture with precision. See ante, at 18. I use the word "significant" because the word "substantial" implies a somewhat narrower power than recent precedent suggests. See, e.g., *Perez v. United States*, 402 U.S. 146, 154 (1971); *Daniel v. Paul*, 395 U.S. 298, 308 (1969). But, to speak of "substantial effect" rather than "significant effect" would make no difference in this case.

Second, in determining whether a local activity will likely have a significant effect upon interstate commerce, a court must consider, not the effect of an individual act (a single instance of gun possession), but rather the cumulative effect of all similar instances (i.e., the effect of all guns possessed in or near schools). See, e.g., Wickard, supra, at 127–128. As this Court put the matter almost 50 years ago:

"[I]t is enough that the individual activity when multiplied into a general practice ... contains a threat to the interstate economy that requires preventative regulation." *Mandeville Island Farms, Inc. v. American Crystal Sugar Co.*, 334 U.S. 219, 236 (1948) (citations omitted).

Third, the Constitution requires us to judge the connection between a regulated activity and interstate commerce, not directly, but at one remove. Courts must give Congress a degree of leeway in determining the existence of a significant factual connection between the regulated activity and interstate commerce – both because the Constitution delegates the commerce power directly to Congress and because the determination requires an empirical judgment of a kind that a legislature is more likely than a court to make with accuracy. The traditional words "rational basis" capture this leeway. See Hodel, supra, at 276–277. Thus, the specific question before us, as the Court recognizes, is not whether the "regulated activity sufficiently affected interstate commerce," but, rather, whether Congress could have had "a rational basis" for so concluding. Ante, at 8 (emphasis added).

I recognize that we must judge this matter independently. "[S]imply because Congress may conclude that a particular activity substantially affects interstate commerce does not necessarily make it so." Hodel, supra, at 311 (REHNQUIST, J., concurring in judgment). And, I also recognize that Congress did not write specific "interstate commerce" findings into the law under which Lopez was convicted. Nonetheless, as I have already noted, the matter that we review independently (i.e., whether there is a "rational basis") already has considerable leeway built into it. And, the absence of findings, at most, deprives a statute of the benefit of some extra leeway. This extra deference, in principle, might change the result in a close case, though, in practice, it has not made a critical legal difference. See, e.g., *Katzenbach v. McClung*, 379 U.S. 294, 299 (1964) (noting that "no formal findings were made, which of course are not necessary"); Perez, supra, at 156–157; cf. *Turner Broadcasting System, Inc. v. FCC*, 512 U.S., (1994) (opinion of KENNEDY, J.) (slip op., at 42) ("Congress is not obligated, when enacting its statutes, to make a record of the type that an administrative agency or court does to accommodate judicial review"); *Fullilove v. Klutznick*, 448 U.S. 448, 503 (1980) (Powell, J., concurring) ("After Congress has legislated repeatedly in an area of national concern, its Members gain experience that may reduce the need for fresh hearings or prolonged debate..."). And, it would seem particularly unfortunate to make the validity of the statute at hand turn on the presence or absence of findings. Because Congress did make findings (though not until after Lopez was prosecuted), doing so would appear to elevate form over substance. See Pub. L. 103–322, 320904(2)(F), (G), 108 Stat. 2125, 18 U.S.C.A. 922(q)(1)(F), (G) (Nov. 1994 Supp.).

In addition, despite the Court of Appeals' suggestion to the contrary, see 2 F.3d 1342, 1365 (CA5 1993), there is no special need here for a clear indication of Congress' rationale. The statute does not interfere with the exercise of state or local authority. Cf., e.g., *Dellmuth v. Muth*, 491 U.S. 223, 227–228 (1989) (requiring clear statement for abrogation of Eleventh Amendment immunity). Moreover, any clear statement rule would apply only to determine Congress' intended result, not to clarify the source of its authority or measure the level of consideration that went into its decision, and here there is no doubt as to which activities Congress intended to regulate. See ibid.; id., at 233 (SCALIA, J., concurring) (to subject States to suits for money damages, Congress need only make that intent clear, and need not refer explicitly to the Eleventh Amendment); *EEOC v. Wyoming*, 460 U.S. 226, 243, n. 18 (1983) (Congress need not recite the constitutional provision that authorizes its action).

II

Applying these principles to the case at hand, we must ask whether Congress could have had a rational basis for finding a significant (or substantial) connection between gun-related school violence and interstate commerce. Or, to put the question in the language of the explicit finding that Congress made when it amended this law in 1994: Could Congress rationally have found that "violent crime in school zones," through its effect on the "quality of education," significantly (or substantially) affects "interstate" or "foreign commerce"? 18 U.S.C.A. 922(q)(1)(F), (G) (Nov. 1994 Supp.). As long as one views the commerce connection, not as a "technical legal conception," but as "a practical one," *Swift & Co. v. United States*, 196 U.S. 375, 398 (1905) (Holmes, J.), the answer to this question must be yes. Numerous reports and studies – generated both inside and outside government – make clear that Congress could reasonably have found the empirical connection that its law, implicitly or explicitly, asserts. (See Appendix, infra at 19, for a sample of the documentation, as well as for complete citations to the sources referenced below.)

For one thing, reports, hearings, and other readily available literature make clear that the problem of guns in and around schools is widespread and extremely serious. These materials report, for example, that four percent of American high school students (and six percent of inner-city high school students) carry a gun to school at least occasionally, Centers for Disease Control 2342; Sheley, McGee, & Wright 679; that 12 percent of urban high school students have had guns fired at them, ibid.; that 20 percent of those students have been threatened with guns, ibid.; and that, in any 6-month period, several hundred thousand school-children are victims of violent crimes in or near their schools, U.S. Dept. of Justice 1 (1989); House Select Committee Hearing 15 (1989). And, they report that this widespread violence in schools throughout the Nation significantly interferes with the quality of education in those schools. See, e.g., House Judiciary Committee Hearing 44 (1990) (linking school violence to dropout rate); U.S. Dept. of Health 118–119 (1978) (school-violence victims suffer academically); compare U.S. Dept. of Justice 1 (1991) (gun violence worst in inner city schools), with National Center 47 (dropout rates highest in inner cities). Based on reports such as these, Congress obviously could have thought that guns and learning are mutually exclusive. Senate Labor and Human Resources Committee Hearing 39 (1993); U.S. Dept. of Health 118, 123–124 (1978). And, Congress could therefore have found a substantial educational problem – teachers unable to teach, students unable to learn – and concluded that guns near schools contribute substantially to the size and scope of that problem.

Having found that guns in schools significantly undermine the quality of education in our Nation's classrooms, Congress could also have found, given the effect of education upon interstate and foreign commerce, that gun-related violence in and around schools is a commercial, as well as a human, problem. Education, although far more than a matter of economics, has long been inextricably intertwined with the Nation's economy. When this Nation began, most workers received their education in the workplace, typically (like Benjamin Franklin) as apprentices. See generally Seybolt; Rorabaugh; U.S. Dept. of Labor (1950). As late as the 1920's, many workers still received general education directly from their employers – from large corporations, such as General Electric, Ford, and Goodyear, which created schools within their firms to help both the worker and the firm. See Bolino 15–25. (Throughout most of the 19th century fewer than one percent of all Americans received secondary education through attending a high school. See id., at 11.) As public school enrollment grew in the early 20th century, see Becker 218 (1993), the need for industry to teach basic educational skills diminished. But, the direct economic link between basic education and industrial productivity remained. Scholars estimate that nearly a quarter of America's economic growth in the early years of this century is traceable directly to increased schooling, see Denison 243; that investment in "human capital" (through spending on education) exceeded investment in "physical capital" by a ratio of almost two to one, see Schultz 26 (1961); and that the economic returns to this investment in education exceeded the returns to conventional capital investment, see, e.g., Davis & Morrall 48–49.

In recent years the link between secondary education and business has strengthened, becoming both more direct and more important. Scholars on the subject report that technological changes and innovations in management techniques have altered the nature of the workplace so that more jobs now demand greater educational skills. See, e.g., MIT 32 (only about one-third of hand-tool company's 1,000 workers were qualified to work with a new process that requires high-school-level reading and mathematical skills); Cyert & Mowery 68 (gap between wages of high school dropouts and better trained workers increasing); U.S. Dept. of Labor 41 (1981) (job openings for dropouts declining over time). There is evidence that "service, manufacturing or construction jobs are being displaced by technology that requires a better-educated worker or, more likely, are being exported overseas," Gordon, Ponticell, & Morgan 26; that "workers with truly few skills by the year 2000 will find that only one job out of ten will remain," ibid.; and that

> "[o]ver the long haul the best way to encourage the growth of high-wage jobs is to upgrade the skills of the work force. ... [B]etter-trained workers become more productive workers, enabling a company to become more competitive and expand." Henkoff 60.

Increasing global competition also has made primary and secondary education economically more important. The portion of the American economy attributable to international trade nearly tripled between 1950 and 1980, and more than 70 percent of American-made goods now compete with imports. Marshall 205; Marshall & Tucker 33. Yet, lagging worker productivity has contributed to negative trade balances and to real hourly compensation that has fallen below wages in 10 other industrialized nations. See National Center 57; Handbook of Labor Statistics 561, 576 (1989); Neef & Kask 28, 31. At least some significant part of this serious productivity problem is attributable to students who emerge from classrooms without the reading or mathematical skills necessary to compete with their European or Asian counterparts, see, e.g., MIT 28, and, presumably, to high school dropout rates of 20 to 25 percent (up to 50 percent in inner cities), see, e.g., National Center 47; Chubb & Hanushek 215. Indeed, Congress has said, when writing other statutes, that "functionally or technologically illiterate" Americans in the work force "erod[e]" our economic "standing in the international marketplace," Pub. L. 100–418, 6002(a)(3), 102 Stat. 1469, and that "our Nation is ... paying the price of scientific and technological illiteracy, with our productivity declining, our industrial base ailing, and our global competitiveness dwindling." H. R. Rep. No. 98–6, pt. 1, p. 19 (1983).

Finally, there is evidence that, today more than ever, many firms base their location decisions upon the presence, or absence, of a work force with a basic education. See MacCormack, Newman, & Rosenfield 73; Coffee 296. Scholars on the subject report, for example, that today, "[h]igh speed communication and transportation make it possible to produce most products and services anywhere in the world," National Center 38; that "[m]odern machinery and production methods can therefore be combined with low wage workers to drive costs down," ibid.; that managers can perform "'back office functions anywhere in the world now,'" and say that if they "'can't get enough skilled workers here'" they will "'move the skilled jobs out of the country,'" id., at 41; with the consequence that "rich countries need better education and retraining, to reduce the supply of unskilled workers and to equip them with the skills they require for tomorrow's jobs," Survey of Global Economy 37. In light of this increased importance of education to individual firms, it is no surprise that half of the Nation's manufacturers have become involved with setting standards and shaping curricula for local schools, Maturi 65–68, that 88 percent think this kind of involvement is important, id., at 68, that more than 20 States have recently passed educational reforms to attract new business, Overman 61–62, and that business magazines have begun to rank cities according to the quality of their schools, see Boyle 24.

The economic links I have just sketched seem fairly obvious. Why then is it not equally obvious, in light of those links, that a widespread, serious, and substantial physical threat to teaching and learning also substantially threatens the commerce to which that teaching and learning is inextricably tied? That is to say, guns in the hands of six percent of inner-city high school students and gun-related violence throughout a city's schools must threaten the trade and commerce that those schools support. The only question, then, is whether the latter threat is (to use the majority's terminology) "substantial." And, the evidence of (1) the extent of the gun-related violence problem, see supra, at 5, (2) the extent of the resulting negative effect on classroom learning, see supra, at 5–6, and (3) the extent of the consequent negative commercial effects, see supra, at 6–9, when taken together, indicate a threat to trade and commerce that is "substantial." At the very least, Congress could rationally have concluded that the links are "substantial."

Specifically, Congress could have found that gun-related violence near the classroom poses a serious economic threat (1) to consequently inadequately educated workers who must endure low paying jobs, see, e.g., National Center 29, and (2) to communities and businesses that might (in today's "information society") otherwise gain, from a well-educated work force, an important commercial advantage, see, e.g., Becker 10 (1992), of a kind that location near a railhead or harbor provided in the past. Congress might also have found these threats to be no different in kind from other threats that this Court has found within the commerce power, such as the threat that loan sharking poses to the "funds" of "numerous localities," *Perez v. United States*, 402 U.S., at 157, and that unfair labor practices pose to instrumentalities of commerce, see *Consolidated Edison Co. v. NLRB*, 305 U.S. 197, 221–222 (1938). As I have pointed out, supra, at 4, Congress has written that "the occurrence of violent crime in school zones" has brought about a "decline in the quality of education" that "has an adverse impact on interstate commerce and the foreign commerce of the United States." 18 U.S.C.A. 922(q)(1)(F), (G) (Nov. 1994 Supp.). The violence-related facts, the educational facts, and the economic facts, taken together, make this conclusion rational. And, because under our case law, see supra, at 1–2; infra, at 15, the sufficiency of the constitutionally necessary Commerce Clause link between a crime of violence and interstate commerce turns simply upon size or degree, those same facts make the statute constitutional.

To hold this statute constitutional is not to "obliterate" the "distinction of what is national and what is local," ante, at 18 (citation omitted; internal quotation marks omitted); nor is it to hold that the Commerce Clause permits the Federal Government to "regulate any activity that it found was related to the economic productivity of individual citizens," to regulate "marriage, divorce, and child custody," or to regulate any and all aspects of education. Ante, at 15–16. For one thing, this statute is aimed at curbing a particularly acute threat to the educational process – the possession (and use) of life-threatening firearms in, or near, the classroom. The empirical evidence that I have discussed above unmistakably documents the special way in which guns and education are incompatible. See supra, at 5–6. This Court has previously recognized the singularly disruptive potential on interstate commerce that acts of violence may have. See Perez, supra, at 156–157. For another thing, the immediacy of the connection between education and the national economic well-being is documented by scholars and accepted by society at large in a way and to a degree that may not hold true for other social institutions. It must surely be the rare case, then, that a statute strikes at conduct that (when considered in the abstract) seems so removed from commerce, but which (practically speaking) has so significant an impact upon commerce.

In sum, a holding that the particular statute before us falls within the commerce power would not expand the scope of that Clause. Rather, it simply would apply pre-existing law to changing economic circumstances. See *Heart of Atlanta Motel, Inc. v. United States*, 379 U.S. 241, 251 (1964). It would recognize that, in today's economic world, gun-related violence near the classroom makes a significant difference to our economic, as well as our social, well-being. In accordance with well-accepted precedent, such a holding would permit Congress "to act in terms of economic ... realities," would interpret the commerce power as "an affirmative power commensurate with the national needs," and would acknowledge that the "commerce clause does not operate so as to render the nation powerless to defend itself against economic forces that Congress decrees inimical or destructive of the national economy." *North American Co. v. SEC*, 327 U.S. 686, 705 (1946) (citing *Swift & Co. v. United States*, 196 U.S., at 398 (Holmes, J.)).

III

The majority's holding – that 922 falls outside the scope of the Commerce Clause – creates three serious legal problems. First, the majority's holding runs contrary to modern Supreme Court cases that have upheld congressional actions despite connections to interstate or foreign commerce that are less significant than the effect of school violence. In *Perez v. United States*, supra, the Court held that the Commerce Clause authorized a federal statute that makes it a crime to engage in loan sharking ("[e]xtortionate credit transactions") at a local level. The Court said that Congress may judge that such transactions, "though purely intrastate, ... affect interstate commerce." 402 U.S., at 154 (emphasis added). Presumably, Congress reasoned that threatening or using force, say with a gun on a street corner, to collect a debt occurs sufficiently often so that the activity (by helping organized crime) affects commerce among the States. But, why then cannot Congress also reason that the threat or use of force – the frequent consequence of possessing a gun – in or near a school occurs sufficiently often so that such activity (by inhibiting basic education) affects commerce among the States? The negative impact upon the national economy of an inability to teach basic skills seems no smaller (nor less significant) than that of organized crime.

In *Katzenbach v. McClung*, 379 U.S. 294 (1964), this Court upheld, as within the commerce power, a statute prohibiting racial discrimination at local restaurants, in part because that discrimination discouraged travel by African Americans and in part because that discrimination affected purchases of food and restaurant supplies from other States. See id., at 300; Heart of Atlanta Motel, supra, at 274 (Black, J., concurring in McClung and in Heart of Atlanta). In *Daniel v. Paul*, 395 U.S. 298 (1969), this Court found an effect on commerce caused by an amusement park located several miles down a country road in the middle of Alabama – because some customers (the Court assumed), some food, 15 paddleboats, and a juke box had come from out of State. See id., at 304–305, 308. In both of these cases, the Court understood that the specific instance of discrimination (at a local place of accommodation) was part of a general practice that, considered as a whole, caused not only the most serious human and social harm, but had nationally significant economic dimensions as well. See McClung, supra, at 301; Daniel, supra, at 307, n. 10. It is difficult to distinguish the case before us, for the same critical elements are present. Businesses are less likely to locate in communities where violence plagues the classroom. Families will hesitate to move to neighborhoods where students carry guns instead of books. (Congress expressly found in 1994 that "parents may decline to send their children to school" in certain areas "due to concern about violent crime and gun violence." 18 U.S.C.A. 922(q)(1)(E) (Nov. 1994 Supp.)). And (to look at the matter in the most narrowly commercial manner), interstate publishers therefore will sell fewer books and other firms will sell fewer school supplies where the threat of violence disrupts learning. Most importantly, like the local racial discrimination at issue in McClung and Daniel, the local instances here, taken together and considered as a whole, create a problem that causes serious human and social harm, but also has nationally significant economic dimensions.

In *Wickard v. Filburn*, 317 U.S. 111 (1942), this Court sustained the application of the Agricultural Adjustment Act of 1938 to wheat that Filburn grew and consumed on his own local farm because, considered in its totality, (1) home-grown wheat may be "induced by rising prices" to "flow into the market and check price increases," and (2) even if it never actually enters the market, home-grown wheat nonetheless "supplies a need of the man who grew it which would otherwise be reflected by purchases in the open market" and, in that sense, "competes with wheat in commerce." Id., at 128. To find both of these effects on commerce significant in amount, the Court had to give Congress the benefit of the doubt. Why would the Court, to find a significant (or "substantial") effect here, have to give Congress any greater leeway? See also *United States v. Women's Sportswear Manufacturers Assn.*, 336 U.S. 460, 464 (1949) ("If it is interstate commerce that feels the pinch, it does not matter how local the operation which applies the squeeze"); *Mandeville Island Farms, Inc. v. American Crystal Sugar Co.*, 334 U.S., at 236 ("[I]t is enough that the individual activity when multiplied into a general practice ... contains a threat to the interstate economy that requires preventative regulation").

The second legal problem the Court creates comes from its apparent belief that it can reconcile its holding with earlier cases by making a critical distinction between "commercial" and noncommercial "transaction[s]." *Ante*, at 12–13. That is to say, the Court believes the Constitution would distinguish between two local activities, each of which has an identical effect upon interstate commerce, if one, but not the other, is "commercial" in nature. As a general matter, this approach fails to heed this Court's earlier warning not to turn "questions of the power of Congress" upon "formula[s]" that would give:

> "controlling force to nomenclature such as 'production' and 'indirect' and foreclose consideration of the actual effects of the activity in question upon interstate commerce." Wickard, supra, at 120.

See also *United States v. Darby*, 312 U.S. 100, 116–117 (1941) (overturning the Court's distinction between "production" and "commerce" in the child labor case, *Hammer v. Dagenhart*, 247 U.S. 251, 271–272 (1918)); *Swift & Co. v. United States*, 196 U.S., at 398 (Holmes, J.) ("[C]ommerce among the States is not a technical legal conception, but a practical one, drawn from the course of business"). Moreover, the majority's test is not consistent with what the Court saw as the point of the cases that the majority now characterizes. Although the majority today attempts to categorize *Perez, McClung*, and *Wickard* as involving intrastate "economic activity," *ante*, at 10–11, the Courts that decided each of those cases did not focus upon the economic nature of the activity regulated. Rather, they focused upon whether that activity affected interstate or foreign commerce. In fact, the Wickard Court expressly held that Wickard's consumption of home grown wheat, "though it may not be regarded as commerce," could nevertheless be regulated "whatever its nature" – so long as "it exerts a substantial economic effect on interstate commerce." Wickard, supra, at 125 (emphasis added).

More importantly, if a distinction between commercial and noncommercial activities is to be made, this is not the case in which to make it. The majority clearly cannot intend such a distinction to focus narrowly on an act of gun possession standing by itself, for such a reading could not be reconciled with either the civil rights cases

(McClung and Daniel) or Perez in each of those cases the specific transaction (the race-based exclusion, the use of force) was not itself "commercial." And, if the majority instead means to distinguish generally among broad categories of activities, differentiating what is educational from what is commercial, then, as a practical matter, the line becomes almost impossible to draw. Schools that teach reading, writing, mathematics, and related basic skills serve both social and commercial purposes, and one cannot easily separate the one from the other. American industry itself has been, and is again, involved in teaching. See supra, at 6, 9. When, and to what extent, does its involvement make education commercial? Does the number of vocational classes that train students directly for jobs make a difference? Does it matter if the school is public or private, nonprofit or profit-seeking? Does it matter if a city or State adopts a voucher plan that pays private firms to run a school? Even if one were to ignore these practical questions, why should there be a theoretical distinction between education, when it significantly benefits commerce, and environmental pollution, when it causes economic harm? See *Hodel v. Virginia Surface Mining & Reclamation Assn., Inc.*, 452 U.S. 264 (1981).

Regardless, if there is a principled distinction that could work both here and in future cases, Congress (even in the absence of vocational classes, industry involvement, and private management) could rationally conclude that schools fall on the commercial side of the line. In 1990, the year Congress enacted the statute before us, primary and secondary schools spent $230 billion – that is, nearly a quarter of a trillion dollars which accounts for a significant portion of our $5.5 trillion Gross Domestic Product for that year. See Statistical Abstract 147, 442 (1993). The business of schooling requires expenditure of these funds on student transportation, food and custodial services, books, and teachers' salaries. See U.S. Dept. of Education 4, 7 (1993). And, these expenditures enable schools to provide a valuable service – namely, to equip students with the skills they need to survive in life and, more specifically, in the workplace. Certainly, Congress has often analyzed school expenditure as if it were a commercial investment, closely analyzing whether schools are efficient, whether they justify the significant resources they spend, and whether they can be restructured to achieve greater returns. See, e.g., S. Rep. No. 100–222, p. 2 (1987) (federal school assistance is "a prudent investment"); Senate Appropriations Committee Hearing (1994) (private sector management of public schools); cf. Chubb & Moe 185–229 (school choice); Hanushek 85–122 (performance based incentives for educators); Gibbs (decision in Hartford, Conn., to contract out public school system). Why could Congress, for Commerce Clause purposes, not consider schools as roughly analogous to commercial investments from which the Nation derives the benefit of an educated work force?

The third legal problem created by the Court's holding is that it threatens legal uncertainty in an area of law that, until this case, seemed reasonably well settled. Congress has enacted many statutes (more than 100 sections of the United States Code), including criminal statutes (at least 25 sections), that use the words "affecting commerce" to define their scope, see, e.g., 18 U.S.C. 844(i) (destruction of buildings used in activity affecting interstate commerce), and other statutes that contain no jurisdictional language at all, see, e.g., 18 U.S.C. 922(o)(1) (possession of machine guns). Do these, or similar, statutes regulate noncommercial activities? If so, would that alter the meaning of "affecting commerce" in a jurisdictional element? Cf. *United States v. Staszcuk*, 517 F.2d 53, 57–58 (CA7 1975) (en banc) (Stevens, J.) (evaluation of Congress' intent "requires more than a consideration of the consequences of the particular transaction"). More importantly, in the absence of a jurisdictional element, are the courts nevertheless to take Wickard, 317 U.S., at 127–128, (and later similar cases) as inapplicable, and to judge the effect of a single noncommercial activity on interstate commerce without considering similar instances of the forbidden conduct? However these questions are eventually resolved, the legal uncertainty now created will restrict Congress' ability to enact criminal laws aimed at criminal behavior that, considered problem by problem rather than instance by instance, seriously threatens the economic, as well as social, well-being of Americans.

IV

In sum, to find this legislation within the scope of the Commerce Clause would permit "Congress ... to act in terms of economic ... realities." *North American Co. v. SEC*, 327 U.S., at 705 (citing *Swift & Co. v. United States*, 196 U.S., at 398 (Holmes, J.)). It would interpret the Clause as this Court has traditionally interpreted it, with the exception of one wrong turn subsequently corrected. See *Gibbons v. Ogden*, 9 Wheat., at 195 (holding that the commerce power extends "to all the external concerns of the nation, and to those internal concerns which affect the States generally"); *United States v. Darby*, 312 U.S., at 116–117 ("The conclusion is inescapable that *Hammer v. Dagenhart* [the child labor case], was a departure from the principles which have prevailed in the interpretation of the Commerce Clause both before and since the decision. ... It should be and now is overruled"). Upholding this legislation would do no more than simply recognize that Congress had a "rational basis" for finding a significant connection between guns in or near schools and (through their effect on education) the interstate and foreign commerce they threaten. For these reasons, I would reverse the judgment of the Court of Appeals. Respectfully, I dissent.

APPENDIX C

Partial List of Federal Law Enforcement Agencies and Types of Officers They Employ

U.S. Capitol
U.S. Capitol Police (police officers)

U.S. Department of Agriculture
U.S. Forest Service (rangers and special agents)

U.S. Department of Commerce
Office of Export Enforcement (special agents)
NOAA Fisheries Office of Law Enforcement (patrol officers and special agents)

U.S. Department of Defense
Air Force Office of Special Investigations (special agents)
Army Criminal Investigation Division (special agents)
Department of Defense Police (police officers)
Naval Criminal Investigative Service (special agents)

U.S. Environmental Protection Agency
Criminal Investigation Division (special agents)

U.S. Health and Human Services
Office of Criminal Investigation (special agents)

U.S. Department of the Interior
Bureau of Indian Affairs (police officers and special agents)
Bureau of Land Management (rangers and special agents)
Bureau of Reclamation (police officers)
Fish and Wildlife Service (rangers and special agents)
National Park Service (rangers and special agents)
U.S. Park Police (police officers)

U.S. Department of Justice
Bureau of Alcohol, Tobacco, Firearms and Explosives (special agents)
Drug Enforcement Administration (special agents)
Federal Bureau of Investigation (special agents)
U.S. Marshals Service (marshals and deputy marshals)

U.S. Department of Homeland Security
Customs and Border Protection (inspectors)
Federal Air Marshal Service (air marshals)
Federal Protective Service (police officers, LESOs, and special agents)
Immigration and Customs Enforcement (special agents)
U.S. Secret Service (police officers and special agents)
U.S. Coast Guard (security officers and special agents)
U.S. Border Patrol (border patrol agents)

U.S. Department of the Treasury
Bureau of Engraving and Printing Police (police officers)
Internal Revenue Service (special agents)
U.S. Mint Police (police officers)

U.S. Department of State
Bureau of Diplomatic Security (special agents)

U.S. Department of Veterans Affairs
VA Police (police officers)

U.S. Postal Service
Postal Inspection Service (postal inspectors)
Postal Service Police (police officers)

U.S. Supreme Court
U.S. Supreme Court Police (police officers)

National Railroad Passenger Corporation
Amtrak Police (police officers)

Smithsonian Institution
Smithsonian Police (police officers)

Tennessee Valley Authority
TVA Police (police officers)

Offices of Inspector General
(all agencies listed below employ special agents/criminal investigators)
Agency for International Development
Amtrak
Appalachian Regional Commission
Central Intelligence Agency
Commodity Futures Trading Commission
Consumer Product Safety Commission
Corporation for National and Community Service (Americorps)
Corporation for Public Broadcasting
Department of Agriculture
Department of Commerce
Department of Defense (Defense Criminal Investigative Service)
Department of Education
Department of Energy
Department of Health and Human Services
Department of Homeland Security
Department of Housing and Urban Development
Department of the Interior
Department of Justice
Department of Labor
Department of State
Department of Transportation
Department of the Treasury
Department of Veteran Affairs
Environmental Protection Agency
Equal Employment Opportunity Commission
Export-Import Bank of the United States
Farm Credit Administration
Federal Communications Commission
Federal Deposit Insurance Corporation

Federal Election Commission
Federal Housing Finance Board
Federal Labor Relations Authority
Federal Maritime Commission
Federal Reserve Board
Federal Trade Commission
General Services Administration
Government Printing Office
Legal Services Corporation
National Aeronautics and Space Administration
National Archives and Records Administration
National Credit Union Administration
National Endowment for the Arts
National Endowment for the Humanities
National Labor Relations Board
National Science Foundation
Nuclear Regulatory Commission
Office of Personnel Management
Peace Corps
Pension Benefit Guaranty Corporation
Railroad Retirement Board
Security and Exchange Commission
Small Business Administration
Smithsonian Institution
Social Security Administration
Tennessee Valley Authority
Treasury Inspector General for Tax Administration
U.S. International Trade Commission
United States Postal Service

APPENDIX D

Table of Contents of the USA Patriot Act

(Signed into law on October 26, 2001)

AN ACT

To deter and punish terrorist acts in the United States and around the world, to enhance law enforcement investigatory tools, and for other purposes. *Be it enacted by the Senate and House of Representatives of the United States of America in Congress assembled.*

SECTION 1. SHORT TITLE AND TABLE OF CONTENTS

(a) SHORT TITLE – This Act may be cited as the 'Uniting and Strengthening America by Providing Appropriate Tools Required to Intercept and Obstruct Terrorism (USA PATRIOT ACT) Act of 2001'.

(b) TABLE OF CONTENTS – The table of contents for this Act is as follows:

Sec. 1. Short title and table of contents.
Sec. 2. Construction; severability.

TITLE I—ENHANCING DOMESTIC SECURITY AGAINST TERRORISM

TITLE II—ENHANCED SURVEILLANCE PROCEDURES

TITLE III—INTERNATIONAL MONEY LAUNDERING ABATEMENT AND ANTI–TERRORIST FINANCING ACT OF 2001

Subtitle A—International Counter Money Laundering and Related Measures

Subtitle B—Bank Secrecy Act Amendments and Related Improvements

Subtitle C—Currency Crimes and Protection

TITLE IV—PROTECTING THE BORDER

Subtitle A—Protecting the Northern Border

Subtitle B—Enhanced Immigration Provisions

Subtitle C—Preservation of Immigration Benefits for Victims of Terrorism

TITLE V—REMOVING OBSTACLES TO INVESTIGATING TERRORISM

TITLE IX—IMPROVED INTELLIGENCE

TITLE X—MISCELLANEOUS

APPENDIX E

Selected Events in the Chronology of Federal Law Enforcement

1772 Colonial Postmaster Benjamin Franklin creates the position of "surveyor" to assist regulating and auditing postal operations (ancestor of the Postal Inspectors).

1787 U.S. Constitution adopted at a constitutional convention in Philadelphia, Pennsylvania.

1789 U.S. Constitution takes effect.

1789 Congress passes the Judiciary Act of 1789, which creates the federal court system, federal judicial districts, the office of U.S. Attorney, and the U.S. Marshals.

1789 Tariff Act signed into law which creates a federal Customs agency.

1790 Congress authorizes construction of 10 warships for the Treasury Department's Revenue Cutter Service (a direct ancestor of the U.S. Coast Guard).

1790 Congress appoints a commission to manage federal buildings and property in Washington, DC. The commission in turn appoints 6 night watchmen to protect federal property.

1791 Bill of Rights ratified.

1792 U.S. Postal Service established as a federal agency.

1794 Whiskey Rebellion occurred in Pennsylvania; a U.S. Marshal and a revenue collector were captured by rebels but later escaped. The rebellion was eventually put down by federalized militia troops.

1798 Alien and Sedition Acts are signed into law.

1801 Postal surveyors officially change their working title to "special agents."

1808 First of many federal anti-slave trade laws passed.

1812 America goes to war against Britain. U.S. Marshals called upon to combat British espionage.

1820 Law passed making international slave trading a federal capital offense akin to piracy.

1828 Congress authorizes the creation of a Capitol police force.

1849 Department of Interior is established.

1850 Fugitive Slave Act passed which required the U.S. Marshals to return escaped slaves found in the North to slave owners in the South.

1853 Mounted customs inspectors patrol the border with Mexico to collect duty on cattle coming into the United States.

1862 Legal Tender Act of 1862 (and in 1863) is passed authorizing the United States Government to print standard paper currency in an effort to curb rampant counterfeiting.

1865 U.S. Secret Service is created with the primary mission of combating counterfeiting.

1866 Civil Rights Act of 1866 passed making it a federal offense to deny basic citizenship rights to former slaves.

1868 14th Amendment of U.S. Constitution ratified.

1870 Force Act (along with Civil Rights Act of 1871) made it a federal criminal offense to wear hoods or masks for the purpose of intimidating minorities.

1870 Department of Justice is established.

1870 Congress passes legislation creating the "Special Agency Service," an investigative unit with the Treasury Department's Customs Division.

1874 U.S. Customs personnel are given the responsibility of enforcing the first federal copyright act.

1875 Isaac Parker (known as the "hanging judge") began his famous 21-year tenure as a U.S. District Judge in Ft. Smith, Arkansas.

1880 Postal special agents are officially renamed "Postal Inspectors."

1891 Congress passes the Immigration Act of 1891 which creates a Bureau of Immigration, staffed by federal immigration inspectors, as a part of the U.S. Treasury Department.

1894 Secret Service provides limited protection to President Grover Cleveland as a result in the wake of death threats made against the president by disgruntled subjects of a Secret Service criminal investigation.

1896 U.S. Marshals and Deputy U.S. Marshals begin to receive a federal salary in lieu of fees for service.

1903 Bureau of Immigration moved to the newly-established U.S. Department of Commerce.

1905 U.S. Forest Service is established. Forest Service employees are given federal arrest authority.

1906 Secret Service officially given responsibility for presidential protection in the wake of the 1901 assassination of President William McKinley.

1908 U.S. Justice Department creates a detective bureau by transferring into it several Justice Department employees and 8 Secret Service agents.

1909 U.S. Justice Department's detective bureau officially named the "Bureau of Investigation."

1910 Mann Act is passed which made White-Slave trafficking a federal crime.

1911 Emma Jentzer becomes the first female special agent to serve with the Bureau of Investigation.

1914 Harrison Act is passed which amounts to the first serious federal effort to regulate opiates and cocaine.

1915 Congress changes the name of the Revenue Cutter Service to the "U.S. Coast Guard and assigns to it life-saving at sea as one of its primary missions.

1916 Postal inspectors successfully investigate and arrest perpetrators of America's last known stage-coach robbery.

1916 The National Park Service is established as a part of the U.S. Interior Department.

1917 Recent law school graduate J. Edgar Hoover joins the U.S. Justice Department's General Intelligence Division.

1919 U.S. Treasury Department's Commission for Internal Revenue creates an Intelligence Unit to investigate tax fraud (ancestor of the IRS-CID).

1919 Congress passes legislation making the theft of motor vehicles across state lines a federal criminal offense.

1919 18th Amendment prohibiting the possession and manufacture of alcohol is ratified.

1922 White House police force created (ancestor of Secret Service Uniformed Division)

1924 U.S. Border Patrol is established as a part of the Bureau of Immigration.

1924 J. Edgar Hoover becomes the director of the U.S. Justice Department's Bureau of Investigation.

1924 Bureau of Investigation established an Identification Division which would serve as a clearinghouse for fingerprint records obtained by all levels of law enforcement throughout the country.

1925 Special Agent Edwin Shanahan becomes the first Bureau of Investigation agent murdered in the line of duty. He is shot and killed during the attempted arrest of a car thief.

1927 Bureau of Prohibition is established within the U.S. Treasury Department.

1928 The Bureau of Investigation establishes a training school for new agents (the precursor to what would become the FBI Academy)

1930 Treasury Department's Prohibition Unit is transferred to the Justice Department.

1930 White House Police become part of the Secret Service.

1930 The Justice Department's Bureau of Investigation is authorized by Congress to collect uniform crime statistics for the nation. To this day, the FBI is responsible for compiling the data that goes into the Uniform Crime Report each year.

1931 Chicago gangster Al Capone is convicted on charges of federal tax evasion.

1932 Infant son of Charles Lindbergh kidnapped in New Jersey. Several federal agencies assist the state and local police in the investigation.

1932 Congress passes legislation making the kidnapping of victims across state lines a federal criminal offense.

1933 President Franklin Roosevelt designates the Justice Department's Bureau of Investigation as the lead federal agency on the Lindbergh kidnapping case.

1933 Bureau of Immigration is renamed the Immigration and Naturalization Service and is transferred to the U.S. Department of Labor.

1934 Bureau of Investigation special agents are given full federal law enforcement authority, including the power to make arrests and carry firearms.

1934   Bank robbery becomes a federal criminal offense.

1934   Public Enemy #1 John Dillinger is shot dead by Bureau of Investigation special agents in Chicago.

1934   The Prohibition Unit is transferred from the Justice Department back to the Treasury Department and is renamed the "Alcohol Tax Unit."

1934   National Firearms Act is passed providing for the taxing and registration of certain types of firearms.

1935   Creation of a U.S. Customs academy for uniformed inspectors and plainclothes officers.

1935   Bureau of Investigation renamed "Federal Bureau of Investigation."

1935   Creation of the FBI National Academy whose purpose is to help train and professionalize local law enforcement leadership.

1936   U.S. Customs creates a Division of Laboratories to support the agency's law enforcement efforts.

1939   FBI is given primary jurisdiction for investigating acts of espionage and sabotage.

1940   Smith Act is passed making it a federal crime to advocate the violent overthrow of the U.S. Government. FBI is given jurisdiction.

1940   The Immigration and Naturalization Service is transferred to the U.S. Department of Justice.

1940   Postal Inspectors establish their own crime laboratory.

1948   Congress authorizes the establishment of a police force consisting of uniformed and plainclothes officers to protect federal buildings.

1950   FBI agents arrest Julius and Ethel Rosenberg for giving American nuclear secrets to the Soviet Union. The Rosenbergs are eventually convicted and executed.

1951   The Treasury Department's Alcohol Tax Unit is renamed the "Alcohol and Tobacco Tax Division."

1953   Bureau of Internal Revenue renamed "Internal Revenue Service."

1962   Secret Service given the responsibility to protect the Vice President.

1962   The U.S. Department of Agriculture creates the first modern Office of Inspector General in the wake of the Billy Sol Estes scandal. The USDA OIG would later serve as a model for the creation of other OIGs.

1963   President John F. Kennedy was assassinated by Lee Harvey Oswald. The FBI was placed in charge of the investigation by President Lyndon Johnson. Eventually, the FBI was given statutory responsibility for investigating presidential assassinations and attempts.

1964 The FBI led the investigation of 4 murdered civil rights workers in Mississippi. Several members of the Ku Klux Klan were convicted in federal court for violating the civil rights of the murdered workers.

1967 U.S. Coast Guard is transferred from the Treasury Department to the newly-created U.S. Department of Transportation.

1968 Establishment of the Bureau of Narcotics and Dangerous Drugs as a part of the U.S. Department of Justice.

1970 Passage of the Controlled Substances Act which serves to this day as the foundation of American drug enforcement laws and drug classification.

1970 Postal Reorganization Act of 1970 renames of the Office of the Chief Postal Inspector the "Postal Inspection Service" and also established a uniformed police force to protect postal facilities.

1970 Treasury Department creates a consolidated law enforcement training academy in Washington DC.

1970 The Racketeer Influenced and Corrupt Organizations Act is passed which provide federal law enforcement with enhanced tools for going after Organized Crime.

1971 Secret Service given the responsibility of protecting visiting heads of state and other foreign dignitaries.

1971 U.S. Marshals Service establishes the Witness Protection Program.

1971 *Bivens v. 6 Unknown Narcotics Agents*—Supreme Court Case which eliminated immunity for federal agents when their official actions are deemed to "shock the conscience" of reasonable people. As a result of this case, citizens may sue federal agents for damages under the Federal Tort Claims Act.

1971 First female special agents of the U.S. Customs Service are sworn in.

1972 First female special agents to be sworn into the modern FBI.

1972 The Alcohol and Tobacco Tax Division within the IRS becomes a stand-alone Treasury Department agency and is renamed the "Bureau of Alcohol, Tobacco and Firearms."

1973 Bureau of Narcotics and Dangerous Drugs is renamed the "Drug Enforcement Administration."

1973 Customs Bureau is renamed "U.S. Customs Service."

1975 Treasury Department's training academy is relocated to a former navy installation in Brunswick, Georgia. The academy is renamed the "Federal Law Enforcement Training Center."

1976   The first statutorily-created Office of Inspector General is established in the U.S. Department of Health, Education, and Welfare.

1978   The Internal Revenue Service's Intelligence Unit is renamed the "Criminal Investigation Division."

1978   Congresses passes the Inspector General Act of 1978 which creates statutory Offices of Inspector General in cabinet-level agencies.

1981   U.S. Department of Agriculture's Office of Inspector General is the first OIG to be given full statutory law enforcement authority for its special agents.

1984   Secret Service given statutory authority to investigate credit card fraud.

1992   Ruby Ridge incident. A deputy U.S. Marshal and the son of federal fugitive Randy Weaver were killed in a shoot-out at Weaver's cabin near Ruby Ridge, Idaho. During the stand-off, Weaver's wife is shot and killed by an FBI sniper. The whole incident became a rallying cry for anti-government zealots.

1993   First act of Middle East terrorism on U.S. soil occurs with the bombing of the World Trade Center. 6 people were killed; over 1,000 injured. At the time, it resulted in the largest federal criminal investigation in U.S. history.

1993   4 special agents of the Bureau of Alcohol, Tobacco and Firearms are killed during a raid on the Branch Davidian compound in Waco, Texas. A stand-off ensued for which the FBI asserted primary jurisdiction to resolve. After 51 days of impasse, the FBI began to insert tear gas into the compound. In response, Branch Davidians set the compound buildings on fire. Ultimately, 80 Branch Davidians were killed, including 19 children.

1995   *U.S. v. Lopez*–Supreme Court strikes down federal Gun Free School Zone Act thereby setting limits on the scope of the Interstate Commerce Clause of the Constitution.

1995   The Alfred P. Murrah Federal Building in Oklahoma City, Oklahoma, is destroyed by a truck–bomb, killing 168 people. Anti-government zealot Timothy McVey was convicted in federal court for killing 8 federal agents (who were among the 168 killed). He was charged with killing federal agents so that the government could secure the death penalty upon conviction, which it did.

2001   The terrorist hijackings of four airliners, three of which were flown into each of the World Trade Center towers and the

Pentagon, results in the death of over 3,000 people and the destruction of the World Trade Center. This was the most deadly act of non-state terrorism in history and resulted in several reforms and adjustments of American federal law enforcement authority and organization.

2001   USA PATRIOT Act is passed giving federal law enforcement expanded authority to investigate terrorist organizations and suspects.

2002   Congress passes the Homeland Security Act of 2002 which creates the Department of Homeland Security.

2002   As a result of the Homeland Security Act of 2002, broad federal law enforcement authority is given to those Offices of Inspector General which did not already statutorily possess it.

2002   The Homeland Security Act renames the ATF as the "Bureau of Alcohol, Tobacco, Firearms and Explosives" and transfers that agency from the Treasury Department to the Justice Department.

2003   22 federal agencies are transferred to the newly-created Department of Homeland Security, including the U.S. Customs Service, the Immigration and Naturalization Service, the Federal Protective Service, the Transportation Security Administration, the Secret Service, the Coast Guard, and others.

2006   Controversial sunset provisions of the USA PATRIOT Act are extended but not made permanent.

Notes

CHAPTER 1

1. Thomas Dye, *Politics in America* (Upper Saddle River, NJ: Prentice Hall, 2001).

2. James Madison, "General View of the Powers Conferred by the Constitution" [Federalist 41], *Independent Journal*, January 19, 1788.

3. James Madison, "Alleged Dangers from the Powers of the Union to the State Governments Considered" [Federalist 45], *Independent Journal*, January 26, 1788.

4. Alexander Hamilton, "Certain General and Miscellaneous Objections to the Constitution Considered and Answered" [Federalist 84], *Independent Journal*, July 16, 1788.

5. Chief Justice William Rehnquist writing for the majority in *United States v. Lopez*, decided April 26, 1995.

6. Ibid.

7. Chief Justice John Marshall writing for the Court in *Gibbons v. Ogden*, decided March 2, 1824.

CHAPTER 2

1. Joel Samaha, *Criminal Justice* (Belmont, CA: Wadsworth, 1994).

2. Frank Schmallager, *Criminal Justice Today* (Englewood Cliffs, NJ: Regents/Prentice-Hall, 1993).

3. Ibid.

4. Ibid.

5. T.J. Deacon, *Police Professionalism: The Renaissance of American Law Enforcement*. (Springfield, IL: Charles C. Thomas Publisher, 1988).

6. Samuel Walker, *A Critical History of Police Reform* (Lexington, MA: Lexington Books, 1977).

7. Kenneth Peak and Ronald Glensor, *Community Policing & Problem Solving: Strategies and Practices* (Upper Saddle River, NJ: Prentice-Hall, 1996).

8. Walker, 1977.

9. Ibid.

10. Anne Saba, "U.S. Customs Service: Always There...Ready to Serve." *U.S. Customs Today*. (February 2003).

11. Ibid.

12. Ibid.

13. Ibid.

14. U.S. Coast Guard, *U.S. Coast Guard: An Historical Overview*. (Washington DC: USCG Historian's Office, 2002).

15. Ibid.

16. Ibid.

17. U.S. Postal Service. "History of the United States Postal Service 1775–1993," http://www.usps.com/history/his1_5.htm

18. Ibid.

19. U.S. Senate Historian. "The Capitol Police," http://www.senate.gov/artandhistory/history/common/briefing/Capitol_Police.htm

20. U.S. Federal Protective Service. "FPS Fact Sheet," http://www.ice.gov/graphics/fps/index.htm

21. U.S. Senate Historian.

22. U.S. Congress. *Records of the U.S. House of Representatives*. HR 158, 20th Congress, April 29, 1828, RG 233.

23. U.S. Senate Historian.

24. Barry Mackintosh, *The United States Park Police: A History* (Washington DC: NPS History Division, 1989).

25. Ibid.

26. David Turk, *United States Marshals Service: Historical Perspective* (Washington DC: USMS Historian Office, 2005).

27. U.S. Marshals Service. *The Office of the United States Marshal* (Washington DC: Government Printing Office, 1981).

28. Federick Calhoun, *The Lawmen: United States Marshals and Their Deputies, 1789–1989* (Washington DC: Smithsonian Institution Press, 1989).

29. Turk.

30. "Judiciary Act of 1789," 1 Stat. 73, Section 27, adopted September 24, 1789.

31. Robin Langley Sommer, *The History of the U.S. Marshals: The Proud Story of America's Legendary Lawmen* (Philadelphia, PA: Courage Books, 1993).

32. Ibid.

33. Ibid.

34. "CHAP. CXIII. An Act to continue in force "An act to protect the commerce of the United States, and punish the crime of piracy," and also to make further provisions for punishing the crime or piracy," adopted May 28, 1820.

35. Sommer.

CHAPTER 3

1. Herbert Johnson and Nancy Wolfe, *History of Criminal Justice* (Cincinnati, OH: Anderson Publishing, 2003).

2. Ibid.

3. Ibid.

4. Sommers, 33.

5. "CHAP. LX. An Act to confiscate Property used for Insurrectionary Purposes," adopted August 6,1861.

6. Sommer.

7. Donald Jackson, "Bicentennial of the U.S. Marshals." *The Smithsonian*, April (1989).

8. "Act to Establish the Department of Justice," Ch.150, 16 Stat. 162, 1870.

9. Philip Melanson, *Secret Service: The Hidden History of an Enigmatic Agency* (New York, NY: Carroll and Graf Publishers, 2002).

10. Patricia Faust (ed), *Historical Times Illustrated Encyclopedia of the Civil War* (New York, NY: Harper and Row, 1991).

11. Ibid.

12. Melanson.

13. Frederick Kaiser, "Origins of Secret Service Protection of the President: Personal, Interagency, and Institutional Conflict," *Presidential Studies Quarterly* Winter (1988).

14. Ibid.

15. Congressional Record, 2275, 1902, 35.

16. Kaiser.

17. House Committee on the Judiciary, "Protection of the President and the Suppression of Crime Against Government," 57th Cong., 1st sess., H. Rep. 1422, 13 (1902).

18. U.S. Secret Service. "United States Secret Service: History" Timeline Fact Sheet. http://www.secretservice.gov/history.shtml

19. U.S. Forest Service. "Law Enforcement and Investigations" Fact Sheet. http://www.fs.fed.us/lei/

20. James Kieley, *A Brief History of the National Park Service*. (Washington, DC: U.S. Dept. of Interior, 1940).

21. Ibid.

22. TRAC Syracuse University. "IRS At Work—IRS History." http://trac.syr.edu/tracirs/atwork/current/irsHistory.html

CHAPTER 4

1. John Fox, *The Birth of the Federal Bureau of Investigation* (Washington DC: Office of Public/Congressional Affairs, 2003).

2. U.S. Department of Justice, *Annual Report of the Attorney General*, Washington, DC, 1907.

3. Charles Bonaparte to Theodore Roosevelt, 14 January 1909, *A Letter to U.S. President Theodore Roosevelt concerning the need for a Justice Department investigative agency.*

4. Fox.

5. Clair Bond Potter, *War on Crime: Bandits, G-Men, and the Politics of Mass Culture* (New Brunswick, NJ: Rutgers University Press, 1998).

6. Don Whitehead, *The FBI Story: A Report to the American People* (New York, NY: Random House, 1956).

7. 71. Smith Act of 1940, 54 Stat. 670, 671, Title I, Sections 2–3, adopted June 28, 1940.

8. Fox.

9. Federal Bureau of Investigation. "J. Edgar Hoover Fact Sheet," http://www.fbi.gov/libref/directors/hoover.htm.

10. Johnson and Wolfe.

11. Ibid.

12. Fox.

13. Johnson and Wolfe.

14. Edward Peykar (ed), *The FBI: Past, Present, and Future* (Hauppauge, NY: Nova Science Publishers, 2005).

15. Richard Lindberg, "No More Greylords?" *Illinois Police and Sheriff News* Summer (1994).

16. Peykar.

CHAPTER 5

1. Federal Bureau of Investigation, "Facts and Figures Fact Sheet" http://www.fbi.gov/priorities/priorties.htm.

2. Turk.

3. U.S. Marshals Service. "United States Marshals Service 2004 Fact Sheet" http://www.usms.gov

4. Ibid.

5. Ibid.

6. U.S. Immigration and Naturalization Service. *Retiring to a New Beginning: An Illustrated History of the Immigration and Naturalization Service* (Washington DC: Government Printing Office, 2003).

7. U.S. Customs and Border Protection. "Populating a Nation: A History of the Immigration and Naturalization Service," *CPB Today*, June/July (2003).

8. U.S. Immigration and Naturalization Service.

9. Joseph Nevins, *Operation Gatekeeper: The Rise of the "Illegal Alien" and the Making of the U.S. Mexico Boundary* (New York, NY: Routledge, 2002).

10. U.S. Immigration and Naturalization Service.

11. U.S. Customs and Border Protection, "U.S. Border Patrol Overview." http://www.cbp.gov/xp/cgov/border_security/border_patrol/overview.xml

12. Ted Gest, *Crime and Politics: Big Governmentís Erratic Campaign for Law and Order* (Oxford, England: Oxford University Press, 2001).

13. U.S. Drug Enforcement Administration, *Tradition of Excellence: The History of the DEA from 1973 to 2003.* (Washington DC: DEA Publications, 2004).

14. George Cole and Christopher Smith, *The American System of Criminal Justice* (Belmont, CA: Wadsworth, 2001).

15. U.S. Drug Enforcement Administration, "DEA Highlights Year's Accomplishments (2005)" http://www.dea.gov/pubs/pressrel/pr122805.html.

16. U.S. Drug Enforcement Administration, "DEA Mission Statement" http://www.dea.gov/agency/mission.htm

17. Saba.

18. Ibid.

19. U.S. Customs and Border Protection, "U.S. Customs—Over 200 Years of History" http://www.customs.gov/xp/cgov/toolbox/about/history/history.xml

20. William Vizzard, *In the Crossfire: A Political History of the Bureau of Alcohol, Tobacco, and Firearms* (Boulder, CO: Lynne Rienner Publishers, 1997).

21. Franklin Zimring, "Firearms and Federal Law: The Gun Control Acto of 1968," *Journal of Legal Studies*, Issue 475, (1975): 133–198.

22. Vizzard.

23. George Kurian, *A Historical Guide to the U.S. Government* (Oxford, England: Oxford Univesity Press, 1998).

24. Vizzard.

25. Samuel Walker, *Sense and Nonsense About Crime and Drugs* (Belmont, CA: Wadsworth, 1998).

26. U.S. Bureau of Justice Statistics, *National Crime Victimization Survey Report for 2003* http://www.ojp.usdoj.gov/bjs/guns.htm

27. U.S. Bureau of Alcohol, Tobacco, Firearms and Explosives, "ATF Online: ATF Program Fact Sheets" http://www.atf.gov/about/programs/

28. U.S. Department of the Treasury, "About IRS Criminal Investigation" http://www.treas.gov/irs/ci/ci_structure/index.htm

29. U.S. Internal Revenue Service, "Criminal Investigation (CI) at a Glance" http://www.irs.gov/irs/article/0,,id=98398,00.html

30. Ibid.

31. 111. U.S. Treasury Inspector General for Tax Administration. "TIGTA Fact Sheet" http://www.treas.gov/tigta/about_what.shtml

CHAPTER 6

1. Melanson.

2. David Clary and Joseph Whitehorne, *The Inspectors General of the United States Army 1777–1903* (Washington DC: Government Printing Office, 1987).

3. Paul Light, *Monitoring Government: Inspectors General and the Search for Accountability* (Washington DC: Brookings, 1993).

4. Genevieve Nowolinski, "A Brief History of the HHS Office of Inspector General" http://oig.hhs.gov/reading/history/ighistory.pdf

5. Ibid.

6. Light.

7. Ibid.

8. Ibid.

9. Glenn Fine, "The New Statutory Law Enforcement Authority for OIG Criminal Investigators" *Journal of Public Inquiry*, Spring/Summer (2003): 15–22.

10. Light.

11. Fine.

12. Ibid.

13. Ibid.

14. President's Council on Integrity and Efficiency. *An Introduction to the Inspector General Community* (Washington DC: PCIE, 2004).

CHAPTER 7

1. U.S. Department of Housing and Urban Development. *HUD Inspector General Semi-Annual Report to Congress, Oct '04–Mar '05* (Washington DC: HUD, 2005).

2. U.S. Forest Service, "Law Enforcement and Investigations Fact Sheet" http://www.fs.fed.us/lei/

3. Ibid.

4. U.S. NOAA Marine Fisheries, "Office for Law Enforcement Fact Sheet" http://www.nmfs.noaa.gov/ole/ole_about.htm

5. U.S. Army, "CID Mission" http://www.cid.army.mil/mission.htm

6. U.S. Naval Criminal Investigative Service, "About NCIS" http://www.ncis.navy.mil/about.cfm

7. Ibid.

8. U.S. Air Force, "Air Force Office of Special Investigations" http://www.af.mil/factsheets/factsheet_print.asp

9. U.S. Environmental Protection Agency, "Compliance and Enforcement" http://www.epa.gov/compliance/basics/criminal.html

10. U.S. Food and Drug Administration, *Investigations Operations Manual* (Washington DC: FDA, 2005).

11. U.S. Federal Protective Service, "FPS Fact Sheet" http://www.ice.gov/graphics/fps/index.htm

12. U.S. Coast Guard, *U.S. Coast Guard: An Historical Overview* (Washington DC: USCG Historian's Office, 2002).

13. Ibid.

14. U.S. Bureau of Land Management, *Year-End Review 2004* (Washington DC: BLM, 2004).

15. U.S. Bureau of Land Management, "BLM Law Enforcement" http://www.blm.gov/nhp/pus/brochures/law

16. Ibid.

17. U.S. Department of Interior, "DOI Bureaus" http://www.doi.gov/bureaus/html

18. Wesley Clark, "Enforcing Criminal Law on Native American Lands" *FBI Law Enforcement Bulletin*, April (2005): 22–31.

19. Fran Mainella, *Director's Order #9: Law Enforcement Program* (Washington DC: National Park Service, 2004).

20. Ibid.

21. U.S. Fish and Wildlife Service, *FWS 2004 Annual Report* (Washington DC: Fish and Wildlife Service, 2004).

22. Ibid.

23. Amtrak. "Amtrak Background and Facts 2005" http://www.amtrak.com

24. Ernest Frazier, *Testimony of Amtrak Police Chief Ernest Frazier before House Transportation and Infrastructure Subcommittee on Railroads*, 05 May 2004.

25. Ibid.

26. U.S. Department of State. "Bureau of Diplomatic Security" http://www.state.gov/m/ds

27. Ibid.

28. Ibid.

29. Thomas Ackerman, *Guide to Careers in Federal Law Enforcement* (East Lansing, MI: Hamilton Burrows Press, 1999).

30. U.S. Tennessee Valley Authority, "TVA Police Fact Sheet" http://www.tva.gov/abouttva/tvap/index.htm

31. Ibid.

32. U.S. Bureau of Justice Statistics, *Federal Law Enforcement...by the Numbers* (Washington DC: BJS, 2003).

33. U.S. Postal Inspection Service. "Who We Are" http://www.usps.com/postalinspectors/

CHAPTER 8

1. Thomas Dye, *Understanding Public Policy* (Upper Saddle River, NJ: Prentice-Hall, 1998).

2. George Cole, Marc Gertz, and Amy Bunger, *The Criminal Justice System: Politics and Policies* (Belmont, CA: Wadsworth, 2002).

3. John Kingdon, *Agendas, Alternatives, and Public Policies* (Boston, MA: Little, Brown, and Co., 1984).

4. Dianne Rahm, *United States Public Policy* (Belmont, CA: Wadsworth, 2004).

5. John Crank and Patricia Gregor, *Counter-terrorism After 9/11: Justice, Security and Ethics Reconsidered* (Cincinnati, OH: Anderson Publishing, 2005). See also—Lee Tien, *Foreign Intelligence Surveillance Act* (Electronic Frontier Foundation, 2003).

6. American Civil Liberties Union, *Civil Liberties After 9/11: A Historical Perspective on Protecting Liberty in Times of Crisis* http://www.aclu.org. See also— American Library Association, *A Resolution on the USA PATRIOT Act and Related Measures that Infringe on the Rights of Library Users* (2003) http://www.ala.org.

7. Paul Light, *Testimony of Paul Light before the Senate Judiciary Committee, Subcommittee on Technology, Terrorism, and Government Information*, 25 June 2002.

8. U.S. Department of Homeland Security, "History: Who Became Part of the Department?" http://www.dhs.gov/dhspublic.

9. Anonymous ICE Agents, *Comments posted by anonymous ICE agents at 911jobforums.com*, 2004.

10. Edgar Schein, *Organizational Culture and Leadership* (San Francisco, CA: Jossey-Bass, 1992).

APPENDIX B

1.   The term "school zone" is defined as "in, or on the grounds of, a public, parochial or private school" or "within a distance of 1,000 feet from the grounds of a public, parochial or private school." 921(a)(25).

2.   See also Hodel, 452 U.S., at 311 ("[S]imply because Congress may conclude that a particular activity substantially affects interstate commerce does not necessarily make it so") (REHNQUIST, J., concurring in judgment); Heart of Atlanta Motel, 392 U.S., at 273 ("[W]hether particular operations affect interstate commerce sufficiently to come under the constitutional power of Congress to regulate them is ultimately a judicial rather than a legislative question, and can be settled finally only by this Court") (Black, J., concurring).

3.   Under our federal system, the "'States possess primary authority for defining and enforcing the criminal law.'" *Brecht v. Abrahamson*, 507 U.S., (1993) (slip op., at 14) (quoting *Engle v. Isaac*, 456 U.S. 107, 128 (1982)); see also *Screws v. United States*, 325 U.S. 91, 109 (1945) (plurality opinion) ("Our national government is one of delegated powers alone. Under our federal system the administration of criminal justice rests with the States except as Congress, acting within the scope of those delegated powers, has created offenses against the United States"). When Congress criminalizes conduct already denounced as criminal by the States, it effects a "'change in the sensitive relation between federal and state criminal jurisdiction.'" *United States v. Enmons*, 410 U.S. 396, 411–412 (1973) (quoting *United States v. Bass*, 404 U.S. 336, 349 (1971)). The Government acknowledges that 922(q) "displace[s] state policy choices in...that its prohibitions apply even in States that have chosen not to outlaw the conduct in question." Brief for United States 29, n. 18; see also Statement of President George Bush on Signing the Crime Control Act of 1990, 26 Weekly Comp. of Pres. Doc. 1944, 1945 (Nov. 29, 1990) ("Most egregiously, Section [922(q)] inappropriately overrides legitimate state firearms laws with a new and unnecessary Federal law. The policies reflected in these provisions could legitimately be adopted by the States, but they should not be imposed upon the States by Congress").

4.   We note that on September 13, 1994, President Clinton signed into law the Violent Crime Control and Law Enforcement Act of 1994, Pub. L. 103–322, 108 Stat. 1796. Section 320904 of that Act, id., at 2125, amends 922(q) to include congressional findings regarding the effects of firearm possession in and around schools upon interstate and foreign commerce. The Government does not rely upon these subsequent findings as a substitute for the absence of findings in the first instance. Tr. of Oral Arg. 25 ("[W]e're not relying on them in the strict sense of the word, but we think that at a very minimum they indicate that reasons can be identified for why Congress wanted to regulate this particular activity").

Selected Bibliography

Ackerman, Thomas. (1999). *Guide to Careers in Federal Law Enforcement*. East Lansing, MI: Hamilton Burrows Press.

American Civil Liberties Union. *Civil Liberties After 9/11: A Historical Perspective on Protecting Liberty in Times of Crisis*. http://www.aclu.org.

American Library Association. (2003). "A Resolution on the USA PATRIOT Act and Related Measures that Infringe on the Rights of Library Users." http://www.ala.org.

Amtrak (2005). "Amtrak Background and Facts." http://www.amtrak.com.

Anonymous ICE Agents (2004). Comments posted by anonymous ICE agents at www.911jobforums.com.

ATF Online. ATF Program Fact Sheets. http://www.atf.gov/about/programs/.

Bumgarner, Jeffrey (2004). Profiling and Criminal Justice in America. Santa Barbara, CA: ABC-CLIO.

Bailey, James (2003). *Hype, Headlines, and High Profile Cases: J. Edgar Hoover, Print Media and the Career Trajectories of Top North Carolina G-Men, 1937–1972*. University of Wales, Swansea: Unpublished Doctoral Dissertation.

Bonaparte, Charles (1909). *Letter to U.S. President Theodore Roosevelt concerning the need for a Justice Department investigative agency*. Dated January 14, 1909.

Bonaparte, Charles (1907). *Annual Report of the Attorney General*. Washington DC: U.S. Department of Justice.

Calhoun, Frederick (1989). *The Lawmen: United States Marshals and Their Deputies, 1789–1989*. Washington DC: Smithsonian Institution Press.

Clark, Wesley (2005). "Enforcing Criminal Law on Native American Lands," *FBI Law Enforcement Bulletin*, pp. 22–31, April.

Clary, David and Joseph Whitehorne (1987). *The Inspectors General of the United States Army 1777–1903*. Washington DC: Government Printing Office.

"Coast Guard Investigative Service" (1996). *Coast Guard*, pp. 24–25. December.

Cole, George and Christopher Smith (2001). *The American System of Criminal Justice. Belmont, CA: Wadsworth.*

Cole, George, Marc Gertz, and Amy Bunger (2002). *The Criminal Justice System: Politics and Policies*. Belmont, CA: Wadsworth.

Crank, John and Patricia Gregor (2005). *Counter-terrorism After 9/11: Justice, Security and Ethics Reconsidered*. Cincinnati, OH: Anderson Publishing.

Deacon, TJ (1988). Police Professionalism: The Renaissance of American Law Enforcement. Springfield, IL: Charles C. Thomas Publisher.

Dye, Thomas (2001). *Politics in America*. Upper Saddle River, NJ: Prentice-Hall.

Dye, Thomas (1998). *Understanding Public Policy*. Upper Saddle River, NJ: Prentice-Hall.

Faust, Patricia (ed.) (1991). Historical Times Illustrated Encyclopedia of the Civil War. New York, NY: Harper and Row.

Federal Bureau of Investigation. "J. Edgar Hoover" Fact Sheet. http://www.fbi.gov/libref/directors/hoover.htm.

Federal Bureau of Investigation. "FBI History." http://www.fbi.gov/fbihistory.htm.

Federal Bureau of Investigation. "Facts and Figures" Fact Sheet. http://www.fbi.gov/priorities/priorities.htm.

Fine, Glenn (2003). "The New Statutory Law Enforcement Authority for OIG Criminal Investigators," *The Journal of Public Inquiry*, pp .15–22, Spring/Summer.

Fox, John (2003). *The Birth of the Federal Bureau of Investigation*. Washington DC: Office of Public/Congressional Affairs.

Frazier, Ernest (2004). *Testimony of Amtrak Police Chief Ernest Frazier before House Transportation & Infrastructure Subcommittee on Railroads*. May 5.

Gest, Ted (2001). *Crime & Politics: Big Government's Erratic Campaign for Law and Order*. Oxford, England: Oxford University Press.

Glenn, John (2004). *The Inspectors General Story*. A video produced by the President's Council on Integrity and Efficiency, Washington DC.

Gorelick, Jamie (1995). Memorandum entitled "Instructions on Separation of Certain Foreign Counterintelligence and Criminal Investigations," U.S. Justice Department.

Hancock, Barry and Paul Sharp (2004). *Public Policy, Crime, and Criminal Justice*. Upper Saddle River, NJ: Prentice-Hall.

Jackson, Donald (1989). "Bicentennial of the U.S. Marshals," *The Smithsonian*. April.

Johnson, Herbert and Nancy Travis Wolfe (2003). *History of Criminal Justice*. Cincinnati, OH: Anderson Publishing.

Kaiser, Frederick. (1988). "Origins of Secret Service Protection of the President: Personal, Interagency, and Institutional Conflict," *Presidential Studies Quarterly*, Winter.

Kemp, Roger (ed.) (2003). *Homeland Security: Best Practices for Local Government*. Washington DC: ICMA.

Kieley, James (1940). *A Brief History of the National Park Service*. Washington DC: U.S. Department of Interior.

Kingdon, John (1984). *Agendas, Alternatives, and Public Policies*. Boston, MA: Little, Brown, and Co.

Kurian, George (1998). *A Historical Guide to the U.S. Government*. Oxford, England: Oxford University Press.

Lee, Matthew (2003). *Crime on the Border: Immigration and Homicide in Urban Communities*. New York, NY: LFB Scholarly Publishing.

Light, Paul (2002). *Testimony of Paul Light before the Senate Judiciary Committee, Subcommittee on Technology, Terrorism and Government Information*, June 25, 2002.

Light, Paul (1993). *Monitoring Government: Inspectors General and the Search for Accountability*. Washington, DC: The Brookings Institution.

Lindberg, Richard (1994). "No More Greylords?" *Illinois Police and Sheriff News*, Summer.

Mackintosh, Barry (1989). *The United States Park Police: A History*. Washington DC: NPS History Division.

Magana, Lisa (2003). *Straddling the Border: Immigration Policy and the INS*. Austin, TX: University of Texas Press.

Mainella, Fran (2004). "Director's Order #9: Law Enforcement Program. Washington, DC: National Park Service.

Maxwell, Lawrence (2003). *Testimony of the Inspector Maxwell Before the U.S. Senate Judiciary Committee*, October 15, 2003.

Melanson, Philip (2002). *Secret Service: The Hidden History of an Enigmatic Agency*. New York, NY: Carroll and Graf Publishers.

National Archives. "Creation of the U.S. Capitol Police." http://www.archives.gov/legislative/features/capitol-police/.

Nevins, Joseph (2002). *Operation Gatekeeper: The Rise of the "Illegal Alien" and the Making of the U.S. Mexico Boundary*. New York, NY: Routledge.

Nowolinksi, Genevieve (2001). "A Brief History of the HHS Office of Inspector General." http://oig.hhs.gov/reading/history/ighistory.pdf.

Peak, Kenneth and Ronald Glensor (1996). *Community Policing & Problem Solving: Strategies and Practices*. Upper Saddle River, NJ: Prentice-Hall.

Peykar, Edward (ed.) (2005). *The FBI: Past, Present, and Future*. Hauppauge, NY: Nova Science Publishers.

President's Council on Integrity and Efficiency (2004). "An Introduction to the Inspector General Community." Washington DC: PCIE.

Potter, Clair Bond (1998). *War on Crime: Bandits, G-Men, and the Politics of Mass Culture*. New Brunswick, NJ: Rutgers University Press.

Powers, Richard (2004). *Broken: The Troubled Past and Uncertain Future of the FBI*. New York, NY: Free Press.

Rahm, Dianne (2004). *United States Public Policy*. Belmont, CA: Wadsworth.

Saba, Anne (2003). "U.S. Customs Service: Always ThereÖReady to Serve," *U.S. Customs Today*. February.

Samaha, Joel (1994). Criminal Justice. St. Paul, MN: West Publishing.

Schein, Edgar (1992). Organizational Culture and Leadership. San Francisco, CA: Jossey-Bass.

Schmalleger, Frank (1993). *Criminal Justice* Today. Englewood Cliffs, NJ: Regents/Prentice-Hall.

Sommer, Robin Langley (1993). *The History of the U.S. Marshals: The Proud Story of America's Legendary Lawmen*. Philadelphia, PA: Courage Books.

Theodoulou, Stella and Chris Kofinis (2004). *The Art of the Game: Understanding American Public Policy Making*. Belmont, CA: Wadsworth.

Tien, Lee (2003). "Foreign Intelligence Surveillance Act," Electronic Frontier Foundation.

TRAC Syracuse University. "IRS At Work – IRS History." http://trac.syr.edu/tracirs/atwork/current/irsHistory.html.

Turk, David (2005). *United States Marshals Service: Historical Perspective*. Washington DC: USMS Historian Office.

U.S. Army. "CID Mission" Fact Sheet. http://www.cid.army.mil/mission.htm.

U.S. Air Force (2005). "Air Force Office of Special Investigations" Fact Sheet. http://www.af.mil/factsheets/factsheet_print.asp.

U.S. Air Force. "About OSI." http://public.afosi.amc.af.mil/about.asp.

U.S. Bureau of Land Management (2004). *Year–End Review 2004*. Washington DC: BLM.

U.S. Bureau of Land Management. "BLM Law Enforcement" Fact Sheet. http://www.blm.gov/nhp/pubs/brochures/law/.

U.S. Bureau of Justice Statistics (2004). *National Crime Victimization Survey Report*. http://www.ojp.usdoj.gov/bjs/guns.htm.

U.S. Bureau of Justice Statistics (2003). *Federal Law Enforcement–By the Numbers*. http://ojp.usdoj.gov/bjswelcome.htm.

U.S. Bureau of Justice Statistics (2001). *Federal Law Enforcement Officers, 2000*. Washington DC: BJS Bulletin.

U.S. Coast Guard. "Coast Guard Investigative Service" Fact Sheet. http://www.uscg.mil/hq/g-o/g-o-cgis/cgis.htm.

U.S. Coast Guard (2002). *U.S. Coast Guard: An Historical Overview*. Washington DC: USCG Historian's Office.

U.S. Customs and Border Protection (2006). "U.S. Border Patrol Overview." http://www.cbp.gov/xp/cgov/border_security/border_patrol/overview.xml.

U.S. Customs and Border Protection. "U.S. Customs–Over 200 Years of History," http://www.customs.gov/xp/cgov/toolbox/about/history/history.xml.

CBP Today (2003). "Populating a Nation: A History of Immigration and Naturalization." June/July.

CBP Today (2003). "Protecting Our Sovereign Borders." June/July.

U.S. Department of Commerce OEE. "Export Enforcement" Fact Sheet. http://www.bis.doc.gov/complianceandenforcement/EnforcementHome.htm.

U.S. Department of Homeland Security. "History: Who Became Part of the Department?" Fact Sheet. http://www.dhs.gov/dhspublic.

U.S. Department of Homeland Security. "Department Subcomponents and Agencies" Fact Sheet. http://www.dhs.gov/dhspublic.

U.S. Department of Housing and Urban Development (2005). *HUD Inspector General Semi-Annual Report to Congress*, Oct '04– Mar '05.

U.S. Department of Interior. " DOI Bureaus" Fact Sheet. http://www.doi.gov/bureaus.html.

U.S. Department of Labor, Office of Inspector General. "The OIG's Labor Racketeering Program" Fact Sheet. http://www.oig.dol.gov/laborrac-program.htm.

U.S. Department of State. "Bureau of Diplomatic Security" Fact Sheets. http://www.state.gov/m/ds.

U.S. Drug Enforcement Administration (2005). "DEA Highlights Year's Accomplishments," http://www.dea.gov/pubs/pressrel/pr122805.html.

U.S. Drug Enforcement Administration. "DEA Mission Statement," http://www.dea.gov/agency/mission.htm.

U.S. Drug Enforcement Administration (2004). *Tradition of Excellence: The History of the DEA from 1973 to 2003*. http://www.dea.gov/pubs/history/index.html.

U.S. Environmental Protection Agency. "Compliance and Enforcement" Fact Sheets. http://www.epa.gov/compliance/basics/criminal.html.

U.S. Federal Protective Service. FPS Fact Sheet. http://www.ice.gov/graphics/fps/index.htm.

U.S. Fish and Wildlife Service (2004). *FWS 2004 Annual Report*. Washington DC: Fish and Wildlife Service.

U.S. Food and Drug Administration. "Office of Criminal Investigations" Fact Sheet. http://www.fda.gov/ora/hier/hfc300.html.

U.S. Food and Drug Administration (2005). *Investigations Operations Manual*. http://www.fda.gov/ora/inspect_ref/iom/.

U.S. Forest Service (2004). "Law Enforcement and Investigations" Fact Sheet. http://ww.fs.fed.us/lei/.

U.S. Immigration and Naturalization Service (2002). *A Career with the INS: Not Your Average Desk Job*. Washington DC: Government Printing Office.

U.S. Immigration and Naturalization Service (2003). *Retiring to a New Beginning: An Illustrated History of the Immigration and Naturalization Service*. Washington, DC: Government Printing Office.

U.S. Internal Revenue Service. "Criminal Investigation (CI) At a Glance." http://www.irs.gov/irs/article/0,,id=98398,00.html.

U.S. Marshals Service (2005). "United States Marshals Service 2004 Fact Sheet." http://www.usms.gov.

U.S. Marshals Service (1981). *The United States Marshals Service: Then and Now*. Washington DC: Government Printing Office.

U.S. Marshals Service (1981). *The Office of the United States Marshal*. Washington, DC: Government Printing Office.

U.S. Naval Criminal Investigative Service. "About NCIS." http://www.ncis.navy.mil/about.cfm.

U.S. NOAA Marine Fisheries. "Office for Law Enforcement" Fact Sheet. http://www.nmfs.noaa.gov/ole/ole_about.htm.

U.S. Postal Inspection Service. "Who We Are" Fact Sheet. http://www.usps.com/postalinspectors/.

U.S. Postal Service. "History of the United States Postal Service 1775–1993."http://www.usps.com/history/his1_5.htm.

U.S. Secret Service (2002). "United States Secret Service: History" Timeline Fact Sheet. http://www.secretservice.gov/history.shtml.

U.S. Senate. "The Capitol Police." http://www.senate.gov/artandhistory/history/common/briefing/Capitol_Police.htm.

U.S. Tennessee Valley Authority. "TVA Police" Fact Sheet. http://www.tva.gov/abouttva/tvap/index.htm.

U.S. Treasury Department. "About IRS Criminal Investigation." http://www.treas.gov/irs/ci/ci_structure/index.htm.

U.S. Treasury Inspector General for Tax Administration (2004). TIGTA Fact Sheet. http://www.treas.gov/tigta/about_what.shtml.

Vizzard, William (1997). *In the Crossfire: A Political History of the Bureau of Alcohol, Tobacco and Firearms*. Boulder, CO: Lynne Rienner Publishers.

Walker, Samuel (1998). *Sense and Nonsense About Crime and Drugs*. Belmont, CA: Wadsworth.

Walker, Samuel (1977). *A Critical History of Police Reform*. Lexington, MA: Lexington Books.

White, Jonathan (2004). *Defending the Homeland: Domestic Intelligence, Law Enforcement, and Security*. Belmont, CA: Wadsworth.

Whitehead, Don (1956). *The FBI Story: A Report to the American People*. New York, NY: Random House.

Zimring, Franklin (1975). "Firearms and Federal Law: The Gun Control Act of 1968," *Journal of Legal Studies*, Issue 475, pp. 133–198.

Index

About the Author

JEFFREY B. BUMGARNER is an Associate Professor of Criminal Justice at Texas Christian University. He is the author of *Profiling and Criminal Justice in America* and the forthcoming *To Protect and Serve: An Introduction to Law Enforcement*. He is also a former federal agent with several years of experience in federal and local law enforcement.